THE TOUGHEST GANG IN TOWN

Police Stories From Old San Francisco

Kevin J. Mullen

NOIR PUBLICATIONS
NOVATO, CALIFORNIA

ISBN 0-926664-09-3

First printing July 2005

Front cover photo: www.sanfranciscohomicide.com

Book design and layout: Chris Carlsson, Cloverleaf Productions, San Francisco

Printed in the United States of America

Noir Publications
448 Ignacio Blvd. #202
Novato Ca 94949

For Jeannie, who continues to put up with my nonsense. With love.

People can sleep peacefully in their beds at night because rough men are willing to go out and fight on their behalf.

—GEORGE ORWELL

He was a cop when the San Francisco Police Department was "the toughest gang in town."

—SGT. ED FOWLIE on the tenure of his father, Sgt. Charlie Fowlie, in the 1940s.

CONTENTS

INTRODUCTION

Every decade or so, someone puts together an anthology of famous San Francisco criminal cases. First, and perhaps still the best, was Police Captain Thomas Duke's 1910 *Celebrated Criminal Cases in America*. In his book, which is still in print, Duke discusses a large number of notable nineteenth and early twentieth century criminal cases from all over the United States, including some San Francisco criminal cases and other stories related to the police. In an earlier era it was a standard reference work for students of criminal justice, both lofty and profane.[1]

In 1929, Peter Fanning, another San Francisco police officer, published his *Great Crimes of the West* which also summarized a number of police related stories including murders and other prominent crimes which occurred in San Francisco, adding some that took place after Duke published. Joseph Henry Jackson, prominent San Francisco author and reviewer, followed up in 1947 with his *San Francisco Murders*. The bodice ripper cover on John Carpenter's 1967 *San Francisco Babylon* masks some really good old San Francisco crime stories.

In 1974 Dean Dickensheet published his *Great Crimes of San Francisco*. The most recent entry is Charles F. Adams *Murder by the Bay*, published this year. To a surprising degree the stories in all the books repeat those laid down by Captain Duke in 1910. Most have accounts of the 1895 "Crime of the Century" in which Theodore Durrant murdered two young women and secreted their bodies in a Mission District church for his later pleasure. Several also include an account of the trials of J. Milton Bowers who, in 1885, was accused of poisoning the third of his three young wives to die an untimely death.

As with Duke and Fanning, the stories in this book, most of

---

1. Dashiell Hammet's Continental Op kept a copy of Duke's book on his night-stand.

which have been published previously in a variety of magazines and newspapers, are informed by my 26 years of experience in the San Francisco Police Department in which I served in every rank and position from patrolman to Deputy Chief. But this book takes a decidedly different approach from the others. For one thing, I've looked for cases the others, for the most part, have not included.

In his selection of crimes to fit the dramatic model for his *San Francisco Murders*, Joseph Henry Jackson bypassed the first two decades of the city's history to settle on an 1870 case, the murder of A. P. Crittenden, a shining light of the California bar, by a rejected paramour in the presence of his wife and children. Murders were common enough before then, Jackson wrote, but they were not of the sort "that produces an interesting murder case." We begin with a child killing that occurred in Mexican San Francisco in 1828. And there follow a number of cases which occurred long before the Crittenden case in 1870. It will be up to the reader to decide whether they are sufficiently "interesting."

There are other subjects covered in the previous books and elsewhere that could be included as well. The big criminal justice story of Gold Rush San Francisco was the establishment of the famed committees of vigilance which on two occasions bypassed the regular institutions of justice and hanged a handful of criminal miscreants on their own. Many books have been written on the topic, so I include only enough mention to provide a setting for other things I want to say. Similarly, the 1906 disaster by earthquake and fire, the most significant event in the city's twentieth century history, was attended by much reported violence, but again I make little mention of the cataclysm other than to bring in a discussion of the fires, which earlier plagued the city, and to introduce a post-earthquake crime wave.

I do not include the usual incidents which can be found in any number of available books and instead search out the less well known, but, to me at least, equally interesting stories. The same year that Crittenden met his death at the hands of his outraged mistress, a little girl named Maggie Ryan was savagely assaulted and murdered under the Pacific Wharf, a crime that led to a police chase of the perpetrator under the wharves and streets of the city, and almost resulted in his lynching by an outraged populace. Another murder of a young girl by a spurned suitor in 1885 resulted in an assault on the Broadway County Jail reminiscent of the vigilante takeover in 1856. In 1885, however, the police were able to fight off the attack and the perpetrator lived to die by legal execution.

There are many other topics which are not included in the collection, or which receive only a cursory mention. Over the years there were many police corruption scandals. One in 1937 resulted in the resignation of two police commissioners and the dismissal of two district captains and a number of other officers. Neither is there a mention of San Francisco's famed Chinatown Squad which, during the late nineteenth and early twentieth centuries, captured the imagination of the American reading public. Still there is plenty here which has not been presented before, and which also, I trust, readers will find of interest.

Prologue
MAY 1979

In the early morning hours of May 22, 1979—on my orders—police formations marched back-step up Castro Street from 18th to Market, followed by a crowd of jeering demonstrators. As the oddly paired groups passed in front of the Castro Theater where I was standing, one of the crowd broke away and approached within 20 feet of me, where he loudly denounced me as a "pig-faced Irish motherfucker" before scurrying back to the safety of the mob. The irony wasn't lost on me that my withdrawal order, which even then I knew would cost me dearly in the opinion of working cops, had also saved my detractor from getting his butt kicked by some very angry police officers.

The string of incidents leading to what came to be called the White Night Riot can reasonably be traced to events six months earlier. In November 1978, the city was shaken to its psychic roots when San Francisco-based Jim Jones led his People's Temple followers in a mass suicide in Guyana. And when a few days later, on November 27, ex-Supervisor Dan White sneaked into City Hall and summarily executed Mayor George Moscone and Supervisor Harvey Milk, it was almost more than the civic psyche could absorb. At first, though, the city seemed to come together in its grief. That night, more than 25,000 candle-bearing mourners formed up in the Castro, then made their way peaceably down Market Street to City Hall.

There they were greeted by the familiar voice of Joan Baez and the strains of "Amazing Grace." Acting Mayor Dianne Feinstein addressed the group over pre-positioned loudspeakers, as did other civic leaders, including Harry Britt, Milk's political protégé. Harvey's recorded voice, taped three weeks earlier on the defeat of the Briggs amendment which would have prohibited gays from teaching in public schools, was broadcast to the assembled throng. The proceedings closed at 11:30 p.m. with a Felix Mendelssohn hymn sung by the Gay Men's Choir.

White had been arrested shortly after the killings and in April 1979 was placed on trial in Superior Court on what most saw as a double premeditated first degree murder. It looked like a slam dunk. To the extent that we thought about it at all, we expected some type of peaceful demonstration when the verdict came in, perhaps a replay of the march six months earlier. When the manslaughter verdict—with a top sentence of imprisonment for eight years—was announced on May 21, San Francisco's gay community, along with many straights, was stunned beyond belief. There would be no Mendelssohn that night.

The verdict was announced shortly after 5 p.m., inconveniently just after the entire police department day watch had reported off duty. Without any firm knowledge about when the jury deliberations would end, we had no plan in place. (Since the Los Angeles riots following the verdict in the Rodney King beating case, the announcements of jury verdicts in potentially volatile cases are often delayed until police can make the necessary arrangements.)

A group formed up at Castro and Market, as they had so many times before, and proceeded to march to City Hall. There were reports along the line of march that the crowd was mostly peaceable with some violent elements. Photographs taken at the time, which I viewed later, showed signs saying "Avenge Harvey Milk." Had I known of the signs at the time perhaps I would have done things differently. But I think not; by then it was too late anyway. When the marchers arrived at the Polk Street side of City Hall and found nothing to distract them from their outrage, they began to attack the face of the building. We called up reserve forces and made impromptu efforts to engage the mob with speakers sympathetic to their cause. It didn't work.

Some questioned whether events could have played out differently. "There's nothing that could have been said that would have placated that crowd," said Supervisor Tom Ammiano, then chairman of the Gay Teacher's Coalition. "Emotions were running too high." According to another view though, that of an injured demonstrator, "Harvey Milk was a street-fighter. . . . he could get that bullhorn and slow that crowd down. That's what we lacked tonight." Whether Harvey could have turned the crowd is open to debate, but I can't help but think that if things had gone differently at several turns that night the outcome would have been different.

In the late 1960s, in the midst of the anti-war demonstrations of that era, the department acquired a surplus military loudspeaker called a loudhailer. The self-contained, battery-operated unit could be heard a mile away. The unit also had a "curdler" feature which, when cranked up to full volume, was supposed to make listeners within hearing range defecate. Early in the disorder, I put in a call for the loudhailer to be delivered to City Hall. As luck would have it—again bad—nobody on duty knew where it was stored. It was found at 3 a.m. the next day, neatly nestled in its place in the Tactical Division Headquarters.

In the meantime, we asked Supervisor Carol Ruth Silver to address the mob from the balcony in front of the Mayor's Office with a police bullhorn. I joined her there and so as not to incite the mob with the appearance of my uniform, I hunched down behind the balustrade and extended my hand holding a lighted butane cigarette lighter above the rail. To the crowd below, the sudden appearance of a small disembodied flame from the embattled ramparts of the enemy citadel must have seemed like a sign from beyond the grave. Immediately, the shouting and rock throwing stopped and a reverent hush fell over the crowd.

Lighted candles, first a few and then more and more, began to appear among the crowd. Who, I wondered, brings candles to a riot? Supervisor Silver, a sympathetic figure to those below, began to speak. The crowd applauded respectfully. For a time peace held the upper hand. In the end, the bullhorn was too feeble to be heard below, and the lighter became too warm to hold alight. The rock throwing resumed. The violence built until almost 11 p.m., when several police cars parked along McAllister Street were set afire by rioters. It was only then that we swept Civic Center Plaza and chased rioters as they trashed shop windows on Market Street and in the surrounding area. Early May 22, a squad of police officers entered the Elephant Walk bar at 18th and Castro and routed the patrons in what many saw as a retaliatory "police riot." The events of the night were capped by a police withdrawal from the Castro, dubbed "Mullen's Retreat" in my honor by officers who would have preferred a different outcome.

The White Night Riot has evolved into one of the founding legends of modern gay San Francisco—sort of a West Coast version of New York's Stonewall riot. If Harvey Milk's assassination was the Boston Massacre, White Night was Concord Bridge. Much of the after-action criticism centered on tactics and timing as the reasons for what went wrong. Some said we moved against the crowd too late, unnecessarily endangering officers who were forced to stand in formation in front of the rock-throwing mob. Others complained that when we did move, officers used excessive force. There could be no way of reconciling the views of those at opposite ends of the opinion spectrum.

Still, tactics and timing aside, the tensions that characterized events in the late 1970s – from the Guyana mass suicide to the White Night Riot—can be viewed in a broader sense as the inevitable eruption in a long-simmering conflict between the San Francisco that had been, and city that was about to be—the death throes of the old San Francisco, you might say, amid the birthing pains of the new.

In a sense, the riot was a fitting conclusion to what had been a truly troubled and troubling decade, both for the city and its police department. The year 1970 – the first of the decade and the deadliest for officers in the city's history – opened with the New Year's morning murder of a police officer in a seedy Tenderloin doorway. A few months later, another officer was assassinated while sitting in his marked police vehicle writing a parking citation; yet another was killed in a gun duel with a bank robber at 6th Avenue and Clement Street.

The cop killers were even coming into the stations after us. In February, Sergeant Brian McDonnell was killed by a bomb set against the window to the assembly room at Park Station by leftist political radicals. The following year Black Guerrilla Army murderers invaded Ingleside Station and killed Sergeant Jack Young at his desk. As we stood in respectful formation in front of St. Brendan's church at the funeral for Inspector Harold Hamilton, killed in the Clement Street bank shootout, a pipe bomb set against the church's outer wall exploded; they wouldn't even let us bury our dead in peace. Is it any wonder that multigenerational police families advised their sons against coming into the department?

Every officer who lived through that time has his own set of remembered experiences. Some of us were luckier than others. I was on my way to work as captain at Taraval Station one morning in 1974 when Patty Hearst and her Symbionese Liberation Army companions robbed the Hibernia Bank on Noriega Street three blocks from my route. If I had come along five minutes later I would have driven into the trap they'd set to take out police officers responding to the bank alarm. The next year, we found an undetonated bomb on the roof at Mission Station; another was found under a car in the parking lot. We also learned of a plan to attack the station with a rocket launcher from the balcony of a school across the street from the station's business office which didn't come off only because the launcher failed to fire.

George Moscone's 1975 election as mayor, supported by a co-alition of leftist minorities, gays and perhaps, as former Chicago Mayor Richard Daly might put it, "a little help" from the members of Reverend Jim Jones' Peoples' Temple, was viewed by many as a victory of the very forces against which we had been arrayed for the preceding murderous decade. Nowhere was the pain felt more acutely than in the police department. Moscone's outsider Chief of Police Charles Gain—from benighted Oakland, of all places— was thought at the very least, to harbor dangerously liberal ideas about how police affairs should be managed.

Over the next few years the department was in a state of low-intensity insurrection. Sworn to enforce the law and obey their superiors, the officers of the department did their job, albeit sometimes grudgingly. It was the same officers who weathered the assaults of the late 60s and early 70s who stood on the line on White Night taking rocks from the mob.

In later years, friends trying to justify my decision to withdraw from the Castro pointed to other instances – more common than is supposed – when officers have withdrawn from the field in the face of overwhelming odds. That wasn't the case that night at all. Embattled and besieged by more than a decade of assaults on their values and their lives, the officers' blood was up. It wasn't a question of protecting the officers from the crowd. In truth, it was the reverse. When the dust settled, Chief Gain was out of a job and any chance of my further advancement in the department was out of the question. No matter. I suppose I didn't realize it at the time but I was already set on a different course.

In November 1978, at the start of the events leading to the White Night Riot, I was driving to the Hall of Justice one Saturday morning to catch up on paperwork when the car radio announced the first seemingly incomprehensible news of the mass suicide in Guyana. And when Mayor Moscone and Supervisor Milk were mur-

9

dered a week or so later, it seemed to me, along with just about everyone else in town, that the world had truly gone mad.

That Christmas I asked for a copy of Margaret Miller Rocq's *California Local History* and returned to a long time interest in the history of San Francisco and its police department. I was not alone in my desire to flee from the madness of the time. Twenty-five years earlier I had attended high school with San Francisco writer John VanderZee. We didn't have much of anything to do with each other at school, and later went our separate ways, meeting with a nod and a pleasantry at occasional class reunions. John, it so happened was on jury duty in City Hall when Mayor Moscone and Supervisor Milk were fatally shot and thus present to observe at first hand the manifestation of civic madness. In the introduction to his *Imagined City* written thereafter, John wrote of his reaction to the events of that week: "One feels the tug of twin temptations: to withdraw into one's own affairs, dissociating oneself from this city and all cities as doomed, antiquated life forms, or to accept the widespread condemnation of an entire community as final – to subside rather than to persevere," he wrote. "So, I withdrew into . . . the insulated order of library stacks. . . ."

Unaware of John's sentiments at the time, I too withdrew into my own set of stacks. During the day, I would do with whatever part of the crazy civic drama came under my responsibility. But each night after work, like some sort of third-rate Nicolo Macchiavelli, I would divest myself of my work-a-day attire, and like the author of *The Prince*, join the inhabitants of what I saw as earlier, nobler times. And also like him, I found that while times change and people come and go, the human impulses which bring on fits of social madness remain constant. Buried in the musty archives of the city of long ago, I found all the same passions and turmoil, the shootings and chicanery, the messiness and down right evil from which I was trying to remove myself in the present.

What follows is some of what I found.

One

MURDER IN MEXICAN SAN FRANCISCO

The old inhabitants maintain that California was a perfect paradise be-
fore the foreign immigration set in to corrupt patriarchal customs; then
robbery and assassination were unheard of, blasphemy rare, and fraudu-
lent creditors unknown.

—ZOETH SKINNER ELDREDGE

B y most accounts, there was little crime in Mexican
California—so little in fact, that there was no need for a
criminal justice establishment. "There were then no jails,
no juries, no sheriffs, law processes or courts," wrote historian
Hubert H. Bancroft, looking back from a bloodier time, "conscience
and public opinion were law, and justice held an evenly balanced
scale." In truth there was a criminal justice system of sorts, under
the authority of the military governor, and probably as much crime
as one would expect in any small homogenous community cut off
from outside influences. If there was less crime than modern urban
dwellers have become accustomed to, it was not because of any
intrinsic moral superiority of our Hispanic predecessors but rather
because there was less opportunity to commit crime and get away
with it. In the words of an old African tribal aphorism "The problem
is not how to steal the king's bugle but where to play it."

Surviving records, while not complete, do suggest that conditions were other than the crime-free paradise suggested by Bancroft.
Some of the behaviors considered grist for the criminal justice mill in
those days would now be considered as matters to be resolved between consenting adults. In 1821 a soldier at San Francisco's Presidio
was sentenced to public works at San Blas for adultery with his sister-in-law. The woman was sentenced to exposure in the plaza with
a shaven head.

But there were also matters of more conventional concern to the justice system. The next year four Indian boys, from nine to eleven years of age, killed one of their companions by strangling him, jumping on his stomach and throwing stones at him. They buried his body but were found out when wild animals dug it up. A few months later five adult mission Indians were tried for the murder of three others. In December 1822, two soldiers were sentenced to two years of hard labor at Monterey for a robbery at San Francisco.

In May 1823 an infantryman at San Francisco was sentenced to two years at hard labor for theft. And in June another infantryman who killed a fellow soldier was sentenced to six years on the chain gang. In 1824 Pomponio, a runaway mission Indian from San Francisco who had mounted a murderous crime wave from San Rafael to Santa Cruz, was executed by firing squad in Monterey. In 1828 a soldier was convicted of rape of a little girl at San Francisco. The murder that same year of two small children at the San Francisco Presidio would culminate in a political revolution that cost the governor his job.

Europeans first settled in San Francisco in the mid-1770s with the establishment of a presidio on the south side of what came to be called the Golden Gate to prevent incursions by foreigners into the bay, and a mission a few miles inland, where female Indian "neophytes" would be at a distance from the improper attentions of the soldiery. A year after the founding of the Presidio and Mission Dolores, a civil *pueblo* (town) was established in the south bay by civilian settlers to grow foodstuffs for the Presidio.

The settlements on the San Francisco peninsula were founded out of military necessity, and not because of any intrinsic desirability of the site for settlement. And they never did prosper in Hispanic times. Few residents of Mexico or sunny Baja California wished to move to the remote northern outpost, and in the end the authorities resorted to recruitment from Mexican prisons and foundling homes to make up settlement parties and their military escorts for Alta California. For one thing, the cold, damp climate near the windy strait was considered inhospitable by the sun-loving Latins. When the settlements in Alta California failed to turn a profit, Spanish authorities lost interest in the enterprise.

Under the prevailing policy of neglect, the Presidio at San Francisco fell into a state of disrepair and military unpreparedness. According to Alexander Forbes, who observed the settlement firsthand during the Mexican period, "They [the presidial soldiers] were always badly clothed and worse paid, so that their appearance was that of tattered ragamuffins; and from their undisciplined state and idle habits they were good for nothing except to retake any miserable Indians who might escape from the missions. . . ." By 1828, the presidial population amounted to about 500 people residing in 120 dwellings around the presidial square and down toward the old Spanish anchorage, in front of what is now Crissy Field.

On August 15, 1828, the usual summer fog that creeps in from the Pacific to blanket the San Francisco Presidio had turned into a cold drizzle. Life at the forlorn military outpost of Mexican California was

1-1 AUTHOR'S COLLECTION. The Presidio at San Francisco in 1816. The Marin Headlands are at the right beyond the anchorage. By the late 1820s, settlers had spread out from the presidial compound and erected private dwellings in the foreground.

13

bleak at any time, and the inhabitants took their entertainment where they could find it. Perhaps that's why soldier Ignacio Olivas and his wife, Ildefonsa, left their children untended in the family dwelling that night when they went to a fandango a few houses away.

When the parents returned home the following dawn, they found that their 5 year-old daughter, Maria Antonia, and their infant son, Blas De Jesus, had both been strangled. The little girl had been raped. Suspicion quickly turned toward 26 year-old Francisco Rubio, a soldier at the Presidio, nicknamed *El Coyote*, designating him as a mulatto of Mexican birth. Rubio was arrested for the crime and at his trial, which followed soon afterward, it was shown that he had a previous record of sexual abuse of Indian females at the Sonoma Mission where he had served as a guard.

On the night of the Olivas murders, Rubio had been present in the Olivas residence before the party and had inquired about whether the children were to be left there. Later he was seen in the vicinity of the Olivas house just before the children were found, and his shoe matched a print found in the moist earth at the point of entry to the house. An Indian testified that Rubio tried to trade shirts with him on the night of the murder and another soldier said that a serape he had loaned Rubio on the day of the fandango was returned the following day with a fresh blood stain. The testimony taken, the case was put on hold for the next two years, not an unusual occurrence under the easygoing criminal justice practices of the time.

With his trial suspended during 1829 and 1830, Rubio remained under nominal arrest but seems to have spent his time working as a servant at the Presidio. (One wonders what the Olivas must have thought about the accused murderer of their children going about the small community.)

The reason for the delay was rooted in Mexican governmental policies. In early 1820s, after a decade of revolt, Spanish colonies in New Spain had broken away from the mother country. The settlements in Alta California no longer looked to the old world but to Mexico as the ultimate source of governmental authority. During the decade of revolt, Alta California, far from the center of activity, had been even more neglected than in the past, and the native *Californios*, or *hijos del pais* (children of the land), had learned that they could not depend on outside resources for support. Some began to question why they should even answer to Mexico.

A succession of Mexican governors was appointed to rule the province during the 1820s, and in 1828, Jose Maria Echeandia sat in the governor's chair. Echeandia was an easygoing official who established his government in San Diego, not in the nominal capital at Monterey, because he preferred the warmer climate—and the girls, it was said—at the southern location. It was during his term of office that the Olivas children were murdered.

In 1830, Manuel Victoria, a man of sterner stuff than Echeandia, was appointed military governor of California by a newly installed conservative regime in Mexico. Whatever else his problems, it is unlikely that Victoria, of Peruvian Indian stock, would have been embraced by *Californio* establishment who considered themselves, whatever their origins were, as descended from those of pure Castillian blood.

Victoria was a strict law-and-order man, and in his view his predecessor had been negligent in his duty, causing crime conditions in Alta California to get out of hand. Soon after his arrival, Victoria had shocked the *Californios* by ordering the execution of an Indian convicted of burglary at Monterey.

He also ordered a rehearing in the Olivas case. No new evidence was adduced in the defendant's behalf and the second tribunal found Rubio guilty as charged. On the governor's order, he was taken to the rear of the Olivas house at 11:30 a.m. on August 1, 1831, and shot to death by firing squad. Rubio's conviction and execution marked not only the first celebrated murder case in San Francisco but also the first of a long list in which it was debated about whether the accused was guilty in the first place. Many prominent *Californios* claimed that the governor had executed the wrong man.

Victoria's appointment as governor had caused consternation among leading *Californios* who had become accustomed to managing their own affairs during the war of independence. The appointment of *Californio* Luis Arguello as Governor following the success of the revolution suited them nicely. And Echeandia, though from Mexico, did not much interfere with their interests. Furthermore, Echeandia advanced the course of mission secularization by means of which prominent *hijos del pais* were eventually to profit mightily. Victoria, on the other hand, suspended the process of secularization on his arrival and knocked their plans into a cocked hat.

To counter their political enemy, prominent *Californios* circulated the story that Victoria had executed the Indian at Monterey for stealing a few buttons. That was not exactly the case. When Victoria took office the burglary trial of Atanasio, an 18-year-old Indian, had been pending since the previous year. Victoria ordered the trial to proceed. It was shown that Atanasio had stolen more than $200 worth of goods from a warehouse and it was his use of some buttons taken in the theft as gambling chips that led to his arrest. The prosecutor recommended leniency but the court ordered that the defendant be executed. (Though draconian by current standards, the penalty was in line with existing law. In January 1824, *Californio* Governor Luis Arguello had proclaimed the death penalty for all thefts exceeding $25. The guilty one's body was to be quartered in cases where force or false keys were used.)

In the same way, Victoria's political enemies regarded the Rubio execution as a case of judicial murder. For years thereafter various alternative explanations for the deaths of the Olivas children were put forth. It was pointed out that the rapist convicted of abusing another young girl that year could well have committed the crime.

The rumor also circulated that in 1833 an Indian at the San Rafael Mission confessed to the crime and was executed on the orders of the local military commander. Another version had it that a coyote had gained access to the house and killed the children. The leading Californios of the day were unanimous in their belief that Rubio was the victim of Victoria.

In the end, after stirring up public sentiment against the governor, the leading *Californios* revolted against Victoria and ran him out of Alta California. Whether Rubio was actually guilty of the murders lies obscured by the mists of time and muddied by the political disagreements of the day. But to Bancroft, who listened sympathetically to the *hijos del pais* when preparing his history, "Though circumstantial, the proofs [of Rubio's guilt] were strong," sufficiently so, he thought, "to justify the severest penalty."

Two

A BIBULOUS BEGINNING

W hen U. S. forces seized the Port of San Francisco in July 1846, Mexican officials buried the town cannon, gave the Mexican flag and town records to a sympathetic foreigner for safekeeping, and, in keeping with long-standing plans in the event of invasion, fled inland. With the Mexican officials gone, U.S. military authorities appointed officials of their own to govern the town. Washington A. Bartlett, a bilingual naval lieutenant assigned to the USS Portsmouth, was appointed *alcalde* (mayor/judge) for the District of San Francisco and Lieutenant Henry B. Watson was assigned with a detachment of 24 Marines to the Mexican customhouse on the plaza (soon to be renamed Portsmouth Square) as a military garrison and as "the chief police of the town."

Immediately after the flag-raising, the garrison was called upon for peacekeeping duties of a sort. The "assembled crowd of free and enlightened citizens of Mexico," wrote Joseph T. Downey, a Portsmouth sailor who later recalled they "at last forced into their brains that they had by some magical proceeding suddenly been metamorphosed into citizens of the United States, and unanimously wanted to go where liquor could be had, and drink a health and long life to that flag." "The Indians consequently rushed frantically to one pulperee," Downey recounted, "Capt. Leidesdorff and the aristocracy to Bob Ridley's bar-room, and the second class and the Dutch [Germans] to Tinker's." The noisy celebration lasted for several hours until the military commandant sent a guard to tell the revellers that the town was under martial law and ordered them to their homes. "But few," said Downey, "were able to do so, and the greater part of them either slept in Tinker's Alley or on the grass in the plaza, and only woke with the morning's first beams, to wonder what was the cause of yesterday's spree."

Thereafter, conditions settled into a more orderly routine. A military curfew was established and town residents were organized into a militia force to defend against a feared Mexican counterattack. According to the later reminiscence of one resident of the time, there wasn't much in the way of regular law enforcement business to occupy the town police. "The peace and quiet of the town was undisturbed," related the town's first newspaper editor years later, "by anything more serious than the arrest of a few of the Portsmouth's men for disorderly conduct and one or two causeless alarms."

One of those alarms was brought on by the antics of the little settlement's first "chief of police." According to John Henry Brown, who kept a hotel on what is now Clay Street near Kearny, Lieutenant Watson—who of course was exempt from the curfew—showed up nightly at Brown's hotel where he "made it a rule . . . to fill his flask with good whiskey." Watson would rap on his window, said Brown, and give the password: "The Spaniards are in the brush." Brown would get up, fill the flask with whiskey, and the "Chief" would then go about his duties.

On one occasion, Brown recalled later, he was particularly tired, having spent the previous night entertaining a group at an all-night party which included Watson and some visiting ship captains. So Brown took to his bed early and was sleeping soundly when "Chief" Watson came and tapped on the window shutters to order up his nightly portion. "I did not hear them," Brown recounts, "and as Watson, who had been imbibing freely, found the raps did no good, he fired off one of his pistols, and sang out at the top of his voice, 'The Spaniards are in the brush!'"

The sentry at the custom house, hearing the cry and shot, fired off his own weapon to sound the alarm. The guard was called out, the militia was assembled, and a force sent ashore from the Portsmouth. For the rest of the cold, damp night, every able-bodied man in San Francisco stood watch against the attack which did not come.

VIEW OF SAN FRANCISCO, FORMERLY YERBA BUENA, IN 1846-7
BEFORE THE DISCOVERY OF GOLD

2-1 *AUTHOR'S COLLECTION.* View of Yerba Buena (San Francisco) from the harbor shortly after Watson's foul-up. The "police" were housed in the building identified as a calaboose to the left of the custom house on the plaza. The saloon where "Chief" Watson caused the ruckus is at the southeast corner of Clay and Kearny Streets. The ship *Portsmouth* (in the foreground) is marked with an "A."

"Chief" Watson called on Brown the next morning and told him that if he ever mentioned what had happened the night before, he would be a dead man.

After the excitement, military authorities ordered the construction of a log blockhouse at Clay Street and Dupont (Grant Avenue) to fend off further "attacks" by Mexican forces from the scrub oak "brush" above Dupont. Mexicans forces never did attack and after the war, the blockhouse was used for a time by civilian authorities as a town jail for pre-Gold Rush San Francisco.

Three

THE FIRST MURDER IN AMERICAN SAN FRANCISCO

The occurrence of last Sunday evening must startle this community from their (sic) fancied security. One of our most quiet citizens, an innocent victim, is shot down in a general quarrel originating in a grog shop.

— THE SAN FRANCISCO CALIFORNIAN, NOVEMBER 17, 1847

At the time of the American conquest, the little settlement of Yerba Buena—from which the city of San Francisco would grow—was a little hamlet of 200 permanent residents dwelling in the 50 or so buildings scattered along the slope fronting the shoreline at what is now Montgomery Street. The settled portion of the town was bounded roughly by the future lines of Pacific, California, and Dupont streets, and the waterfront at Montgomery. Down by the beach were commercial warehouses and grogshops to slake the thirst of visiting seafarers. More saloons, and a sailors' boarding house, were located over by the deep water landing place (embarcadero) at Broadway and Battery streets.

To the south of California Street, a trail led through the sand dunes to the mission, and on the north a few residences straggled off through the *puertosuelo,* the cleft between Telegraph and Russian Hills, which ran toward the Presidio. Almost at once after the American flag was raised, the previously somnolent little settlement took on new life. A few weeks later the population of the town more than doubled at a stroke with the arrival of the Mormon ship *Brooklyn,* with 200 immigrant settlers. The town received another spurt of growth with the arrival of Colonel Jonathan Stevenson's regiment of New York volunteers at the end of March 1847.

The regiment had been formed earlier in New York and sent to California to assist in the Mexican War. By the time the regiment arrived in San Francisco, however, hostilities had ended in California,

21

so the various companies were distributed on garrison duty around the newly acquired territory. Two companies were assigned to the Presidio at San Francisco and a detachment was detailed to the old Mexican custom house on the plaza at Yerba Buena as a town police. By mid-summer of 1847 the town had a population of 459, not counting military personnel and residents of the mission. Men, most of them under 40 years of age, outnumbered women by two to one, and about twenty percent of the population was identified as Indian, African-American, or Sandwich Islander (Hawaiian).

By the fall, with hostilities at an end, the military authorities began to turn over the reins of government to civil authorities. A civilian town council was elected in September and the military guard was replaced by two constables charged with keeping the peace and enforcing the law in the little settlement. Among those who served in Stevenson's regiment in San Francisco was Private McKenzie Beverly. The former seaman signed on with the regiment in San Francisco in May. At first he had been placed on detached duty in San Jose, where he got in trouble almost immediately and he was sent to Monterey under arrest. He escaped from custody there, though, and returned to San Francisco, where he was rearrested in early November. Testimony at later proceedings supported the contention that Beverly was subject to depressive episodes involving violent outbursts directed at himself and others, all of which, no doubt, had an affect on events which followed.

On Sunday afternoon, November 14, 1847, a motley group of sailors, townsmen, and soldiers from the volunteer regiment were in John Ellick's grocery/saloon at what is now Pacific Street, just west of Montgomery. About 7:30 p.m., a young sailor on shore leave from the ship *Confederacion,* anchored in the nearby cove, jostled his way to the bar to get a drink. William Landers, a member of the volunteer regiment, punched him in the head and announced that he could "whip any son of a bitch in the house," always a dangerous claim in a room full of drunks. Just then, David Ward, a mate

22

from the *Confederacion,* who was rounding up his fellow shipmates to take them back to the ship after shore leave, entered the saloon. Ward took Landers up on his challenge, and gave him a sound whipping, but when he tried to shake hands after the fight, the soldier declined. Instead Landers left the saloon, but returned almost immediately, insulted Ward verbally, and went back outside again. Ward followed him out, whereupon Landers picked up a rifle leaning against the porch railing and tried to aim it at the mate.

Ward disarmed his adversary and, to avoid further trouble, took the rifle for safekeeping to George Denike's bakery/saloon down the hill on the beach near the current intersection of Sansome and Pacific Streets. The rifle, as things turned out, belonged to Private Beverly. Aroused to action by the loss of his rifle, Beverly armed himself with a rifle belonging to another soldier and made his way down to Denike's, goaded on by about 30 of his fellow revelers. Once there, he stood outside and demanded the return of his rifle, threatening to shoot if the weapon was not forthcoming. Ward, from inside the saloon, refused the demand and closed the door in Beverly's face.

Beverly fired through the door and struck a cigar maker named Charles Dornte—the inevitable innocent bystander—who was standing at the end of the bar. Dornte fell soundlessly to a table, mortally wounded, and Ward handed out the requested rifle. A group of bystanders seized Beverly and hustled him immediately before Alcalde George Hyde. The recently appointed constables don't seem to have become involved in any part of the proceedings. Hyde immediately convened a preliminary examination at which Beverly's responsibility for the shooting was established, but since the defendant was a military man, he turned the case over to the military authorities for trial on a charge of murder.

Beverly's trial before a military courts martial commenced at the Presidio on December 18, 1847. It was clear from the evidence that Beverly had shot Doernte under the circumstances described, despite testimony elicited by the defense that some of the prosecution witnesses were drunk and that their testimony was thus of questionable value. The main efforts of the defense were directed at creating the impression that Beverly was suffering from a severe form of mental disease. Several of his fellow soldiers were called to testify that he was subject to frequent convulsions after which he would act "perfectly crazy, talking to himself and calling on others who were not present."

The witnesses recounted several previous instances during which Beverly had become uncontrollably violent for no apparent reason, and said he had tried to kill himself several times while in a state of depression. Regimental physicians testified that they had observed Beverly while going through convulsions, and concluded that the man's mind was seriously impaired. San Franciscans of that day were not yet ready for insanity defenses—the staple of the defense arsenal of tools of a later time—and no one at the time seems to have wondered why a man with a well documented mental problem, and awaiting trial for military desertion, was allowed to go about armed with a loaded rifle and to visit drinking saloons in the first place.

The military court found Beverly guilty of murder, and sentenced him to fifteen years of penal servitude. He was incarcerated in the guardhouse at Clay and Dupont streets. A few nights later, however, Beverly somehow escaped, and another soldier, Henry Woolard, was later court-martialed for aiding him in his escape and concealing his departure from the officer of the guard. Woolard was acquitted at trial.

Less than a month after Beverly's conviction, gold was discovered on the American River, setting in motion the great California Gold Rush. In the excitement which followed, Beverly was lost to history, and to any punishment the courts could exact. There were later stories that he was operating with a band of brigands near San Jose, but no one seems to have felt compelled to go after him. Ironically, had Beverly been able to remain in San Francisco, he might have become a wealthy man. In 1847 he acquired title to a lot at Montgomery and Pine streets for $12. A few years later, similar lots there sold for between $30,000 and $50,000, and those who held the land still longer made great fortunes. There are quietly wealthy San Francisco families today who live comfortably on the earnings from lots bought in the same sale at the same location. But since Beverly was not around to make the improvements on his lot as required by the terms of the sale, title reverted to the city, and the property was resold to others.

William Landers, the man who started the whole mess, later served for a time as Sheriff of San Francisco.

Four
MALACHI FALLON, FIRST CHIEF OF POLICE

W hen the steamship *California* landed at San Francisco in the flush of the Gold Rush year of 1849, it brought the first wave of a flood of argonauts from the Atlantic states. As described in the *Annals of San Francisco*, the men were "largely composed of the rowdy and the knavish class," able quickly to leave "the States" for California because they "required no long time to make preparation for the voyage. Their baggage was on their back, and their purse in every honest man's pocket." Among the passengers who jammed the decks and cabins of the first Pacific Mail steamer arriving that spring was Malachi Fallon, the man who, as San Francisco's first chief of police, would be charged with imposing order on the gold-maddened boom town.

Reminiscing much later, Fallon was more generous in his appraisal of his fellow gold seekers: "San Francisco's population was then made up of rough young men with adventurous spirits, excited by the discovery of gold. They needed a strong and experienced hand to keep them in control. Many of them were of the cowboy class, while the worst were deserting whalemen coming from all parts of the world. They were not men of evil principles but they felt the excitement of the time and enjoyed the lack of restraint in a town where there was no social organization or adequate legal control. Outside of this looseness of moral forces at the time, they were good fellows."

Clearly there was little law and less order to be found in the town at the time of Fallon's arrival, for news of the gold strike on the American River had resulted in the prompt abandonment of such rudimentary institutions of government and criminal justice as existed.

As the news of the strike spread, the next to head for California, according to the *Annals*, were "the most daring and clever adventurers of blemished reputation" from Pacific ports and "stray vagabonds" from Australia, "where had been collected the choice of the convicted felons of Great Britain." In San Francisco they joined in common purpose with the dregs of the New York regiment of volunteers, sent to California during the Mexican War as soldier-settlers, and with failed miners who found work in the placers too arduous for their taste.

As shipload after shipload of gold seekers descended on the town and swelled the population, most of the "good" citizens neglected public affairs and scrambled to make a pile; others vied among themselves for control of the town government.

4-1 COURTESY OF S. F. HISTORY CENTER. Malachi Fallon. The Irish-born New Yorker who became San Francisco's first chief of police.

Against this backdrop of public apathy and political confusion, the rowdy elements of the town banded together into a loose-knit criminal alliance called "The Hounds" and filled the governmental vacuum. Encouraged by an opinion voiced by the newly arrived military commander, Persifor Smith, that Latino immigrants were not entitled to mine gold in American territory, the Hounds set about harassing the Latino residents of San Francisco. On the pretext of raising revenue to support their self-appointed law enforcement efforts, they brutally extorted money and goods from Latinos.

Unchallenged by the disorganized citizenry, the Hounds soon extended their exactions to non-Latino merchants, demanding and receiving free food and drink from saloons and restaurants of the town under the guise of payment for police services. On Sunday afternoons, the sole day of rest in Gold Rush San Francisco, the Hounds would parade through the streets of the town to the accompaniment of fife and drum, in drunken and defiant parody of a military parade, while the cowed citizenry averted their eyes.

Then, on July 15, 1849, the Hounds went too far. After a drunken Sunday excursion to the *Contra Costa*, or eastern shore of San Francisco Bay, they returned to town, where, worked up into a retaliatory frenzy by the recent shooting of an American by a Chilean defending his tent, they raged through "Chiletown" on the slopes of Telegraph Hill for an entire night, tearing down tents, stoving in boats, and shooting at the inhabitants of the hill.

The next morning the citizens of the town finally roused themselves to action. Forming themselves into a volunteer police force, they established the first of the popular tribunals for which Gold Rush San Francisco would become famous, and in the following days, they arrested, tried, and convicted the leaders of the Hounds, effectively bringing the group's reign of terror to an end.

While the trial of the Hounds was proceeding, a group of merchants, who recognized that predatory crime will grow in an enforcement vacuum and that something had to be done to ensure order, approached 35-year-old Malachi Fallon and asked him to organize a police department in San Francisco.

Born in 1814 in Athlone, Ireland, Malachi Fallon had been taken as a young boy to New York and apprenticed as a saddler. As an adult, he seems to have had some connection with a political saloon, and he served for a time on the New York Police Department as a keeper at the Tombs Prison. It was to this "former connection with police matters" that Fallon later ascribed his selection by the San Francisco merchants to establish a police department.

On Christmas Eve of 1848, in the great mania that seized the eastern seaboard following President James K. Polk's announcement of the gold strike in California, Fallon took ship from New York on the steamer *Falcon*. He steamed to the Isthmus of Panama and crossed to the Pacific side where he embarked with 350 other hopeful argonauts on the steamer *California*. Before the gold excitement had erupted in the East, the *California* had made its way around the Horn, with most of its seventy five passenger berths empty, to establish a mail service on the West Coast between Panama and the recently acquired territory of California.

Upon landing in San Francisco in February 1849, Fallon left for the gold regions, where he set up a mining partnership in the Jamestown region of Tuolumne County. It was during a business trip to San Francisco a few months later, during the trial of the Hounds, that he was asked by a group of merchants to become San Francisco's chief of police.

The political and social confusion that characterized San Francisco in the first months of 1849 was brought to a temporary end by an election. Proclaimed by the military governor and held on August l, the election brought in a new town government headed by *Alcalde* (Mayor) John Geary and a 12- member *ayuntamiento* (council). Prompted to action by the affair of the Hounds, the *ayuntamiento*, composed largely of town merchants, appointed Fallon the first chief of police on August 13, 1849. In the following weeks, Fallon in turn appointed an assistant chief, three sergeants, and thirty police officers as the first members of the department. Establishing themselves in a station house at the head of Portsmouth Square, they set about policing the town.

From the beginning of his tenure as chief, and despite the claims of some apologists for events which occurred, Fallon was faced with only a moderate amount of that sort of crime which could be expected in a Gold Rush town. On August 20, 1849, he had to arrest a Frenchman, Joseph Daniels, who had murdered his partner for his poke near the road to Mission Dolores. In October, a Chilean stabbed a black "servant" to death in a drinking tent. In November, the trussed-up body of a John Doe murder victim was found on the beach on the east side of town, and in mid-December Rueben Withers killed Arthur "Bones" Reynolds in the Bella Union Saloon. The year ended with the discovery of the body of Thomas Browne, mutilated with twenty-four stab wounds in the bushes near the road to the mission.

4-2 *ANNALS OF SAN FRANCISCO.*
The Hounds riot on Telegraph Hill, July 15, 1849.

Still, despite the exceedingly heavy rains of the winter of 1849-50 which restricted miners to their tents and the saloons of San Francisco and other settlements, Fallon was relatively unbothered by those predations which would in a short time cause the rise of the Vigilance Committee, eclipse the activities of the police department, and end Fallon's brief police career.

In reporting that only three arrests had been made in the preceding three days, the *Daily Alta California* remarked on January 18,1850, "We believe there is no place in the world with the same amount of population, where crime exists less than in San Francisco at the present time." And as late as November of that year, the paper warmly complimented the police department as "equal to any in the world, "saying it would be hard to find a "set of men their superiors as regards gentlemanly conduct and intelligence."

But in the summer of 1850, after the establishment of a chartered city government following an election at which Geary had been chosen mayor and Fallon chosen city marshal (chief of police), Fallon's problems began to multiply. The city began to experience a very real increase in predatory crime, as the incidence of murder doubled, and housebreakings and robberies — crimes less tolerated in those times before urban populations had retired behind iron grillwork— increased alarmingly. Press and public opinion toward the authorities gradually began to harden in the face of a crime wave thought to be the work of Australian ex-convicts unintimidated by the criminal justice apparatus.

Taking their cue from the more sparsely populated mining regions about the territory, where, in the absence of adequate criminal justice facilities, summary justice had been administered to those who preyed on their fellows, and urged on by promptings from the press, private citizens moved to take matters into their own hands. On several occasions, even in instances of relatively minor crimes, groups of citizens tried to take prisoners from Fallon's officers and deal with them summarily. On January 6, 1851, the *Evening Picayune*, while allowing that the police department was too small to be everywhere, reported on the well-known fact that "out of the vicinity of the drinking saloons, a policeman is scarce ever to be found, day or night." Then it openly endorsed the idea of volunteer patrols as long as the volunteers were "permitted to take their own way in the treatment of public offenders."

By late February 1851, the people were ready to act on their own. The occasion of the beating and robbery of a popular merchant threw the town into a three-day frenzy. Because of the widespread belief that regular institutions of justice were incompetent to handle the matter, "the people" at a series of angry mass meetings formed a popular court. There followed several abortive rushes to take the two suspects from Fallon and his officers. But the sentiment favoring a trial, albeit an extra-legal one, prevailed. Fortunately for the defen-

LYNCH LAW IN CALIFORNIA.—SCENE OF THE FIRST EXECUTION IN SAN FRANCISCO, ON JUNE 10. *1851*
ON THE PLAZA

4-3 ANNALS OF SAN FRANCISCO.. The hanging of Australian John Jenkins from a beam of the custom house by the first Committee of Vigilance in June 1851.

dants, the jury could not agree on their guilt, and they were eventually released, and later shown to have been innocent.

Dissatisfaction with crime conditions were quieted for a time but not dispelled. Next the disgruntled citizenry turned to the ballot box. In the municipal election at the end of April, Fallon and his fellow Democrats were turned out of office in a rousing Whig victory. The Whig mayoral candidate bested the Democrat by a margin of 414 out of 6,000 votes cast. Robert G. Crozier, the Whig candidate for city marshal, defeated Fallon by 1,709 votes, receiving 64 percent of the vote to Fallon's 36 percent, a landslide by any definition to the term.

For a time the people and the press believed that conditions would improve with the change of officials. But on the very day the new city government was to be sworn in, San Francisco was devastated by the fifth and greatest of a series of fires thought by many to have been set by arsonists. As luck would have it—bad luck for the new police—there followed a series of escapes from the station house. For the most part, flimsy construction of the jailhouse was at fault, but it was thought at the time that the breaks were the result of police incompetence or collusion with the criminals.

Even with Fallon out of office, the press kept up a steady drumbeat of criticism of the town authorities, and in early June 1851, when the trial of an Australian arrested for setting fire to his rooming house on Central Wharf (Commercial Street) was postponed for what was considered a trivial technicality, "the people" had had enough. A group of prominent citizens formed themselves into a Committee of Vigilance, vowing in their hastily composed constitution that "no thief, burglar, incendiary assassin shall escape punishment either by the quibbles of the law, the insecurity of prison, the carelessness or corruption of the police, or a laxity of those who pretend to administer justice."

The committee had hardly organized itself when an Australian thief named Jenkins (or Simpton) was arrested on the evening of June 10 by nearby boatmen while burglarizing a shipping office on Central Wharf. At the suggestion of a member of the Vigilance Committee, he was turned over to that body rather than to the police. The committee was assembled by the prearranged tolling of fire bells, and in the next few hours Jenkins was tried by the secret tribunal, convicted of burglary, and sentenced to death by hanging. In the early morning hours, he was escorted to Portsmouth Square with a rope around his neck and hanged from a beam of the custom house, to the general approval of the press and public. In the months which followed, the committee, in secret conclave, conducted a number of hearings. Testimony taken from suspected criminals and others resulted in the execution of three more Australian criminals and the banishment of a number more.

In the social turbulence that attended the vigilante eruption, information was uncovered which supported the belief that some police officers were on the take and that Marshal Fallon had been part of it. Some chroniclers present in San Francisco at the time of Fallon's tenure during the Vigilante uprising would characterize Fallon as "a good officer and an honest man." But other information suggests a different conclusion.

Though Fallon had been out of office for a month by the time the secret tribunal was convened, the Vigilance Committee had occasion to scrutinize and review his conduct while in office. In testimony before the committee in July, Thomas Ainsworth (aka Tommy Roundhead), an Australian with an extensive criminal record, charged that Fallon had tried to set him up in business as a burglar, and, when he refused to cooperate, caused his repeated arrest. Ainsworth was on a first-name basis with other members of the criminal band from Australia, and as the sole witness against Fallon before the committee, his testimony was not enough to sustain a charge of corruption against the marshal.

But there was more. Even as San Francisco seethed with vigilante turmoil, the governor of the state granted a one-month reprieve to a man in Sacramento who had been sentenced by the regular courts to hang for highway robbery. An enraged mob seized the man from the authorities and promptly hanged him. But before he died, with his neck in the noose, he was said to have made "grave charges" against the mayor of Sacramento and Marshal Fallon of San Francisco. The establishment press, which supported the Vigilance Committee and missed no opportunity to discredit its opponents among officialdom, was quick to discount allegations as sensationalism. With more important fish to fry than an out-of-office marshal, the committee never called Fallon to testify regarding the charges made against him, and the papers of the committee (which contained the charges made against him) were kept solely within the committee for more than twenty years. As a result, Fallon did not have the opportunity to officially refute the allegations at the time.

Historian Mary Williams, whose *History of the San Francisco Committee of Vigilance of 1851* and *Papers of the San Francisco Committee of Vigilance of 1851* are the definitive treatment of the 1851 committee, includes four San Francisco police officers on a list of criminals implicated by other members of the gang infesting San Francisco in the summer of 1851. Three of the officers are shown as being important members of the gang; Malachi Fallon is the fourth.

In later years when the aging Fallon was interviewed, he never hesitated to speak of his work in the Tombs in New York, and he regaled listeners about the rowdy days of Gold Rush San Francisco. However, he avoided discussing any specifics of his term of office in San Francisco and made no mention of any charges of misconduct laid against him decades before. The matter must stand, then, where Mary Williams left it.

After his removal from office in the April election of 1851, Fallon never again worked in law enforcement. He opened a saloon, the Rip Van Winkle, on the corner of Pacific Wharf and Davis Street and later moved to the Knickerbocker House at Central Wharf and Battery. In 1852, he left the city forever and moved to a seventeen-acre parcel he had purchased on the Peralta grant on the *Contra Costa*. There he lived near Seventh and Fallon streets in Oakland until his death in 1899, at the age of 85. Today, his connection with the criminal justice system of an earlier age is remembered, symbolically at least, by the presence of the Alameda County Courthouse on Fallon Street, just down the road from his former residence.

Five

TORCHING OLD-TIME SAN FRANCISCO

F ire—frequent, terrifying and all-consuming—and what San
Franciscans did about it, form one of the prominent themes
in the exciting history of the city that the Gold Rush built.
Six times in little more than 18 months between December 1849
and June 1851, the city was devastated by major fire disasters. One
legend inextricably bound up in early San Francisco lore is that the
fires were set by Australian criminals bent on looting the town in the
attendant confusion. "Many of the fires were believed to have been
raised by incendiaries," declared editors of contemporary *Annals
of San Francisco* "solely for the opportunity which they afforded for
plundering." The fires did not come to an end, according to the
legend, until the famed Vigilance committee of the 1850s drove the
criminal predators from the city.

Today's mass media helps perpetuate this fanciful legend. According to one modern version in *The San Francisco Examiner*, there
were several gangs during the Gold Rush time which would "torch"
shops and buildings if the owners didn't pay "protection" money.
"Worst among these groups was the 'Sydney Ducks,' a group of
former Australian convicts. It is believed they were responsible for
a large majority of the six fires that swept the city between 1849 and
1851." A neat explanation, but it didn't happen exactly that way.

In 1849, San Francisco, "the city that was never a town," exploded
into existence as the port of entry for men and goods headed for the
recently discovered California gold-fields. Argonauts rushed to San
Francisco from all parts of the world and the town quickly became a
roiling, round-the-clock madness of business, speculation, gambling
and carousing as nearly all its inhabitants simultaneously sought to
wring a quick fortune out of the boomtown on San Francisco Bay.

Australians of dubious reputation were among the first of those who made their way to the California goldfields. Australian ex-convicts figured prominently in the criminal annals of the city, but whether they were responsible for starting the fires that repeatedly burned down San Francisco is another question. As a matter of fact, most of San Francisco's great fires were probably set by accident, and it was the city's merchants and property owners who gained by the disasters.

The first of the major fires in Gold Rush San Francisco broke out in the early morning hours of December 24, 1849 in a building at the corner of Kearny and Washington streets. The fire started at 5:45 a.m. in the second floor of Dennison's Exchange Saloon and spread quickly to nearby buildings. Before the disorganized citizenry could mount an assault on the fire, 50 buildings valued at $1,000,000 lay in smoking ruins, and in the confusion of the fire, criminal opportunists took advantage to loot where they could. Seventy thieves, many of them recent Australian immigrants, were arrested for stealing salvaged goods which no doubt lent a measure of believability to the idea that they were in the habit of setting fires so they could steal. But for this fire at least, the evidence points in another direction.

According to John Henry Brown (a highly regarded observer and the only contemporary who seems to have left an account with a specific explanation for the origin of the December 1949 fire), it was an unwritten rule in Gold Rush San Francisco saloon society that a black man could be served one drink—but just one—in a white saloon. He was then expected to depart. In December 1849, a southerner named Thomas Battle (or Battelle) took over Dennison's saloon at Kearny and Washington streets. Evidently Battle didn't subscribe to the custom about blacks in white saloons, for when a black man entered and ordered a drink, the new owner beat him senseless, according to Brown. The beating victim vowed vengeance and was seen in the vicinity of the saloon on several occasions just before the fire. He bided his time, and then, on Christmas Eve morning, 1849, he burned the place down along with a good part of the rest of the town.

In less than a year, four more major fire disasters visited the city:

• In the early morning hours of Saturday, May 4, 1850, the U.S. Exchange saloon, erected on the site of Dennison's Exchange, burst into flame. Again the fire spread rapidly despite efforts to contain it until, by mid-day, an area three times the size of that burned in the December fire was engulfed. This time, $4,000,000 worth of property was destroyed.

• On June 14, 1850, major fire broke out just before 8 a.m. supposedly started in a defective chimney in the Sacramento House (on Kearny Street between Sacramento and Clay). In this third (and so far largest) fire, 400 buildings burned before the flames were extinguished.

• On September 17 the fourth great fire struck, beginning in the Philadelphia Saloon on Jackson between Dupont and Kearny streets, it destroyed 150 buildings before it was put out. (Shortly after the fire, *the San Francisco Picayune* claimed that most of the city's ruinous conflagrations probably resulted from carelessly arranged flues and stove pipes.)

• The 270-pound fire bell installed in March of 1851 in the Monumental Engine Company at the head of Portsmouth Square rang on the evening of May 3, heralding the start of the fifth and greatest fire that would afflict San Francisco until the disaster of 1906. This fire started in the upstairs room of a paint store on Clay Street across from Portsmouth Square, and spread quickly to nearby buildings even before the Monumental Company could drag its pumper the few feet across the plaza. By the time the fire had burned itself out, 20 square blocks (three-quarters of San Francisco's business section) were in ruins and between 20 and 100 people—the exact number has never been established—were killed.

The papers seemed pretty sure they knew who was responsible. In January 1850, the *Alta* blamed one fire (fortunately stopped before it had gotten out of hand) on one of the "most desperate scoundrels who have been serving the queen," or an Australian. Similarly, after the May 1850 fire, the *Alta* only echoed the prevailing rumor that it was caused by arson: "There [is] no doubt whatever that the fire was the base act of incendiaries." And although the earliest press reports blamed the June 1850 fire on a faulty chimney in the bakery where it started, once again the story was soon circulating that arson was behind it. In the immediate aftermath of the May 1851 fire, its cause was attributed to accident. But as the magnitude of the conflagration became known, public wrath grew, and stories circulated that the police had been investigating plots to burn down the town. In just a few days the belief had crystallized that (as expressed by the *Alta*) the fire doubtless had been set "by an incarnate fiend for the purpose of robbery." The competing *Courier* narrowed down the "incarnate fiend" category a few days

5-2 *AUTHOR'S COLLECTION*.   The Great Fire of May 1851. The brig *Euphemia* had been removed from its berth in front of the Apollo Saloon shortly before the image was made.

later, specifying that "immigrants from Sydney have been able to burn the city over our heads four or five times. . . ." (A year later, after tempers had cooled, *Parker's Directory* commented that "this fire, though by some ascribed as usual to design, is now generally charged to accident or carelessness").

By the time of the May 1851 fire, San Francisco's social conditions had been deteriorating for months. Predatory crime of all types — in addition to all the alleged arson—had been increasing and, as many saw it, the local authorities were unable to bring the problem under control. The final straw came in early June. After having been evicted from his lodgings in a rooming house on Central Wharf, an Australian immigrant named Lewis returned and set his old bed on fire. The fire was promptly put out and Lewis was arrested by a police officer, but when the district court judge postponed his trial until July on a legal technicality, the "people" decided to take the law into their own hands.

In June a group of citizens led by some of the most prominent merchants of the city formed themselves into a committee that had as one of its stated objectives the elimination of "incendiaries" from the city. In the following three months, the first of San Francisco's vigilance committees shoved the regular authorities aside and effectively took over the administration of justice in San Francisco. Before disbanding in the fall, they hanged four Australian criminals, banished a number more, and frightened still more away from the city.

But even the vigilance committee's actions didn't stop the fires — not entirely surprising if Australians had not been setting them. Despite widespread fear that fire would break out on the anniversary of June 14 fire of the year before, that day came and went without one, but on June 22 at 10:30 a.m., smoke was seen issuing from under the eaves of a house at Pacific and Powell streets. Before it was put out, that fire destroyed the previously untouched northwest quarter of the city. Arson was immediately suspected (there supposedly had been no fire in the house where the conflagration started) and the Committee of Vigilance conducted an investigation that turned up several theories but no chargeable suspects resulted.

If arson was indeed the cause of the city's great fires, however, there is somewhere else we can look besides at Australian criminals. Scholars of fire as crime have isolated a number of motivations behind its commission. Some arsons conceal other crimes; many are set for revenge, some are set by clinically defined pyromaniacs; some by" heroes" who might want to be firefighters and seek to prove themselves and still others by sexual deviates. But by far the most common motive for arson, according to criminal investigator Charles O'Hara—far more frequent than all the other reasons combined — is economic gain, either from insurance fraud or to get rid of overstocked or obsolescent goods. The incidence of arson fires varies, says O'Hara, between from five to 10% during good business times and as much as 40% when business conditions are unsettled.

Viewed one way, the California Gold Rush migration can be seen as the movement of a great number of customers from all parts of the world to the west coast of North America. Eastern merchants, sensing correctly that great profits were to be made in the goldfield economy of scarcity, shipped massive amounts of goods to California in anything that would float. Not knowing what was needed, they sent anything, everything. If they guessed right and sent wanted items that were scarce, there were fortunes to be made. The economic history of Gold Rush San Francisco is the story of boom and bust: when goods were scarce and miners had full pockets, business was good and fortunes were made on a single voyage. But when, as often happened, several ships showed up bearing the same goods, they were a drug on the market and there were fortunes to be lost.

Eastern shippers sent much of the merchandise on consignment. If goods sold at above cost, the profit was shared by the eastern shipper and the San Francisco commission merchant. If goods sold below cost, or they were lost at sea on the way, or destroyed before they could be sold, the San Francisco merchant was not out of pocket.

According to the *Annals of San Francisco:*:

> The commerce and imports of San Francisco were very great during 1851—too great indeed for profitable trade. . . most kinds of goods were a dead loss to the owner. In the palmy days of '48 and '49, all were purchasers, at any price: now everybody sought to sell, at no matter what sacrifice. . . . Enormous losses were sustained during 1850, and especially1851, by foreign shippers. The commercial people in San Francisco generally acted as agents on commission for others, and didn't often import as merchants on their own account.

Explained the *Alta:* "a vast amount of the property destroyed [in the June 1850 fire] was in the hands of commission merchants and heavy losses will fall on shippers in New York and New England." Vincente Perez Rosales, a Chilean merchant who kept a store in San Francisco until he was burned out and returned home, explained in his memoirs "Nobody, however, was discouraged [by bad business conditions]. Even the lowest-priced items could be given scarcity value by arranging for convenient fires. We saw such fires break out all over town day after day, posing the danger of a general conflagration."

Not all San Francisco journalists were as naive (or deceptive) about the causes of the fires as the establishment *Alta. California Police Gazette* publisher George Wilkes, who was present in San Francisco during all but one of the great fires in the1850s, observed with disgust:

> The warehouses of San Francisco were glutted to the roofs; but the precious commission merchants of San Francisco could not make returns to their Atlantic shippers, and then came the terrible conflagrations which gave them a clear balance sheet . . . "Thieves, thieves, incendiaries'"

shouted the merchants. "Hang them! Hang them!" echoed the ignorant and timid—"they have set our city on fire." And they did seize and hang several poor devils . . . though nobody benefited but the merchants of San Francisco.

The only certain case of a fire being set by an Australian—the disgruntled and ejected lodger Lewis—fell within the personal revenge category of arson motives and seems unconnected to any larger plot to burn down the town.

Whatever the original causes of the fires, their spread can best be explained by the absence of adequate fire protection measures. Large urban fires on a scale incomprehensible to modern city dwellers were a terrifying reality to pre-twentieth century urban Americans, not just in San Francisco but elsewhere. At the beginning of the nineteenth century, no more than 250,000 Americans (5% of the total population) were urban dwellers and the nineteenth-century concept of urban fire service was still rooted in rural and small-town American experience, largely based on volunteer fire companies whose members would drop whatever else they were doing when the fire alarm sounded and hurry together to put it out.

As America became more urban, fire companies were organized in large cities by neighborhood, each functioning independently of the other. The companies might get together to elect a chief engineer, but there was really no coordinating authority to assure that the member companies worked harmoniously to extinguish fires. Competition and conflict, rather than cooperation, were often the rule. As a result, large fires commonly ran out of control.

In August, 1849, one Argonaut wrote from San Francisco to his wife back East:

> I consider the risk alone of fire here exceedingly great. The town is but one great tinder box, and a fire once commenced at the windward side would be certain to burn the whole of it to ash, and this I predict will sooner or later be its fate. The material is all of combustible, very dry pine, with

a large proportion of canvas roofs; no engines, I mean fire engines; no hooks or ladders; and in fact no water (except in very deep wells) available where it might be most required. Many people have their all at stake under these circumstances. Is it not enough to make a prudent man tremble?

Reporting on the December 1849 fire, one early historian observed that "There was no wind but almost all the houses were mere shells, ceiled and walled with cotton cloth papered or painted, and very inflammable. No fire department or fire company existed; and nothing at all effective to stop the flames [was being] or could be done."

In August 1849 a newly organized town government ordered two fire engines from "the states" and a start was made on building cisterns but nothing was done to enact or enforce anything like a building or fire safety code to restrict dangerous practices. Prodded to action by the first major fire—the Christmas disaster of 1849—the town council appointed Frederick Kohler as fire chief in January 1850 and instructed him to organize a fire department. He assigned the three engines in town to three hastily-organized volunteer companies—Empire, Protection and Eureka—manned by former firemen from eastern cities. But as time went by with no more catastrophic fires, people again became absorbed with their personal affairs and interest in completing the formation of the fire department dwindled.

When the May 1850 fire rekindled that interest, the previously designated volunteer companies were formally organized. An ordinance was passed that required citizens to help at fires, authorized excavating artesian wells and erecting cisterns, and required householders to keep a number of water-filled buckets at the ready. While claiming that incendiaries were responsible for the fire, the *Alta* attributed its spread to "the frail and combustible character of the buildings of the city." With the June 1850 fire as further impetus, the fire department was finally formally organized by charter in July, and in September the volunteer firemen elected Kohler chief engineer of their combined companies. Unfortunately, new chief engineer Kohler and his key staff members were away in Sacramento when the May 1851 fire struck, and no coordinated assault was brought to bear on the conflagration.

By the end of 1851, gold seekers who had come to California intending only to wrest a fortune from the golden land and return, decided to stay. In 1852, the city council created a board of fire wardens under the chief engineer of the fire department with authority to inspect all places where fire was used and impose criminal sanctions on those violating ordinances pertaining to fire safety. Within two years—with more than 50 cisterns in place and 950 proud volunteers serving in 13 engine and three hook-and-ladder companies—"no one any longer apprehends any danger from fire to San Francisco," rejoiced the editor of the *Alta*. "The torch has repeatedly been lighted since June 1851," the editor went on, "and there have been the same high winds to fan the flames to greater fury; but, except in isolated cases, the damage done has been trifling. More—aye, *everything*, is due in this connection to the unrivalled 'Fire Department.'"

Six

WHO KILLED FRANCISCO GUERRERO?

"[Francisco Guerrero] was a man of high standing and well regarded by Americans as well as Californians. . . . [He] was murdered in San Francisco in 1851."

—ZOETH SKINNER ELDREDGE

Francisco Guerrero y Palomares was a man who lived comfortably in two very different worlds. The Mexican native came to San Francisco with an immigrant party in the early 1830s at a time when the peninsula was a sparsely populated pastoral wilderness. At his arrival, the mission and Presidio, founded a half century earlier, were in a state of decline.

Most of the Indians, those who had not already succumbed to disease, had been moved to the San Rafael and Sonoma missions. And shortly after Guerrero's arrival, the Presidio garrison was moved to Sonoma, leaving a corporal's guard at San Francisco to protect the 200 or so non-Indian settlers who remained.

The uninhabited plot of land fronting on Yerba Buena Cove, from which the future city of San Francisco would grow, was used by Candelerio Miramontes and his family to raise potatoes for sale to visiting ships' captains. With the departure of the military garrison, a municipal government was established at the Presidio, moving shortly thereafter to the mission. About the same time, William Richardson founded the commercial settlement at Yerba Buena from which American San Francisco would spring.

During the Mexican era, Guerrero took an active part in local governmental affairs and in 1839 he was appointed *juez de paz* (justice of the peace) for San Francisco. In the following years he served as administrator of customs, and in 1845, as the American conquest threatened, was appointed sub-prefect, the chief executive authority in San Francisco. In 1836, the 25-year-old Guerrero acquired title to several level, well watered acres northwest of the mission complex, centered on what is now the line of Market Street at about 14th Street. For 100 cows and $25 worth of goods, he bought the Rancho Laguna de la Merced in 1837, encompassing several thousand acres in the southwestern portion of what is now San Francisco County and the northern portion of San Mateo. He married Josepha DeHaro, daughter of a prominent San Francisco family, and started a family of his own. In 1844 he was granted title to the Corral de Tierra Rancho at Half Moon Bay.

As increasing numbers of foreign immigrants arrived at San Francisco in the late 1830s and early 1840s, most settled on Yerba Buena Cove. Some Mexican settlers maintained dwellings there, but most, like Guerrero, preferred the more pastoral setting around the old mission.

When American forces seized the port of San Francisco in 1846, sub-Prefect Guerrero was out of office. He went to his rancho but came downtown a few days later to turn over his official papers to the new rulers. He seems to have gotten along well with them, for shortly after the conquest, in September 1846, he was made an inspector of elections at the first vote under American rule.

Following the discovery of gold in 1848, San Francisco—at least the settlement on Yerba Buena Cove—exploded into cityhood as the port of entry for men and goods headed for the gold fields. By the end of 1848 the town's population had grown to 2,000 and by a year later it would increase to 20,000. In August 1849 at an election ordered by the American military governor, Guerrero was elected to the post of sub-prefect.

By 1851 San Francisco was a thriving American metropolis of more than 30,000 permanent residents, with a full-blown municipal government organized according to U.S. governmental forms. By then the town had begun to set aside the rude dress and habits of

47

the earlier years, and the crude tents and shanties of 1849 began to give way to more substantial brick buildings, at least in the downtown core. The Mission District itself, though still thinly populated, was used increasingly as a bucolic weekend retreat by harried city workers. And real estate development South of Market was stimulated generally that year with the construction of a wooden plank road along the line of the old Mission Road from Montgomery Street to the mission.

That same summer, with the organization of the Committee of Vigilance, prominent San Franciscans effectively took the administration of justice out of the hands of the regular authorities to deal with what they saw as intolerable amounts of predatory crime. On Saturday afternoon, July 12, 1851, in the midst of the vigilante ascendancy, Francisco Guerrero, in company with Robert Ridley, another San Franciscan from before the conquest, went downtown to conduct some business. Ridley decided to stay there overnight, so Guerrero returned to the Mission District, leading Ridley's bay horse along the recently constructed plank road. At First and Mission streets at about 3:00 p.m., according to one eyewitness account, Guerrero was seen to permit a man, later identified as Francois LeBras, to mount the bay and accompany Guerrero on his ride toward the mission.

The two were next seen by Mrs. Anne Greene, wife of Alderman William Greene, from her house on the west side of the Mission Road between what are now 11th and 12th streets. Mrs. Greene, according to a contemporary press account, "saw Guerrero and another man riding along as if racing, and saw a striking, as though they were whipping each other's horses, and a sort of scuffle." As they raced along the plank road, Guerrero fell from his horse just about in front of Greene's house.

Harry Josephs, another witness, had a different version of the incident. He was riding out from town to the mission in a buggy with a lady, he said, when he observed Guerrero and LeBras pass him from behind racing along the plank road. He claimed to have seen the entire incident and stated unequivocally that LeBras had not struck Guerrero. LeBras was seen by several witnesses later that afternoon in the area of Stockton and Broadway streets, where he tried unsuccessfully to sell the bay horse. He put it up for the night in a nearby stable and when he returned on Sunday morning to pick it up he was arrested by the Vigilance Committee.

That afternoon, Judge Harvey Brown convened a coroner's inquest at the Mansion House Saloon adjacent to the old Mission Church. The Vigilance Committee was conducting its own inquiry into the matter, but at the judge's request, conveyed LeBras to the inquest under a vigilante guard. Charles J. Maysfield told the jury that he was proceeding toward town from the mission on Saturday afternoon when he first observed the two men off the road up on the hill beyond Alderman Greene's house. "As I saw them, there appeared to be some trouble or controversy between them," he testified. "The one on the bay horse turned it toward Guerrero."

Maysfield turned his eyes away for a moment, he said, at which time he heard "some harsh words from the hill." When he he looked back, he saw the other horseman start to run down the hill, with Guerrero after him, plying his spurs and whip. Suddenly about where he passed in front of Greene's house, Mayfield said, Guerrero dropped his arms, leaned forward, and dropped from his horse.

According to the testimony, LeBras reined in his horse after Guerrero fell, and Maysfield told him to go to the mission for help before turning to assist the dying Guerrero. Instead, according to other testimony, LeBras headed back downtown and talked to several other people along the way without making any mention of the incident on the plank road.

Peter Van Winkle, who was on the scene almost immediately, said that he observed blood on the plank road, about six yards short of where Guerrero lay, suggesting that Guerrero was injured before he fell. Charles Maysfield also testified that he later found blood on the top of the hill where he had seen the disturbance begin. Dr. Peter Smith testified that his examination of the deceased showed that Guerrero had received several injuries to the head, consistent with blows from a slung shot or club. Dr. Charles Hitchcock agreed with Dr. Smith's findings and concurred that the injuries were not consistent with a fall from a horse.

The coroner's jury found "the said Guerrero came to his death in consequence of blows inflicted on the head with some deadly weapon by one Francois LeBras...." Press reaction was divided. The *Alta* endorsed the finding of the coroner's jury and was convinced that the death could not have been an accident. *The San Francisco Herald* disagreed. Disregarding the evidence about blood at the top of the hill and on the plank road in advance of where Guerrero fell from his horse, the paper said that the only evidence to support the murder adduced at the coroner's inquest was the testimony of the physicians which, in the end, amounted only to opinion. *The Herald* chose to accept Josephs' version as the definitive account.

By all accounts, LeBras was a most unlikely candidate to commit a violent murder. He was generally believed to be insane. A

6-1 Courtesy of Bill Secrest. Mission Dolores in the 1850s. The open door of the Mansion House Saloon is shown immediately behind the flagpole.

few days before Guerrero's death, he had reportedly shown up at a house in the mission where he stripped off his clothes and demanded to be hanged. Even the *Alta* which supported the coroner's verdict, was forced to admit that "[he] is a diminutive man who looks as though he possessed scarcely the strength or courage to kill a flea or mosquito."

The Vigilance Committee concluded its deliberations with the finding that the evidence did not tend to convict LeBras, and turned him over to the regular authorities. His trial on a charge of murder was on Saturday, November 15, presided over by Judge Delos Lake. Charles Maysfield repeated the testimony he gave at the coroner's inquest. And Alderman Greene came forward to testify that on the day of the death he examined the area and found blood spots running back from the pool where Guerrero lay at least 20 yards up the hill. Alfred A. Green (no relation), another prominent Mission District resident said that he noticed blood spots 5 to 6 feet apart running back 60 yards toward the top of the hill to where the confrontation had first been observed.

A Dr. Lambert testified to fractures to the skull of the deceased, apparently produced by some smooth, heavy weapon like a slung shot. Testimony was also given connecting LeBras to the bay horse and his later attempts to sell it downtown. At this point the prosecuting attorney asked that the case be adjourned until the following Monday morning so that the testimony of Dr. Smith and Dr. Hitchcock could be obtained. Judge Lake objected, saying that the prosecution had not made its case. The prosecution promptly agreed and since the defense offered no evidence, the matter was turned over to the jury. No doubt taking their cue from the judge, the jury returned a verdict of not guilty without leaving the box. LeBras was released.

On the face of it, the trial was indecently rushed. Neither of the attending physicians was called to testify and according to contemporary accounts, neither Mrs. Greene nor Harry Josephs was called

51

at the inquest or trial, where their statements would have been subjected to cross-examination. Reading between such lines as remain, there is a reason for the seeming contradiction in their statements. Several witnesses testified that the original confrontation occurred off the plank road and up the hill behind Greene's house. Josephs, riding toward the mission as he was, conceivably saw only the second half of the incident and, as did others, concluded that he was looking at a simple horse race, and not the pursuit of his assailant by the severely wounded victim of an assault.

Less understandable is Judge Lake's haste in closing off the matter before hearing all the testimony and apparently disregarding the blood evidence found at the site of the original confrontation and on the plank road in advance of the spot where Guerrero fell. There was, and is, the lingering suspicion that there was more to the hasty resolution of the trial than sloppy Gold Rush jurisprudence. Did someone get away with murder? "It is well known that [Guerrero] was most intimately acquainted with the land titles in this portion of California," commented the *Alta* at the time, "and many parties were interested in having him out of the way."

When American forces seized California in 1846, Commodore John Sloat promised to respect Mexican land titles in effect at the time of the conquest. When American immigrants surged in during the Gold Rush, however, they found—for the first time in their movement into the western frontier—that most of the choicest land was already in private hands, granted in large tracts by the Mexican government. As the U.S. Congress argued over whether the new acquisition would be a slave or free state, California went without a government and the new arrivals simply settled or squatted where they chose, setting the stage for decades of wrangling over land titles. Complicating matters was the realization that Mexican officials had made numerous grants of questionable legitimacy during the waning days of Mexican rule.

In March 1851, after California had been admitted to the Union, the U.S. Congress established a Land Commission to sort out California land claims. (Ironically, the newspaper which carried the account of Guerrero's inquest carried the full text of the law establishing the Land Commission.) As an important public official intimately involved in real estate matters and a significant land holder during the late 1830s and early 1840s, Guerrero was uniquely informed about what grants had been made and to whom, and which were legitimate.

One case in which Guerrero's knowledge would have been invaluable was in the Santillan claim. According to the claim, in February 1846, when the demise of the Mexican regime looked likely, Governor Pio Pico granted three square leagues at the mission (which by 1851 included most of the city and county land south of California Street) to Prudencio Santillan, the pastor of the mission church. By the early 1850s, the claim was owned and advanced by Palmer and Cook, a somewhat sleazy but politically well-connected Anglo banking house in San Francisco.

The Santillan claim was confirmed by the land Commission in 1855, and reconfirmed by the U.S. District Court in 1857. It was not until a final appeal to the U.S. Supreme Court in 1860 that the claim was shown to be fraudulent. It is certain that the fraud wouldn't have gone as far is it did, had Guerrero been alive and willing to testify against it. Considering the stakes, people have been murdered for a lot less.

LeBras, if he was truly as insane as described in contemporary accounts, was an unlikely agent in any scheme to kill Guerrero. But Alfred A. Greene, who had testified about the blood at the trial and who the 1856 Vigilance Committee threatened to hang over a land issue, later wrote that LeBras, "who was supposed to be simple-minded," had in fact been used as a tool by land schemers who wanted Guerrero out of the way.

By now the trail to any murder conspirators is cold, but some of the consequences of the events of the time are known. In the end, burdened by the cost of endless litigation, many land-rich but cash-poor Latinos with legitimate claims lost their family holdings. And maybe, just maybe, Francisco Guerrero lost his life as a consequence as well.

Seven
GOING TO JAIL

T he calaboose in Mexican San Francisco was at what would later be the intersection of Clay and Kearny streets, in a building owned by a Swiss immigrant operator of a saloon farther down Clay Street. Both the saloon—not far from the waterline east of Montgomery Street—and the jail were convenient to the crews of the occasional Yankee merchantmen visiting the tiny Mexican port.

Imprisonment was not the preferred post-sentencing disposition in those times. Except for very serious crimes, fines were usually imposed on Mexicans and Anglos convicted of crimes, while Indians were whipped. Jails were used only for temporary confinement. Running a jail in any age is a labor-intensive business requiring round-the-clock staffing, and the widely scattered settlement of the rancho era had to look to other alternatives. Jails were reserved for pretrial incarceration; sentenced offenders were confined only in the most serious cases.

In the 1830s José Antonio Galindo, member of a pioneer *Californio* family and recipient of the first land grant rancho within what would be the city limits of San Francisco, was accused of murdering his cousin. On Galindo's arrest, San Francisco's *juez de paz* (justice of the peace) asked the governor to send the prisoner to San Jose because there were not enough residents in "downtown" San Francisco to maintain a round-the-clock guard on him. "Happy was San Francisco," commented attorney/historian John Dwinelle, "to whom the 'fact' criminal had not yet suggested the word 'jail': less happy, but more wise San José, whose experience had already advanced to the word and fact of 'prison.'"

But even in the pretrial detention facility that did exist in San Francisco, there were complaints of congestion. In February 1846, just before the American conquest, the settlement's senior public official complained to his superior that there were many prisoners in San Francisco awaiting trial and that the *juez de paz* was moving slowly in trying their cases. The judge must have gotten right to work, because by July, shortly after the American conquest, the common room of the empty jail was used to celebrate the first wedding in American San Francisco.

After the American seizure of San Francisco, the town was governed for a time in 1846 under a form of martial law. The marine guard, replaced early in 1847 by a similar detachment from the recently-arrive Regiment of New York Volunteers, used a calaboose next to the Mexican Custom House to hold the occasional arrestee. Still earlier, in 1846, fearing an invasion from the "wilderness" west of Dupont Street by Mexican forces bent on retaking the town, the American authorities had constructed a sturdy blockhouse near Sacramento and Dupont streets, armed with a large gun from the *Portsmouth*. After the war's end in mid-1848, the blockhouse was used by the civilian *alcalde* as a town jail. From the start, there were problems.

The story is told of a prisoner, "Pete from Oregon," who was being held in the blockhouse jail for cutting the tails off some horses, planning to send them to Queen Victoria to whisk the crumbs from her table. One morning Pete showed up at the *alcalde's* office, carrying on his back the door of the town jail to which he was chained, and demanded his breakfast. He was fed and then released on his own recognizance. Though a start was made on acquiring a suitable civil jail for the town, the effort came to nothing. In March 1848, on the occasion of a double escape from the "hoosegow," *The Californian*, one of the town's first two newspapers, lectured the town council to the effect that money spent on filling in the foot of Clay Street (to build a wharf for the benefit of commercial interests) would have been better spent on the erection of a suitable jail.

With the discovery of gold, San Francisco's embryonic justice system was taxed beyond its limits. Early in 1849, by which time the population of the town had grown to about 2,000, a committee of the recently-elected town council reported that the old blockhouse, in which three convicted prisoners were being held, was not only insecure but also "the most awful and filthy den, perhaps ever beheld by any human being and consequently dangerous to the health of persons there." The committee recommended that other quarters be found or the prisoners be released for the sake of their health.

The Gold Rush influx mushroomed and by mid-summer, after the city's population had again trebled, with nearly everyone scrambling to make their pile in the excited boomtown, newly elected *alcalde* John Geary, in his inaugural address to his *ayuntamiento* (town council), reminded them that among its other municipal deficiencies, the town did not have "the means to confine a prisoner for an hour." For a time jailed prisoners were held in the old one-room schoolhouse on Portsmouth Square, by then a multi-use governmental building. But soon the council asked the military governor for a loan to build a town jail. The governor answered that he was not empowered to lend the town money, but that he would give them the $10,000 if they would match the amount and agree to use it to build a court house and a jail. Instead they chose another source. In October 1849, Councilman Sam Brannan reported on the purchase of the brig *Euphemia* for $3,500—from another member of the town council—to serve as a temporary town jail. After alterations that brought its final cost to almost $8,000, the prison brig in San Francisco was tied to the Sacramento Street wharf at Battery Street to house sentenced prisoners.[2]

Early in 1850, the council acquired a city hall and courthouse through the purchase—again from one of its own members—of a

2. It was about this time that the term "brig" became common usage for "jail" among American seamen.

7-1 Author's collection.
The prison brig *Euphemia* moored at the Battery Street wharf. 1849-1851.

large wooden building at the corner of Pacific and Kearny streets. In the police station of the new city hall was a city jail to hold the accused before trial and some convicted prisoners. This was widely held to be adequate to the needs of the town "for years to come," according to the *Alta* of April 3, 1850. But San Francisco's population—a polyglot mélange of adventurers from all corners of the globe—continued to grow so that by the end of 1850 it had increased to 30,000. Not surprisingly, given the heterogeneous potpourri of humanity where the prevailing attitude was "every man for himself," predatory crime began to increase in the latter part of 1850.

And although the police made increased arrests, the courts—

saddled with a procedural system designed for an earlier, simpler time as well as attitudes that failed to grasp the connection between extended court adjournments and backed-up dockets—couldn't process the load. The jail population swelled, and soon the wooden brig and station house jail were overflowing. Prisoners had their own remedy for the overcrowding problem: until a secure prison was finally built, the newspapers treated San Franciscans to almost daily tales of escapes from the town jails. Eventually the revolving-door policy of escape and recapture that resulted from the authorities' inability to contain their charges behind bars was one of the proximate causes for the establishment of the first San Francisco Committee of Vigilance in 1851.

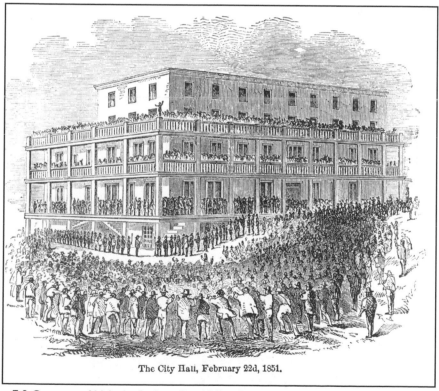

The City Hall, February 22d, 1851.

7-2 Courtesy of Malcolm Barker. City Hall at Pacific and Kearny streets on February 22, 1851. The entrance to the city Jail can be identified by the grilled door at the lowest level. Skilled miners had no trouble digging or auguring their way out of jail.

In 1850, after a county government was formed, construction was begun on what promised to be a secure county jail of brick and stone on the north side of Broadway between Kearny and Dupont. Construction went forward in fits and starts over the next several months, accompanied by charges of judicial misconduct. According to the April 1851 Grand Jury, the members of the Court of Sessions were guilty of "gross and wanton extravagance and unfaithfulness generally in the discharge of their duties" in connection with the construction of the county jail. According to some accounts, as much as $146,000 had been spent on the site but little more than $15,000 worth of work had been done. County Judge Roderick N. Morrison, presiding justice of the Court of Sessions, resigned, but the matter never was cleared up.

And in the meantime, prisoners continued to escape from the existing "wooden sieves." Public indignation over the frequent jail escapes grew; city marshal Malachi Fallon was turned out of office at the end of April by a vote of more than two to one. But in the absence of anything like an adequate jail facility, the change of administration did no good. The escapes continued. On May 1 and 2, attempts to bore through the floor of the Station House were thwarted, but on May 5, five prisoners escaped by making a hole beneath a bed. Then on May 8, more than a dozen prisoners escaped right from under the eyes of their five warders—who were promptly dismissed from the police force. Not quite a week later, the *Alta* reported on the "inexcusable" escape of two men from the prison brig. They had cut a hole through their cell and removed the decking planks on which a guard was supposed to have been posted.

Public attitudes about jail conditions, at least as expressed in the press, were ambivalent. On the one hand, the *Alta* could joke that the town jail was like "the one in Nantucket" where "a prisoner sent the sheriff a formal note that if he didn't keep out the sheep, the prisoner would vacate the premises." But the same paper, a few days later, commented more soberly that the conditions under which 50 people were held in jail were intolerable and inhuman. When heavy rains fell in late November 1850, the basement of the City Hall was flooded to a depth of several inches. And the November grand jury recommended that the prisoners be given blankets and that the marshal be empowered to furnish one substantial meal a week in addition to the usual inmate ration of one pound of bread a day. According to *The San Francisco Courier* in 1850,"our prisons, from the number in them, are regular Calcutta holes."

By early 1851, the six cells in the Station House jail, designed to hold 24 prisoners, contained between 50 and 60 inmates. In the 1850s the young, the old, the alcoholic, the sick and insane—men and women and children shared the same jail. It was said that the noise of one escape was muffled by the screaming of the insane. Criminals as young as 12 and 13 years, awaiting trial on charges of petty theft, were held with the general jail population for as long as four or five months. In August the *Alta* reported that from six to eight prisoners were being held in a cell scarcely large enough for one man and by the following May, the paper reported that 66 prisoners were being held in the Station House cellar under conditions "such as no white man should be incarcerated in."

On the other hand, the sentiment was also expressed that prisoners were being coddled. "We looked in on the gentry in the Station House yesterday," reported the *Alta* on February 27, 1851: "They were smoking, walking about, gathering in groups, chatting, singing, taking siestas in a warm comfortable room, sleeping guarded by kindly officers without fear of being robbed. . . . How many of our honest country men have not one half the comforts of these leprous cancers?" It was this sentiment which seems to have prevailed in late April when the same paper, on the occasion of a mass escape, suggested that all expense of trying criminals would be lost "unless the people take the matter into their own hands and execute summary justice on them."

7-3 Author's collection.   The *Euphemia* as an insane asylum in the mid-1850s.
Located at what is now about Bay Street and Columbus Avenue.

In May 1851, the prison brig *Euphemia,* the temporary expedient of 1849, finally ended its term of service as the town jail. In early April it was sold for $70 to pay a judgment against the city and the prisoners held there were finally moved to the Station House jail. The city reacquired the brig in early June and towed her to North Beach (to the present site Columbus and Bay) where it was employed as a lunatic asylum, thus relieving that pressure from the other jails.

Inmate pressure was reduced further by an act of the State Legislature in April, which awarded a contract to James Estell and Mariano Vallejo to establish a state prison. They converted the bark, *Waban,* to a prison ship and took it later that year to Angel Island with 30 prisoners from the county and city facilities. There they put them to work in a quarry.

In June, 1851, finally fed up with what they considered to be an intolerable amount of crime and the authorities to deal with it, a number of prominent San Franciscans organized the first of San Francisco's famed vigilance committees. It is not surprising that jail escapes declined during the tenure of the Vigilance committee. With a determined group outside the walls waiting for any excuse to hang them without observing all the legal niceties, the inmates no doubt calculated that they were safer in jail.

With the partial completion in June of the Broadway County Jail, for the first time San Francisco finally had a secure place to hold prisoners. By early June, the first 12 prisoners were delivered from the Station House to the new county jail. (And just in time: on June 22, the City Hall and the Station House Jail burned to the ground in the last of the great fires to afflict early San Francisco.) By the end of June, however, the same complaint was heard. The partially completed County Jail building, most of which was still not usable, was congested with 40 prisoners. By September, with funds subscribed by members of the Vigilance committee to finish the work, the jail was put in shape to hold as many as 200 prisoners securely. (With the coming of winter rains, however, the press advised the raising of money to put on a roof.)

From 1852 on, pre-trial prisoners were held in the basement dungeon of the new City Hall Police Station on Kearny and Washington streets. The next year an industrial school was established to get juvenile offenders out of adult jail facilities. In 1872 the Ingleside Jail was established in what was then the hinterlands at the intersection of the San Jose Road and the Ocean House Road. In 1934, the current suburban jail "Bruno," was built in San Bruno and the Ingleside jail was shut down.

Eight

"USE OF FORCE" IN GOLD RUSH SAN FRANCISCO

When a violently drunk Warren Norris punched San Francisco Police Officer James Edgerton in the mouth at the booking counter of the police station on January 24, 1852, the officer disemboweled him with a bowie knife. After a protracted trial, Edgerton was found guilty of manslaughter and was given a four-month jail sentence; he resigned from the force. Apologists for Officer Edgerton no doubt recalled the case of Oliver Dewey two years before, in January 1850, at the height of the Gold Rush excitement. Dewey shot Officer Blackman point blank in the face only to be released by a court a few months later. The officer survived because his assailant's pistol was poorly primed and partially fired. For police officers in boomtown San Francisco, deadly violence was a frequent companion, on both sides of the badge.

A month after the Norris killing, James McDonald, a former "Whig" policeman, who had been removed from office in January after the Democrats took office, stabbed a man to death in a "house" on Dupont Street. Conflicting stories were given during the judicial proceedings but McDonald said he couldn't shed much light on the matter because he was drunk and confused at the time of the incident. Eventually the case fizzled out and when the Whigs regained control of city offices the following fall, McDonald was appointed a captain in the police department. McDonald was acting City Marshal and due to be made permanent at the time of his death in 1856.

All the knife play by officers in those days can be traced to the undependability of nineteenth century firearms, as seen in the Blackman shooting. Though not a part of their regular equipment, most patrolmen carried a sheath knife, "particularly when on morning duty," said an *Examiner* reporter in 1891. "It is during this time he meets many rough characters and frequently finds it necessary to engage in hand to hand fights."

From the beginning, opinion was divided on the use of deadly force by the police. And it didn't do much good to ask the boss. "If a policeman looked to his superiors for support on the question of firearms, he saw only confusion," says police historian David Johnson. "Popular attitudes divided between those who feared that patrolmen would abuse their powers if allowed to carry guns and those who regarded criminals as the greater danger." San Franciscans divided along the same lines. "Several persons have been shot at night by the present police," reported *Alta* on April 20, 1853, "and the consequence is that when a policeman arrests a man, he goes, without a word." "It may be laid down as a rule," the editor said, "that when at night a person whom the policeman wants, runs, and runs too fast for him, the policeman should shoot, and shoot in such a manner that the offender will not run farther, nor shoot back." In such cases, the editor added, "the policeman should be sustained by public opinion and not have a hue and cry raised against him at the very time he should be supported."

Not everyone was so comfortable with the use of police force. A few months later when an officer shot up a "house" on Dupont Street and pistol-whipped several arrestees, Recorder (Police Court Judge) Baker criticized him for his actions and said that he was entirely opposed to the idea of firearms being carried by the police. His idea was that the authorized club was sufficient in most cases as a weapon of defense. Officers were too sensitive, thought the judge, and too ready to misconstrue drunken struggles of a man as resistance to their authority.

In the careless use of force, the officers might have been taking a cue from their own superiors who were as prone to resort to violence as they were. In 1855, City Marshal (Chief of Police) Hampton North challenged Officer John Nugent to a fist fight "in the sand dunes" outside the police office when the officer wouldn't wear his badge as ordered. The next year, Officer (and later Chief of Police) Isaiah Lees pulled a knife on Marshal North, who had ordered his arrest in a disagreement involving the previously mentioned Captain McDonald.

In 1856, the Committee of Vigilance was convened to run criminals out of town and to reform the agencies of municipal government, the police department definitely included. For the next half-century the vigilantes and their philosophical descendants would rule San Francisco. But the reform didn't have much immediate effect on police violence. In June 1858, Ned McGowan, an enemy of the vigilantes who had just posted bail on a charge of criminal libel brought against him by Police Chief James Curtis, left the bail office in the City Hall police station. Officer James Bovee, who was standing by, walked up to McGowan and shot at him point-blank. Fortunately for McGowan, the bullet missed and he was spirited out of town by friends. Bovee was arrested and tried, but let off with a fine. He stayed on the police force.

Nine
ARMING THE POLICE

Saying cops must be able to keep up with crooks' firepower, a Board of Supervisors committee and the Police Commission have come out strongly in favor of arming all San Francisco police officers with semiautomatic weapons.

—*San Francisco Examiner*, December 1, 1994.

In the early days of municipal policing, it was far from certain that police officers should carry firearms at all. According to Sir Robert Peel, upon whose London Metropolitan Police American municipal police departments were modeled, police officers were to be unarmed. And British police officers generally carry no firearms to this day (although in some cases they are now being so equipped to deal with the growing number of armed criminals with whom they are confronted.) It is difficult to get an exact handle on when American police departments began to go armed. As with many controversial policy issues, the bosses couldn't make up their minds, and, in the very violent policy vacuum in which they found themselves in their formative years, officers made the decision on their own. The principal determinant was the long tradition of carrying arms by Americans generally. (At one upper-middle-class assemblage in Philadelphia in 1845, it was discovered that four fifths of the men were carrying firearms.)

And the citizens were not reluctant to use the guns, often against the police. In the late 1850s, four New York City police officers were killed in the line of duty in a single year, and the superintendent of police recommended that his officers be permitted to carry firearms. There was disagreement about the issue, however, and when local politicians failed to act, officers armed themselves. In 1854, Philadelphia's mayor told his officers to buy guns, but a year later the issue was still being hotly debated in the council to no final resolution. In

67

Boston, after an officer was shot to death in the line of duty in 1857, there was some agitation to arm the force. "[I] never knew before," commented the pastor who presided over the officer's funeral, "that the billet of wood which they carry was their only defense against midnight assassins." It was not until 1884 that Boston officers were first issued firearms as part of their regular equipment.

In San Francisco, the issue followed a similar course. Gold seekers heading west to Gold Rush California almost invariably equipped themselves with a pistol to ensure their safety along the way. Once here, they did not dispense with the practice. Wrote a later San Francisco coroner: "There are so many in our midst, and to a great extent (I am sorry to say) among the youth, who do not consider their toilet is complete for an evening's walk or a call upon

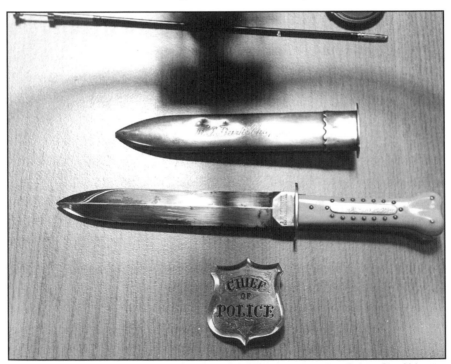

9-1 Courtesy of Robert Chandler. Ceremonial dagger presented to Police Chief Martin Burke by a grateful German community. In an age of uncertain firearms, police officers and "fighting men" regularly supplemented their personal arsenal with large knives.

a friend unless they have a revolver hung to their side."

When some complained in 1853 about indiscriminate shooting by San Francisco police officers, the leading establishment newspaper of the day opined that officers should have no compunction about shooting fleeing suspects. A few months later, though, the recorder (police court judge) chided officers for being too free with the use of force. Furthermore, he continued, he was "entirely opposed to the general system of firearms being carried by the police." "They [are] allowed to carry a stick," he said, "which in most cases was a sufficient weapon of defense." Still the issue was not officially resolved. When the first police rule book was published the same month, it specified when and under what conditions an officer could use force, but made no mention of firearms.

The debate continued. In 1858 The *National Police Gazette* editorialized that police officers were beginning to recognize the folly of going armed, saying that "the plan they adopted to coerce rogues and rowdies into submission, has had a contrary effect, and instead of overawing them, has driven them to deeds of desperate daring, as they are now using the very same weapons most effectively against the policemen" Nonetheless, Chief Martin Burke explicitly resolved the issue in January 1859 by requiring that "all regular officers shall, when on duty, carry a large sized revolver and baton, also a whistle." To allay the concerns of those who feared excesses, he added that "Officers are especially cautioned against using pistols except in cases of emergency."

Ten

FREEDOM OF THE PRESS

On Saturday, February 13, 1858, Police Chief James Curtis and several of his officers confiscated all copies of the next day's issue of Ned McGowan's *Phoenix* newspaper "as unfit for circulation," under the provisions of the city's first obscenity law which had been passed the previous day with the paper in mind. A few days later, when McGowan was in a City Hall office after posting bail on a charge of criminal libel brought by Curtis, Officer James Bovee walked up to the editor and fired at him at point-blank range. Fortunately for McGowan, the shots missed.

The trouble began when the Vigilance Committee of 1856 got together "to cleanse" the town of what it saw as corrupt, mostly Democratic, public officials and their criminal hangers-on. McGowan, a Democratic Party stalwart, happened to be nearby when County Supervisor James Casey shot crusading newspaper editor James King and triggered the vigilante eruption. The vigilantes thought McGowan had engineered the shooting, and while they went about hanging and banishing their political enemies in San Francisco that summer, they also chased McGowan around the state with the clear intention of hanging him if they could catch him.

When the committee disbanded in August, after making sure that the government in San Francisco would be safely in the hands of its political arm, the People's Party, McGowan returned to the Bay Area, to Napa, where he founded the *Phoenix* to expose the vigilantes as the hypocritical scoundrels he thought them to be. In language to make a modern tabloid editor blanch, McGowan set about flaying his vigilante enemies. One of his favorite targets was Chief Curtis, who, if accounts are to be believed, had good reason to fear McGowan's pen.

Curtis, San Francisco's first post-vigilante police chief arrived in

1848, having left Boston to avoid charges that he debauched his own daughter, according to writer Helen Holdredge. He was a member of the 1851 Committee of Vigilance until his past became known. In 1852, Curtis became involved with Liz Moore, a prostitute he "rescued" from a local brothel and set up in a place of her own. The future chief of police, it was said, was not above accepting part of the proceeds for Moore's other "amours."

10-1 Courtesy of Dr. Albert Shumate. Police Chief James Curtis in his Civil War uniform, taken shortly after his tenure as chief.

The Second Vigilance Committee was less discriminating about its membership than its predecessor, and Curtis was accepted with open arms. In fact, he served for a time as the committee's director of police, and in the first election after the vigilance uprising, he was elected chief of police on the People's Party ticket in the fall of 1856. Curtis was still living with "retired bawd" Moore, according to writer Curt Gentry, and it was an exposé about their relationship and the charge that the former prostitute had contributed $3,500 to secure his nomination as chief of police that McGowan published in the *Phoenix* and Curtis confiscated.

After the seizure, the paper continued publishing for a few issues until, after the shooting in City Hall, McGowan closed it down and left the state, fearing, probably correctly, that he might not live to get a fair trial in the courts dominated by his enemies. In the next election, though, the People's Party bypassed Curtis as their candidate for chief and selected Martin Burke, who won the election.

The charges of misbehavior ascribed to Curtis seem out of character with what is known about the rest of his career. Although there is reason to question the veracity of some of McGowan's attack journalism, "after removing the usual patent allegations of race, religion, and physical malfunctions, a surprising number of McGowan's basic charges were elsewhere verified," says Gentry. Whatever the case, Curtis was out of office, and though Bovee was convicted for the attempted assassination of McGowan, he remained on the police force.

Eleven

DUE PROCESS

This morning about 10 o'clock. . . the thieves and vagrants in the Station House were marched out, for the purpose of being shown to the citizens. They were handcuffed and tied, two by two, about six feet apart, to a thick rope, and were taken from the City Hall [at Kearny and Washington] to the public Plaza [Portsmouth Square] . . . one end of the rope was then tied to the Plaza flagstaff, and the other to the iron fence, and the regiment was then kept there guarded by officers and looked at by a constant changing crowd.

—SAN FRANCISO BULLETIN, AUGUST 10, 1857

When municipal police departments were established in nineteenth century cities, they were modeled roughly on Sir Robert Peel's concept of "preventive" patrol. The idea was that uniformed officers would patrol visibly on fixed beats to deter those inclined to commit crimes. Those few who did try to pull something off, it was thought, would be quickly apprehended. The original projectors believed that street crime could be virtually eliminated, if only enough officers were put on patrol.

As a practical matter, no municipality has ever had a large enough tax base to provide enough preventive patrols to eliminate crime by their mere presence. "It would require an increase to the Police Force to an extent which our Common Council could never be brought to sanction," said one observer in 1854, "to amount to anything like complete *protection* of our city. . . . " "It would, in fact require the posting of a Policeman in front of almost every house," he said, "and the *surveillance* that would necessarily result over every citizen . . . would be an annoyance, greater, even, than the evils from which he would be protected."

When the limitations of preventive policing were recognized, the idea of a detective police came under consideration. Prior to the development of regular police forces, crime was not so much looked upon as an offense against the community but rather more as a difficulty between two individuals. In most cases it was up to a victim of a crime to put together a case, secure warrants, and serve them himself, sometimes with the help of a constable who operated on a fee basis.

By the turn of the nineteenth century, a class of constables evolved—"thieftakers"—who, for a fee, usually a portion of stolen goods, would track down criminals. These detective constables would frequent the dives and brothels where criminals tended to congregate. They would develop "snitches" or "stool pigeons" among vice operators and petty crooks, who, for a small fee or promise of immunity from the consequences of their own offenses, would help the detectives with their cases. Very often, when major offenders where finally caught, the case would not be brought to court at all but instead would be resolved by splitting the loot among the victim, the thief, and the constable. The courts did not look too closely at these practices and the victim took what he could get on the theory that half a loaf was better than none. With the adoption of regularly paid municipal police detectives, the system evolved into a semi-formal system of rewards paid by crime victims to spur detectives along in their work.

By mid-century, some large cities began to supplement their preventive patrols with publicly employed detective police whose task it was to "ferret out" criminals. Boston seems to have been the first American city to have employed detective officers in 1846; New York and other eastern cities followed suit sometime later. According to the new departmental configuration, patrol officers would continue to prevent crime by visibly patrolling the streets and making arrests for crimes occurring in their presence. The detectives were expected to follow up to identify offenders and to do the post-arrest evidence collection necessary to secure convictions.

The detectives themselves, according to one contemporary description, were "ordinarily shrewd, active, and courageous men, of long experience in police duty, who have learned the habits and resorts of criminals, and can tell very nearly where to lay their hands on any particular rascal when he is wanted."

The detectives were "able to lay their hands on any particular rascal" at will because from the beginning they had adopted some of the less palatable practices of the thieftakers. The simple fact is that those who most often know the most about crime are criminals themselves. To get at this information, detective officers used stool-pigeons who kept them informed about what was going on in the criminal underworld in return for a "pass" in some case in which they were themselves involved.

The police force established in San Francisco in 1849 was strictly a preventive force, designed to patrol the streets visibly to prevent crime and to make arrests as possible. But by early 1851, as crime was seen to increase, some began to rethink the department's role. In June 1851, the editor of the *Alta* , commented on the release without hearing of "a notorious burglar and bad character," who had been let go even though evidence clearly tied him to the crime. "It is often the case," the editor complained, "that against prisoners thus arrested on suspicion there is no immediate available evidence; but it should be the duty of some one, when notorious thieves are thus arrested, to hunt up evidence and convict the suspected persons, if guilty."

Almost two years later, in February 1853, after a spate of robberies, some of which had gone unsolved, the editor of the *Alta* brought the subject up again. "In connection with this affair," he wrote, "we would suggest the organization of a small 'detective police' of about six men here, who would be selected with the greatest care as to their integrity and capacities." Several months later, in October 1853, according to surviving payroll records, the first detective element was introduced into the department. Almost from the start there was criticism that the detectives resorted to the use of stoolpigeons to get information, and that they would do their work only if rewards were provided.

"The officers of justice [in San Francisco] do not consider themselves under any obligation to ferret out crimes, and punish them," commented the same 1854 observer, "they will not hunt out testimony and summon witnesses. . . . They will be mere machines, of which some private person must turn the crank and feed them, or else they will do nothing."

At the heart of any detective system is the need for a regular means of identifying repeat criminals so that detectives, patrol officer and the public at large, for that matter, can recognize them. One way to circulate information about known criminals in early San Francisco was to put them to work on public projects in a chain gang so that potential victims would be able to identify them later.

A simpler way to identify criminals was provided with the introduction of the daguerreotype camera. From early on, photographic likenesses, compiled in "mug books" of known criminals, were a valuable asset in the detective's arsenal of weapons to fight crime. Then as now they were used by detectives to familiarize themselves with the faces of known criminals or to show to victims in an effort to identify unknown assailants. Photographic mug shots were first employed by the San Francisco police in 1857 by Chief James Curtis, who paid for the images out of his own pocket. It might have been the drain on his personal funds that caused him to suspend the practice temporarily later in the year and revert to earlier methods of identifying criminals to the public.

About the same time detective officers were introduced, police practitioners began to rethink the concept of preventive patrol. In addition to the inability to provide sufficient patrols to cover an entire city, there were limitations to the essentially reactive nature of the process. "An organized band of thieves can," said one observer, "with little difficulty, make themselves acquainted with every member of the Police, ascertain precisely those who are assigned to any particular beat, and by placing a proper watch. . . can pursue their objects without fear of interruption from that quarter." More proactive measures were called for.

So "crime prevention" evolved from simple patrols which, it had been hoped, would prevent crime before it occurred, into proactive efforts directed at those considered most likely to commit crime—the "dangerous classes," in the usage of the time. It was common practice for detectives to keep intense pressure on known criminals and potential criminals in the hope that they would go elsewhere. "Much of the time and labor of the officers," reported Chief Martin Burke in an early annual report, "is devoted to the prevention of crime, by the following up of criminals, and by keeping so strict a sur-

11-1. Courtesy of Bill Secrest.   Isaiah Lees, nonpareil detective. Appointed to the department in 1853, Lees was soon assigned as a detective. He was appointed captain of detectives in 1859 and served in that capacity for most of the rest of the century, becoming involved in every major criminal investigation and forging an international reputation. He was appointed chief of the department in 1897 and served until 1900.

veillance over them, that they prefer leaving the city to submitting to it."

In August 1857, Chief of Police William Curtis set off a huge flap when he rounded up a number of known criminals, tied them together like "onions on a string," according to one contemporary account, and paraded them on Portsmouth Square so that the citizenry would know who they were. Over the next several days, the newspapers were full of acrimonious debate about the chief's tactics. An attempt was made in the Board of Supervisors to censure him. On the one hand were those who considered his methods a reversion to barbaric practices of the past and called for his resignation. Others who defended the chief's display of "notorious scoundrels. . . to show them to the citizens, so that they might be known and guarded against," regretted only the fact that he had rounded them up from the streets and at the time of their display there were no charges against them.

Constitutional considerations aside, the chief was vindicated by ensuing events. Within two days, one of the men paraded on Portsmouth Square was picked up after a man who had seen him there identified him as the perpetrator of a residential burglary. A couple of days later two others who had been put on display were picked up in the commission of a nighttime hot prowl burglary in a rooming house. That's all well and good, commented the editor of *The Spirit of the Times*, who offered a less controversial way of getting information about criminals before the public. "The best plan to make public the faces of *known* burglars and thieves," the editor said, "is that of taking their daguerreotypes . . . and keeping them in the Police Office where on application to the Chief of Police any citizen can inspect them if he so desires." Thereafter, photographing criminals became a regular practice in the San Francisco Police Department and has continued as an important part of the detective function ever since.

In later years there would be other technological advances to help detectives in their work. Late in the nineteenth century, the Bertillion method of body measurements was hailed as a definitive way to identify people. Early in the twentieth century it was replaced by fingerprinting (even now being supplemented by DNA comparisons which make identifications even more certain). Many, if not most, of the major cases worked on by San Francisco police detectives were solved by patient legwork, a bit of luck, and intelligent analysis of the clues. But throughout, and until relatively recently, the old tried and true methods of getting information remained in place. Over the years there would be periodic press exposés of the system of rewards, the stoolpigeon system, and the detectives' heavy-handed methods of "crime prevention," but the crime control practices developed in the 1850s were to continue for more than a century as more or less the standard practice of the detective police.

In the end, Supreme Court decisions would call such practices into question. (For all of that, "trading little ones for big ones" — sometimes with the involvement of the courts, sometimes not — continues as an essential element of bringing criminals to justice. Whoever coined the maxim that it's best not to watch sausage being made if one wants to continue enjoying it, could well have had detective policing in mind.)

And, if asked to justify the practices they used, the old-time detectives would probably point to the fix we now find ourselves in. One common method used by nineteenth-century crime analysts to measure the effectiveness of a police department was to compare the amount of property recovered against that reported stolen. In 1860, Chief Burke was able to report proudly that his department, using the detective methods then in fashion, recovered 81% of the property reported stolen. Furthermore, he claimed, "No crime of any magnitude has gone undetected." As might be expected, the recovery rate fell off as the city grew in size and complexity. By 1865, Chief Burke reported a recovery rate for lost and stolen property of

63%. By the early 1870s, the rate of recovery had declined further to 40%. And in 1956, when detective practices began to change in response to a series of court decisions which forbade the old practices, the department recovered 10% of property reported stolen ($114,000 of the $1.2 million).

The figures comparing stolen to recovered property are still collected in department crime statistics, though understandably they are no longer highlighted as they were in the past. Despite all the wondrous technological advantages of modern times, in one recent year, during which $2.2 million in goods (not counting automobiles) was reported stolen, an infinitesimal $44,000 worth was recovered. In response to our criticism of the methods they used, old-time detectives might reply that they did a better job of "getting the goods."

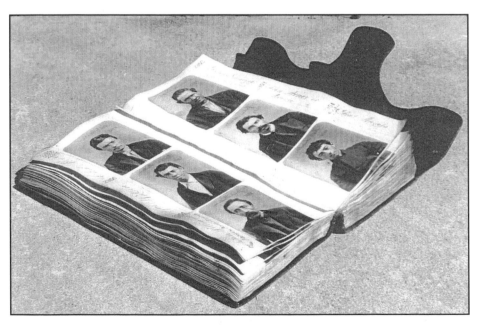

11-2 Courtesy of Bill Secrest. San Francisco Police mug book from the 1870s.

Twelve
ARCHY LEE

The Legislature having passed a bill prohibiting the future immigration of free negroes (sic) to this State, and requiring those already here to register their names . . . the negroes have become highly incensed, and have held meetings at which was discussed the propriety of the colored people withdrawing in a body from the State. . . .

— SAN FRANCISCO BULLETIN, APRIL 1858

The proposed legislation that would have excluded African-Americans from California in 1858—and the threat by African-Americans to leave the state en masse—grew out of the peculiar racial, social, and political climate of the period. But the issue was drawn into sharp relief by the case of Archy Lee. Following the seizure of California from Mexico in 1846, while the U.S. Congress debated whether the new territory should allow slavery, Californians convened a constitutional convention in Monterey in late 1849. According to the constitution fashioned there, slavery was to be prohibited in the new state—not out of any strict sense of racial amity, but rather to prevent Southern entrepreneurs from working the placers with gangs of African-American slaves to the disadvantage of individual white miners. California was admitted to the Union the following year as a free state.

In mid-1857, a young Mississippian named Charles Stovall, accompanied by a family slave named Archy Lee, came to California and settled in Sacramento. When young Stovall decided in January 1858 to send his 18-year-old slave back to Mississippi, Lee had other ideas. Stovall had Lee arrested and lodged in the Sacramento City Jail. Later the same month, County Court Judge Robert Robinson freed the prisoner in response to a petition for habeas corpus filed by African-American supporters, at which point Lee was promptly rearrested on the order of a State Supreme Court justice. A majority of that court, while agreeing with the legal points in favor of Lee's freedom, found that, as Dr. Rudolph Lapp put it, "since Stovall was such a young and inexperienced man, and since this was the first time that the court had faced such a case, the court could show kindness and give Lee back to Stovall and slavery." Stovall took possession of Lee and prepared to return to Mississippi.

Word had it that Stovall intended to take ship from San Francisco with his prize. The African-American community in the city mobilized to stop him by all legal means. With a writ of habeas corpus for Lee from San Francisco County Judge T.W. Freelon in hand, and a kidnapping warrant for Stovall, shifts of African-Americans patrolled the wharves for any sign that Stovall was attempting to spirit Lee aboard an outbound steamer. On March 5 the steamer *Orizaba* left from the Vallejo Street wharf, and unbeknownst to Stovall's supporters on board, the ship also carried San Francisco Police Officer Isaiah Lees and a deputy sheriff with the judge's order.

As the steamer made its way toward the gate, a boat was seen to approach from Angel Island. As the small craft drew alongside, Stovall's confederates on the steamer, who by now were aware of the officers' presence, tried to warn it off. Too late. Officer Lees leaped into the boat "at the risk of jumping through her," seized Lee, who he passed up to his partner on the steamer, and placed Stovall under arrest on the kidnapping warrant. At that point things got tense, but Lees hustled Lee into a whitehall boat brought along for the purpose and rowed with him to the Market Street wharf where he was greeted by a large crowd of cheering African-Americans. Stovall was quickly discharged on the kidnapping charge. When Lee was brought before Judge Freelon on March 17 the court set him free. But again Lee was rearrested right in the courtroom, this time on a charge of violation of the Fugitive Slave Act of 1850, to be brought before U.S. Commissioner George Pen Johnston.

As Lee was escorted back to jail by a U.S. Marshal to await his hearing, tempers ran high and fighting broke out but a riot was averted. On April 14, Commissioner Johnston determined that since Lee had not escaped from his master in Mississippi, the fugitive slave law didn't apply, and set him free once more. Not trusting to the finality of white men's decisions, Lee didn't stick around for the celebration but hightailed it into the sand dunes to await any further developments. Conditions settled down then, and the African-American exclusion act never did pass. But Lee joined a large number of African-Americans who moved to British Columbia voluntarily after his ordeal. He returned to California following the Civil War and died of illness in Sacramento in 1873 at the age of 34.

Thirteen
STREET JUSTICE

O n January 6, 1859, Officer George Rose tried to arrest John Croger "for insulting women on Pacific Street." Croger, "a desperate character when in liquor," according to a contemporary news account, resisted violently. Later there would be controversy about his treatment but there was no disagreement that Croger was generally a bad hat. A year earlier, Croger had stabbed at Officer Isaiah Lees in a dance hall on Pacific Street but escaped before he could be arrested. In March he had cut another African-American man with a razor, but the man left town before he could testify. Croger was fined $40 shortly thereafter "for beating a poor old negro woman." A few months before his run-in with Officer Rose, he had shot at a man on the Presidio Road and hit him in the head with a brick, for which he was sentenced to four months on the chain gang. His term expired on January 6, 1859, and within a few hours he was drunk and insulting female pedestrians when Officer Rose happened upon him.

The arrestee was more than the officer could handle, and passers-by declined the officer's request for help. Finally, Officer John McKenzie showed up and helped get the resisting prisoner to the city jail where again he resisted, according to officers' reports, until Officer John Durkee settled the matter with a well-placed kick. Later, as Croger was being removed from the "dark cell," he made a dash for an open street door and was returned to his cell only after another desperate struggle, according to officers. A non-police witness who happened to be in the jail at the time saw things differently and filed charges of excessive force before the police commission, which, after hearing testimony, dismissed the charge with the comment that "the officers were not restricted to use exertion simply for self-defense but had the right to employ the force necessary to disable the prisoner in order to secure him."

The *Alta* chose the opportunity to criticize the bystanders for not coming to Officer Rose's aid in the first place. *The California Police Gazette*, however, claimed that the Police Commission's prosecution of the officers had been of no avail "for by swearing in favor of each other [the officers] succeeded in having the charge dismissed." The latter version was given support when former Police Captain E.J. Folsom and the two officers assigned to the prison at the time came forward after their removal from office. Croger had indeed made a break for the street door, they said, but was being returned to his cell peacefully when detectives Lees, George Johnson, and Jake Chapelle began to beat the unresisting prisoner. One of the dismissed officers said that he had "informed Chief [Martin] Burke of the affair, "but he did not appear to wish to hear it, and treated me rather coldly." The chief later claimed that the officer had not

INHUMANITY.

12-1 Author's collection. "Inhumanity." From the *California Police Gazette* July 23, 1859 showing police officers beating John Croger. The text says, "The above cut represents several of the favorite policemen in their efforts to show their authority. A negro has been arrested, and when taken to the Station House he was kicked and bruised in a terrible manner. A citizen made complaint against him (sic), which was of no avail, for by swearing in favor of each other they succeeded in having the charge dismissed."

spoken to him about the case.

It would have been difficult to get to the bottom of the case at that point because Croger had been taken from the jail and placed aboard an outbound sailing ship—a common crime prevention technique of the time. There were intimations of racism in Croger's treatment at the time, but it would be difficult to support such a contention against Isaiah Lees, who a year earlier, had put his life on the line to rescue Archy Lee.

And month after the Croger arrest, detectives Lees and Johnson arrested another black man, Moses Tate, for brutally beating to death a white man named Albinius Billman. That the officers managed to imprison Tate without abusing him suggests that Croger's treatment had more to do with his behavior than his race.

In the end, the whistleblowers were out of a job, and Isaiah Lees was appointed captain in Folsom's place. Lees would go on to an illustrious career as captain of detectives for most of the rest of the century, capping his career in 1897 with his appointment as chief of police. Whatever the merits of the case against the officers, San Francisco was well served by Croger's departure, however irregular. A year later he was hanged in the Seychelles Islands by a ship's captain for murdering the second mate on the ship on which he had been banished.

And nineteenth-century San Franciscans seemed satisfied, on the whole, to trade a little due process for a bit of order on the streets. Officer Durkee, the one who had delivered the telling kick, left the department soon after the incident to take other city employment. On the occasion of his death several decades later, his obituarist commented that Durkee was well known in the 1850s as "a brave and fearless policeman." However, continued the obituary, "he was of too peaceful a nature for the duties of the office."

Fourteen

SEX, RACE AND HOMICIDE IN OLD SAN FRANCISCO

Thus ends the farce. But a few weeks since, the whole country was aroused against the perpetrators of one of the most diabolical murders ever recorded, and three persons were arrested . . . . The finale to the whole thing is that one of the parties, a poor, miserable ignorant Negro, has been sent to San Quentin, and the others have been discharged.

—CALIFORNIA POLICE GAZETTE, MAY 14TH, 1859.

In the early morning hours on Sunday February 20, 1859, recently wed Albinius Billman, 28, and his young wife, Mary Ann, 23, were startled awake by a loud knocking on the rear door of their house on Jessie Street near First. When Billman answered the knocking, he was viciously assaulted with a cart rung taken from a nearby wagon. As police pieced things together, they learned that there had been a card game at the Jessie Street residence the night before, attended by the Billmans, a man named James Magness and another named Hayden. Moses Tate, an African-American and sometimes servant to the Billman family, was also present to care for Mrs. Billman's four-year-old daughter.

The game broke up at about 10:00 p.m. and the parties went their separate ways. Mrs. Billman and her husband went to bed; Magness went to his boat, tied up at Mission Wharf a few blocks away; and Tate and Hayden walked up to Sansome Street and then on to Pacific where they parted company. Some cases stink right from the start, and this was one of them. Police suspicions were aroused by Mrs. Billman's curious behavior immediately following the attack. With a maniac presumably loose in the neighborhood, she ran upstairs to her neighbor's apartment and climbed into bed, leaving her four year old daughter alone below.

At 5:00 am, police aroused Magness at his boat, and at 7:00 a.m.

Moses Tate showed up at the Jessie Street house of his own volition. Tate told officers that after separating from Hayden, he had visited a few night spots before going to his lodging house, where he was in bed before midnight. Detectives Isaiah Lees and George Johnson escorted Tate to his lodging house where the landlord remembered things somewhat differently. When Tate first showed up at about 2:00 a.m.—not midnight as he claimed—he was refused a room because of unpaid rent, the landlord said. Tate departed and returned after what seemed about a half hour, offering an iron pot (which turned out to have been taken from the murder scene) in lieu of room rent. The detectives booked Tate into City Prison on a charge of attempted murder.

As they probed farther, detectives discovered that Mrs. Billman had been born Mary Ann Tate in Gurdon, Clark County, Arkansas, in 1836. She had been married there in 1852 to a man named Richard Magness with whom she had a child. Af-ter Magness' untimely death a few years later, she headed for California with her little daughter and a family slave named Moses, who, as was the custom of the time, was given the family's surname as his own. In January 1858, they arrived in San Francisco, where things didn't go well, and Mary Ann, according to a contemporary news account, "became an inmate in several houses of prostitution." In October 1858, James Magness, her deceased husband's brother, found her working in a brothel on Pike Street (now Waverly Place).

14-1 Courtesy of Bill Secrest. Moses Tate. 1859 police mug shots had not yet achieved the uniformity found in later years.

Magness took his sister-in-law out of the brothel and set her up in a lodging house at Vallejo and Dupont streets in North Beach. Shortly thereafter, Magness introduced Mary Ann to Albinius Billman, his partner in a coasting schooner. On Christmas Day 1858, Billman and Mary Ann Magness were married, and a week later she and her daughter moved in with him at the Jessie Street house.

The police theory was that the crime was gotten up between Magness and Mrs. Billman to do away with her husband for his money, and that Tate was the instrument of their plan. Albinius Billman died of his injuries at 7:00 p.m. Sunday evening. Police then arrested Mary Ann Billman and James Magness for murder, and rebooked Tate on the more serious charge. To prevent the arrestees from comparing notes, Tate was placed in the "dark cell," usually reserved for obstreperous prisoners, while Magness and Mary Ann Billman were placed in separate parts of the main jail.

After 24 hours in the dark cell, Tate told officers he was ready to tell all. After Mrs. Billman left the North Beach house to join Billman on Jessie Street, Tate told Detective Johnson, he had twice carried messages from her to a man there named John Kelly. On one occasion, said Tate, Kelly offered him $800 to put strychnine in Albinius Billman's food. At about midnight on February 19, Tate continued, he ran into John Kelly and another man named Michael Kelly, at Broadway and Dupont streets. At their request, he claimed, he accompanied them to the Jessie Street address to point out the Billman house to them. When Billman answered the door to their knock, said Tate, Michael Kelly beat him with the cart rung. Police promptly arrested John and Michael Kelly.

At the coroner's inquest , Tate repeated his story that it had been the Kellys who did the killing, adding that it was their idea for him to pick up the iron pot so that the murder would look like a robbery gone wrong. John Kelly testified that he had indeed known Mrs. Billman at his rooming house. Along with everyone else, he said, he "thought she was a proper lady" until she invited him into her bed. On Christmas, he continued, she returned from a carriage ride with two men and informed him that she had just been married.

That didn't prevent her from spending her wedding night with him, however. She moved out a week later.

Later, Moses Tate, whom he had never seen before, showed up at Kelly's with a note from the now Mrs. Billman saying that she would call on him that afternoon. She told Kelly, he said, that her husband was stingy and asked him for money. He had none to give her. She visited him in his rooms once more, he testified, and told him that she intended to get $6,000 out of her husband, and then return with her brother-in-law to Arkansas. That was the last time he ever saw her, he testified. Kelly also admitted that he and Michael Kelly had indeed run into Tate on Broadway on Saturday night February 19, but said that after a short conversation, he and Michael had gone home and were in bed by 1:00 am.

Tate's story was soon seen for the red herring that it was, and the Kellys were released, no doubt wiser to the ways of a certain type of woman. Other witnesses, mainly neighbors who testified to events immediately following the assault, also took the stand. The Grand Jury indicted Moses Tate, Mary Ann Billman, and James Magness as principals to the murder of Albinuis Billman. Tate's trial began on March 21, 1859 before Judge Myron Norton. Witnesses testified as they had in the coroner's inquest. The most damning testimony was given by Henry Anderson, an African-American who lived immediately adjacent to the Billman house. Anderson related that as he was returning to his own home at about 2:30 a.m. on Sunday morning, he had seen Tate, who he knew as "Arkansaw," coming out of the alley next to the Billman house alone.

But when the prosecution tried to introduce Tate's earlier statements about his involvement, the defense objected. Tate's incarceration in the dark cell, his attorneys contended, constituted coercion, or an inducement to make statements against his own interest in hope of bettering his condition. Detective Johnson denied offering any inducements but did admit the he would not spend 24 hours in the dark cell "for all the money in San Francisco." Chief of Police Martin Burke, called by the defense as a hostile witness, offered as proof that the dark cell wasn't such a bad place the fact that Tate had survived it. The court decided that Tate's admissions to the police—and related testimony at the coroner's inquest—were not admissible. Nonetheless, after deliberating for two hours, the jury returned a verdict of murder in the second degree against Moses Tate.

Mary Ann Billman's trial began in Judge Norton's court on Monday, May 2. Among the first witnesses was the physician who attended Albinius Billman after the attack. He described how Mary Ann had coldly insisted that her dying husband be taken to a hospital so he wouldn't bleed on her bedding. And when asked for rags to make bandages, she only grudgingly surrendered some of her husband's shirts.

On the occasion of Tate's conviction for second-degree murder, the editor of the San Francisco *Bulletin* was puzzled along with everyone else. "The verdict is manifestly unjust, either to the people or the prisoner," he said. Given the circumstances of the crime, it had to be first -degree murder or nothing. In our own time, such an outcome would be easy to understand. Tate's conviction on a lesser charge would lead to a "plea bargain" resulting in the actual killer's testimony against those who put him up to it. But, according to the law then in effect, that couldn't happen.

At the Constitutional Convention at Monterey in 1849, at which the State Constitution was written, delegates specifically excluded slavery from the new state. But the provision had more to do with fears of economic competition from gangs of imported Southern slaves than any sense of racial altruism. For when the first State Legislature devised a criminal code in 1850, testimony of "Indians, Negroes and mulattoes" was specifically excluded in cases involving whites. So, no matter what the inducement, Tate could not have testified against his former mistress. And it wasn't just Tate's testimony that was excluded. In earlier proceedings, Henry Anderson had established the timetable which placed Mary Ann Billman's first cry for help an hour after he saw Tate in the alley. Anderson's testimony would have shown that Mary Ann had delayed raising the alarm to give the actual killer time to flee. But, as an African-American, Anderson's testimony was suppressed also.

The prosecution had to make do with Ann Smith, a white woman living several houses away from the Billmans on Ecker Alley, who testified that she heard people talking in the yard—possibly a woman—and heard a child cry, before it was hushed and taken away. To bolster its case, the prosecution called Catherine Allen, who claimed to have worked with Mary Ann Billman in several brothels. Allen went to visit Mrs. Billman in jail, she testified, and Mary Ann as much as admitted to her that she and Magness had the whole deal cooked up even before she married Billman to get at his money and move back to Arkansas.

Catherine Allen also described how she had once found Mary Ann in a compromising position with Moses Tate, and when she tried to intervene, Mary Ann had pulled a knife on her. In his testimony at the coroner's inquest, Tate admitted that he had had a "criminal intimacy" with Mrs. Billman, "previous to her marriage, but never in this country." The jury was given the case at 6:00 p.m. on May 5. They deliberated all night and then returned to the court for further instructions. The foreman asked the court if they could convict the defendant as an accessory after the fact—in other words, not for instigating or actually committing the crime but for helping the perpetrator to cover up the fact afterward. The court ruled that since the charge of being an accessory after the fact was not included in the indictment, they could not so find.

The jury apparently didn't think much of Allen's testimony: after deliberating for more than 26 hours, they returned a verdict of not guilty. "When the prisoner was taken out of Court," commented the editor of the *Bulletin*, "she absolutely danced with delight to think how she escaped." The press was vociferously outraged at the outcome. Writing about the case much later, by then Captain of Detectives Lees concluded that juries in 1859 were just not ready to convict a woman of murder.

But given the law as charged to them, and the known facts of the case, the jury verdicts in both cases comport with the evidence they were able to consider. It's fairly obvious from the web of circumstantial events that Mrs. Billman most likely wanted to see her husband dead. But that doesn't mean she actually planned the murder as it happened. From the rest of what we know about the calculating Mary Ann Billman, it's hard to conceive of how she would have become involved in such a poorly planned and executed crime. What probably happened is that Tate, knowing of his former mistress' general desire to do away with her husband, took it upon himself to get the job done.

There had been some drinking at the Saturday night card game, and when he left the Billman house, according to Magness' testimony at the coroner's inquest, Magness had given Tate 50 cents to pay for lodging for the night. Instead of going home after parting company with Hayden, Tate went to a Broadway Street saloon, where he drank up the money. Then he went to his lodging house, where he was refused a room because he was broke. It was there, half drunk and broke, with no place to stay, that the brainstorm may have come to him to return to Jessie Street.

Perhaps he was just looking for a place to sleep—it would have been too cold to sleep out-of-doors in February—or maybe he intended to ask for money, or just steal the pot that he knew was in the back yard. Whatever the case, at some point he decided to do away with Billman, and armed himself with the cart rung. And when Billman answered the door he beat him with it. It was probably at that point that Mary Ann Billman first became involved in the matter, not as a principal, but as an accessory who tried to salvage the situation after the fact. According to witnesses who went immediately to the scene, the usually self-possessed Mrs. Billman was rattled. She just was not prepared for the immediate grilling, and acted against her own self-interest.

Given the body of facts the jury was allowed to consider, and the restrictions of the law as interpreted by the court, they pretty much were bound to find as they did. With Mary Ann acquitted, there was little hope of a conviction of James Magness, and he was discharged a few days later. Moses Tate was sentenced to life imprisonment at San Quentin but was released in a general pardon in 1867. The law that kept Tate from testifying against his former mistress was repealed in 1863, too late to have any effect in the Billman case. A few months after her trial, an outraged press reported that Mrs. Billman was back in the prostitution business, this time as proprietor of a house, financed perhaps by her late husband's estate.

All in all, the case asks as many questions as it answers. We don't know what became of the daughter, or, even the little girl's name. Mary Ann eventually made her way back to Arkansas. How much of the story of her San Francisco adventures accompanied her is not known either. One thing we know: When Mary Ann died years later, she was buried in the Tate family plot in Clark County, Arkansas, as the widow Billman.

Another tantalizing question remains: What were the circumstances of the early demise of Mary Ann's first young husband in Arkansas before she left for California? One is compelled to wonder.

Fifteen
MARK TWAIN AND MARTIN BURKE

L egend has it that Mark Twain left town rather hurriedly in the mid-1860s, just one step ahead of the police; not the law or justice, mind you—the police. Twain came to San Francisco in early 1864 and was hired as a general assignment reporter with *The San Francisco Morning Call*. The fledgling humorist selected the San Francisco Police Department as the principal subject of his already formidable satiric skills.

On one occasion Twain is said to have come upon an officer sleeping against a lamppost. Twain fanned him elaborately with a large cabbage leaf, to the great amusement of passersby. "Don't they [the police] take good care of the city?" Twain wrote. "Is not their constant vigilance and efficiency shown in the fact that roughs and rowdies here are awed into good conduct?—isn't it shown in the fact that ladies. . . are safe from insult . . . when they are under the protection of a regiment of soldiers?"

Twain parted company with the *Call* a few months later, according to his later account, after the editor refused to print a story about the assault of a Chinese man by a bunch of hoodlums while a police officer looked on. It was after Twain posted bail for a fellow reporter who had been arrested for assaulting a Howard Street saloon keeper and friend of Police Chief Martin Burke, the story goes, that Twain decided to leave town for his own continued good health, and settled for a time at Jackass Hill in the Mother Lode country.

Whatever the reason for his departure, Twain returned to the city a few months later and redoubled his criticism of the department. He contracted with his former employer at Virginia City's *Territorial Enterprise* to write a series of articles about life in San Francisco. In the next few months Twain supplied the paper with a series of scathing pieces about the San Francisco Police Department which created a public furor in the city and, incidentally, caused "his star to rise in literary circles."

In one article, he criticized Captain of Detectives Lees for detailing four officers to nurse him through a broken leg at a time when "interested parties are always badgering the Supervisors with petitions for an increase of the police force . . ." And when an arrested burglar died unnoticed in a police cell, Twain wrote that the officers probably thought he was merely "sleeping with that calm serenity which is peculiar to men whose heads have been caved in with a club." Twain took a particular interest in department discipline and supported pending legislation which would have limited the chief of police's authority in the disciplinary process. "Chief Burke's Star Chamber Board of Police Commissioners is the funniest institution extant," Twain wrote ". . . . it is all humbug, display, fuss and feathers. The Chief brings his policeman out as sinless as an angel, unless the testimony be heavy enough and strong enough, almost, to hang an ordinary culprit in which case a penalty of four or five days suspension is awarded... Chief Burke appoints all the policemen. . . and feels something of a parent's solicitude for them," Twain continued, "and yet if any charge is brought against them, he is their judge

. . . [and] since every conviction is a reflection on the chief, police officers are seldom convicted." Burke replied with a suit for libel against *The Territorial Enterprise*.

There is reason to question the literal veracity of much of what Twain wrote. In later years he gave several sometimes conflicting versions to the story about the hoodlum assault on the hapless Chinese man. And his editor at the *Call* suggested later that his departure from the paper was occasioned more by his lack of industry than differences over editorial policy. For Twain, the yarn was the thing, and he never let the facts get in the way of a good story, but his enmity against the police department was real enough.

Not surprisingly, officers of the department kept out a watch for any slips on his part and, in January 1866, in the midst of *The Territorial Enterprise* series, Twain spent a night in jail after being arrested for drunkeness by members of the force. (For all his genius, Twain seems to have had problems with authority figures. A year or so later he was arrested by New York City police officers for interfering in an arrest they were trying to make.) Whether his experience with the police contributed to his decision a few months later to leave the city is not known, but in March 1866 he sailed away from San Francisco and on to worldwide acclaim as America's most beloved humorist.

15-2. Courtesy of Bill Secrest.
Police Chief Martin Burke in later years.

Sixteen

HOMELAND SECURITY

I had in view the formation of the Police into a drilled force that can be promptly assembled in case of riot or other emergency.

—CHIEF MARTIN BURKE, 1863

Much of the growth and development of San Francisco in the 1860s, which almost trebled the city's population by the end of the decade, can be attributed to the Civil War. During the early war years, 100,000 easterners came to California to avoid military service. Many settled in San Francisco where they found employment in the expanding manufacturing industries, energized by the war-induced scarcity of imported goods.

San Francisco and California remained loyal to the Union during the Civil War. In February 1861, 14,000 pro-Union demonstrators gathered noisily at Post and Market Streets in support of the Union Cause. A few months later, 25,000 Union supporters assembled in Union Square, thus giving the park its name. Chief of Police Martin Burke, who, like most of the city's establishment, was an ardent Unionist, assembled the entire police department and required them to swear an oath of fealty to the Union. All attended except one special officer who was reported to have departed for the Confederacy.

There was really little to fear from secessionists. Since 1856 the Peoples/Republican Party had dominated the political life of San Francisco. Those banished by the Vigilance Committee were almost all Democrats, who, as the Civil War approached, were thrown into greater disarray by a split along northern and southern lines. With the coming of the war, as establishment politicians coalesced under the banner of the Unionist Party, those who might oppose the war either left town or kept their heads down.

Fears about secessionist activity were given concrete form, however, when in February 1863 authorities got wind that some Southern sympathizers had bought the schooner *Chapman* with which they planned to either seize bullion-carrying ships or blow up the Benicia arsenal. Police and Navy forces kept the schooner under surveillance and at 3 a.m. on March 13, after the *Chapman* left Pacific Wharf, cutters from the warship *Cyane* and the police chase boat stopped the boat in the stream. Going below they found 17 men hiding in the hold along with weapons, including 12 pound cannons, and a substantial amount of ammunition. They also found a letter of marque from Confederate President Jefferson Davis. The *Chapman* was towed to Alcatraz where its crew was placed in the custody of the military commander.

In the public furor following the seizure of the *Chapman*, the Union League, a secret armed society sprung up in California, in

16-1 Courtesy of the San Francisco History Center.
Meeting to support the Union. Post and Market streets ca. 1861.

imitation of chapters formed earlier in the East. San Francisco Police Chief Martin Burke served as grand marshal. The League organized 113 councils in 33 of California's counties which in turn formed Union Clubs, to seek electoral votes and collect "the names of all persons known to be disloyal." For the rest of the time until after the war, the Union League through its agents on the police and the implied threat of mass public action, did a fair job of keeping political dissenters off balance.

As the conflict wore on, however, and the casualty figures began to mount, the demographics of the city changed, and more dissent was heard. Many of those who came to swell the population were working-class Democrats who headed west to avoid service in a war which a rich man could dodge by the payment of $300. (California was to the Civil War what Canada was to the Vietnam War, a place of refuge for those avoiding the war.) By 1864, as the presidential election approached, many San Franciscans were tiring of the carnage, and overt opposition to the war party increased.

Almost nightly there were mass meetings and torchlight parades in San Francisco as pro-Unionists demonstrated for Lincoln while their opponents came out in support of Democrat George McClellan, the "peace" candidate. On September 21, 1864, a thousand of McClellan's "Broom Rangers" tried to disrupt a Unionist meeting at Montgomery and Bush streets even as a few blocks away pro-Unionists establishment leaders met to form a "committee of safety," reminiscent of the Vigilance Committee of a decade before.

Burke was prepared. A year earlier he had formed the first riot squad in the San Francisco police department. "I had in view. . . "he wrote in his annual report, "the formation of the Police into a drilled force that can be promptly assembled in case of riot or other emergency." At the September disorders "Chief Burke was fortunately at hand with a strong force of police," reported the *Alta*, "and threw a line of police across the street, turning back the tide." Several further attempts to bypass his lines were thwarted but somehow a contingent of "Rangers" got around and disrupted the Union meeting.

When on October 6th, McClellan's adherents mounted a procession through the streets, Chief Burke monitored the march closely with his superior force. As the procession broke up, a few of the marchers hissed the police, and Burke, "with the promptness that is so efficient in quelling a turbulent spirit," wrote a sympathetic newspaper reporter, ". . . instantly halted his men, and alone walked through the crowd, inquiring for the hisser, but none dared avow the cowardly act," Burke marched and counter marched his force "through the silenced crowd." (a year earlier "anti-war" protestors had thrown New York City into a week of rioting which dozens were killed.) President Lincoln went on to with the election in San Francisco and the nation, but the chastened Democrats were to remember their treatment at the hands of Chief Burke.

In the midst of the 1864 electoral disturbances, the Board of Supervisors authorized a two month increase in the police force from 62 to 100 men. And with funds supplied by the "Committee in aid of the Public Peace" a paid police battalion of 175 was organized and drilled at the Mechanics Pavilion at Union Square. A further unpaid volunteer force of 3000 men was also organized, four fifths of whom, it was claimed, could be armed and ready on an hours notice.

On the morning Saturday April 15, 1865, news of Lincoln's assassination threw the city into shock. Businesses closed down and angry knots of Union sympathizers gathered in the streets. Chief Burke seemingly had matters well in hand. When he received news of the assassination shortly after 10 a.m., he reacted promptly. Two hundred officers of the regular police and the police battalion were quickly assembled and posted about the city.

Burke's main activity thereafter was directed at finding a way to silence those who might approve of the assassination. "I applied to the courts," Burke later wrote," for information as to whether men who approved of the assassination and announced their views on the street could be arrested to prevent a riot . . . but strange to say the judges could not find a law any law to authorize the arrest. . ." While Burke was looking for ways to arrest those who might applaud the assassination—only one such incident was reported, in which an arrest was promptly made—his own political friends had other fish to fry. By early afternoon a large group of Union sympathizers gathered in the street just a below the City Hall Police Station. At 3 p.m.. they decided to teach a lesson to the "treasonous" *Democratic Press*, (a leading Democratic newspaper which would change its name a few months later to the *San Francisco Examiner*) The paper had supported the "peace" candidate in the recent election, so the group marched to its office a block away, and wrecked its presses, throwing cases of type out the windows into the street.

The cheering crowd then moved on to other anti-Unionist newspapers. Chief Burke was notified of the riot and marched at the head of fifty men down to the scene of the riot. The crowd scattered and, as Burke posted a guard at the *Press*, the mob made its way to the *Newsletter,* another block away which they proceeded to destroy. Again the police showed up and the crowd moved up to the block to the *Monitor* which they also destroyed. In each case the police seemed to arrive at the scene just as the mob moved on.

The crowd then made its way to the French *Echo du Pacifique* on Sacramento Street. Here they met an obstacle. The offending newspaper shared a building with the strongly pro-Unionist *Alta California*, whose editor, knowing that "to attempt to enter the building under such circumstances was to insure the destruction of the *Alta* office as well as the *Echo* . . .," denied them access to the premises.

As the mob hesitated—it was about 4 p.m. by now—Chief Burke showed up at the head of his police force and drew a line across Sacramento Street below Montgomery to protect the newspaper office from assault. Burke called on the US Army for assistance. Forces

16-2 Courtesy of Lincoln Museum, Fort Wayne, Indiana. A rare photographic image of a nineteenth-century urban riot in progress. Sacramento Street east of Montgomery during the course of the disturbance, showing police lined up to thwart the intentions of those bent on destroying a "secesh" newspaper.

103

under General Irvin McDowell arrived by 5 p.m., and the general, while evincing sympathy for the rioters, said anyone who exulted at the assassination would be arrested. He called on the crowds to go home and called out the Militia, 2,000 of whom began clearing the Montgomery Street by 5:30 p.m. By nightfall, 5,000 troops patrolled the streets of San Francisco to maintain the peace.

Later, opponents of Chief Burke would accuse him of dragging his feet in responding to the riot call, and several of the newspapers, some of them too damaged to resume production, filed lawsuits totaling $100,000, charging the police with willful tardiness, one declaring "the police lacked diligence and were cowardly in their slowness." In the end, the cases were settled in favor of the plaintiffs for $21,000.

At the 1867 election, the People's Party withdrew its support from Martin Burke, in part because it was realized that he would not fare well with the growing numbers of Democratic voters who blamed him for his inaction on the occasion of the 1865 riot.

Seventeen
"DUTCH CHARLEY" DUANE

It must be stated that Duane bears the reputation of being an exceedingly bad man. In fact one of the worst in the city. Under no circumstances was he justified in discharging four shots in succession in the public streets, when not assaulted himself.

—*SAN FRANCISCO BULLETIN*, MAY 1866

In the early afternoon of May 23, 1866, Charles "Dutch Charley" Duane approached "Colonel" William G. Ross from behind near the Merchant Street entrance to San Francisco's Police Court. Without a word, Duane shot Ross four times in the back with a self-cocking Dean and Adams five-chambered pistol. The assailant was quickly disarmed and hustled into the nearby police station, along with his heavily armed brother John. Ross was taken to a pharmacy down the street, and from there to St. Mary's Hospital on Rincon Point where he died of his wounds two days later. To anyone who knew anything about Charles Duane, the assault was no surprise, but rather part of a pattern of violence he displayed throughout his life.

Charles P. Duane was born in Tipperary, Ireland in 1829, and moved with his family to Albany, New York, when he was eight. At the age of 15, and big for his age, Duane struck out on his own for New York City where he was apprenticed to a wagon maker. Endowed as he was with superior physical ability, Duane soon made a name for himself in athletic circles, which, in those days before organized sports, revolved around prizefighting. "While not being a professional pugilist," remarked one observer, Duane "was recognized as a man who could make it decidedly interesting for any person with an inclination in that line. . . ." He earned the sobriquet "Dutch Charley" from a German athlete he bested in one early contest.

17-1 Author's collection.
Charles Duane (left) and his brother John (right). The man in the center is unidentified.
The cane dates the photo to sometime after Charles' bout with bad alcohol.

The mid-nineteenth century was a period of dramatic social change in America's growing cities, as hordes of migrating rural Americans were met in urban centers by a flood of European immigrants, all seeking employment in the growing industrial economy. Political arrangements that had served well in the small-town America of the past disappeared. Before the advent of electoral laws designed to curb the worst excesses of party activity, political parties quite literally fought it out at polling places to gain physical control of ballot boxes.

To assist them in their electoral efforts, the politicians engaged gangs of thugs (called "shoulder strikers" because of their usual association with prizefighting) to "help out" at the polls. Exercising the franchise was not an activity for the timid in nineteenth century urban America. Duane joined with a will in the political fray in New York City. When news of the great California gold strike took hold in the East in late 1849, the 20-year-old Duane, like many another adventurous young man, struck out west to make his fortune. He arrived in Gold Rush San Francisco in January 1850, but doesn't seem to have gone to the mines like most other new arrivals, or, for that matter, to have sought any other regular employment. Instead he joined former companions from the "fighting wards" of eastern cities and immersed himself in the exciting political life of the boomtown city. The political connections gained there would get Duane out of one scrape after another.

Duane's name first appeared on the criminal docket in San Francisco in July 1850 when he was hailed before the Recorder's court for assault. The charge was dismissed when the victim failed to appear. In September, Duane was again before the Recorder, this time charged with battery and riotous conduct, but he was again discharged after two police officers testified to his peaceable nature.

Duane's life in San Francisco can be traced through published accounts of his frequent outbursts of physical violence. His common practice was to assault an adversary without warning, to knock him down and stomp him before he had a chance to recover from the initial attack. But Duane was no coward. Violence was his stock in trade, and he just didn't see much sense in giving an adversary an even break.

In December 1850, another police officer tried to cite Duane to court for shooting a dog. Duane responded by choking the officer, knocking him down and stomping on him. Duane told the court he shot the dog because it bit him, and explained the assault by saying he thought the officer was the dog's owner presenting him with a bill. Not explained was how this would have justified the attack. He was fined $100.

On February 17, 1851, Duane committed an assault that foreshadowed the Ross shooting a decade and a half later. Emile Fayolle, proprietor of the French Adelphi Theater on Clay Street, hosted a masked ball—a popular form of entertainment in the largely bachelor boomtown society. Shortly after midnight, Duane, who had been drinking in the downstairs bar room, decided he would attend.

When the doorkeeper at the lower entrance to the ball asked for his ticket, Duane knocked the man down and went up the stairs. And when the attendant at the upper landing tried to delay him, according to a contemporary newspaper account, Duane "seized him by the throat and with his head 'butted' him in the face, bruising it in the most shocking manner."

Following his exertions, Duane went to the bar to refresh himself and when manager Fayolle approached the area shortly thereafter, the young rowdy attacked him as well. He knocked Fayolle down with his right fist, and floored his companion with a left. Duane then proceeded to kick the downed Fayolle unmercifully, and as the Frenchman struggled to his feet to escape, Duane pulled a pistol and shot the man in the back.

At his trial a month later, the jury could not agree, and the matter was set for a new trial on May 5. Several postponements were obtained until Fayolle departed for France, speeded on his way, it was said, by a generous contribution from Duane's political friends. When the matter came to trial on June 26, the victim was not available and the case was dismissed.

On July 21, Duane, again in his cups, showed up at another masked ball on Commercial Street. Also in attendance was Frank Ball, a popular saloon singer who, as a member of the February Grand Jury, had voted to indict Duane in the Fayolle shooting. According to eyewitness accounts, Duane forced his way into the party and beat and kicked Ball into unconsciousness. At first, it was thought that Ball would not survive. This time it appeared as though Duane's timing was badly off. It was during this period that the first of San Francisco's famed Vigilance committees was formed to clean up the town.

With the vigilance committee—of which Frank Ball was a member—looking over their shoulders this time, the courts moved more expeditiously than they had before. On July 27, Duane was found guilty of aggravated assault and sentenced to a year in jail. When it was revealed a few weeks later that the governor had secretly pardoned him, the vigilance committee issued a warrant for his arrest, but by then the fugitive had slipped out of town on a Panama steamer.

After the vigilance committee adjourned and things cooled down, Duane returned to San Francisco, and was next arrested on April 5, 1852, for battery and "mischievous and riotous conduct." The defendant professed "entire repentance and reform" to the court and paid for the damage he had done. The court fined him $50 and bound him to keep the peace.

From his earliest years Duane had "run with the engines" in volunteer fire companies in New York City, then an indispensable precondition to a life in politics. He continued his association with the volunteer fire department in San Francisco as a member of the Manhattan Fire Company. He performed courageously fighting the series of devastating fires which afflicted the Gold Rush city, earning a reputation for unequaled bravery.

Duane apparently took his fire department responsibilities seriously, for on June 6, 1853, as an assistant chief of the department, he entered the jail and stomped and broke the arm of a man who had raised a false fire alarm. In December he was elected Chief Engineer of the department. Not everyone agreed on his suitability for the office, and many of the more "respectable" members of the volunteer fire companies resigned in protest.

In May 1856 a reconvened Vigilance committee again took over the administration of justice in San Francisco. Before adjourning several months later, it hanged four men and banished a number of political thugs, Charles Duane among them, under pain of death should they return.

In the next few years, while the exile order remained in effect, Duane involved himself in politics in the East. At a political meeting in the nation's capital in 1859, Duane was poisoned along with several others, probably by drinking liquor containing wood alcohol. For the rest of his life, Duane would suffer from the crippling effects of that incident.

His disability didn't seem to have dampened his ardor for doing violence, however. In July 1860, after the exile order was lifted, Duane returned to San Francisco, and almost immediately became involved in a fight with a man named Brady. Duane tried to strike Brady with his cane, but his intended victim wrested it away from him and knocked him down with it. "Duane has an affection (sic) in his legs which reduces his power for harm," commented a contemporary news reporter, "otherwise Brady might have been the victim of a brutal attack." As it is," the newspaper account continued, "it shows that Duane has the same mind as formerly for assault, and is only prevented by incapacity from doing harm."

Still, Charley Duane managed to make the news occasionally, usually for some type of assault or other disorderly conduct. And with the May 1866 shooting of Ross, it appeared that he had finally gone too far. The wild and woolly Gold Rush days were in the past, and San Francisco, in the immediate post-Civil War period, was growing rapidly under a reform-minded city government.

The genesis of the problem resulting in Ross' death was a dispute over land ownership. Charles Duane had a history of involvement in the land troubles which plagued the early state. In 1850 he was part of an armed party which hastened the resolution of a land dispute which resulted in the founding of the city of Oakland. On May 28, 1851, while awaiting his second trial in the Fayolle case, Duane managed to get arrested for assault in a squatter dispute in San Francisco. In 1854 Duane claimed title to a tract of land extending beyond the then city limits at Divisadero Street. In 1858, while Duane was out of the state, part of his claimed land was established as Alamo Square Public Park.

In 1860, William Ross settled with his wife and young son on a tract of land claimed also by Duane, at the northwest corner of what is now Fulton and Divisadero streets. By May 1866, the federal government ceded to the city its claim to the land in the area, and it looked as though title might soon be awarded.

On May 22, 1866 Charles Duane and his brother John went to the disputed site, where Ross and some friends were erecting a house. According to eyewitness accounts, Duane got out of his buggy and as he approached, Ross raised a rifle and pulled the trigger but the gun misfired. Witness accounts differ as to whether Duane had a firearm in his hand or not. Anyway, he retreated to the buggy, returned downtown and signed a criminal complaint against Ross. That night the house under construction was burned to the ground. The two adversaries met the next morning in Police Court where they filed cross complaints — for assault and arson. Both were bound to keep the peace. It was while the court was adjourned in the early afternoon that the shooting took place.

Duane's trial began on October 22, 1866. It seemed at first to be cut and dried. The prosecution called several witnesses from among the many who had been present on the street on the day of the shooting who testified that Duane had shot Ross in the back without warning as he stood at the curb line of Merchant Street facing outward, his cane in his left hand and his right hand on his hip.

The defense cross-examined prosecution witnesses closely, to plant the seed of suspicion that Ross may have had a weapon which was spirited away by friends after the shooting. When the prosecution tried to introduce Ross' dying declaration that he had been unarmed and had no idea Duane was behind him, the defense successfully objected.

The defense proceeded to put the victim on trial. Then as now, evidence about a defendant's previous violent behavior is inadmissible against him, except under narrowly prescribed circumstances. No such protection exists for the victim. The defense called witnesses to Ross' reputation for violence. Allegations that he had previously killed three other men were allowed, as was testimony that in 1863 he had broken another man's arm. A stream of defense witnesses characterized Ross as a loud, threatening man who terrified people. Duane knew about this reputation, the defense contended, and had armed himself only after Ross attempted to fire upon him.

It is doubtful that there was anyone in San Francisco in 1866 who was unaware of Duane's violent propensities. Nevertheless, none of that got into the trial. In his closing remarks, the prosecutor tried to cut through the confusion. "Stripped of all the surroundings introduced by the defense for the purpose of confusing the jury," he argued, "and taken aside from the sophistry of counsel, it was an incontrovertible fact that Ross was shot down in open day, in a public street, and in the back, without an opportunity for defense, that he was attacked before he was aware of the presence of his assailant."

The defense rejoined that it didn't matter whether Ross had been armed or not, as long as Duane thought he was, and that he intended to do him harm. It works now, and it worked then. After less than two hours' deliberation, the jury returned a verdict of not guilty.

It might be that the jurors acted responsibly, in accord with their understanding of the law, or perhaps Duane, through his political connections, got to someone on the jury. But there was also another element in play. Duane's defense was able to appeal to a passion then much in the public mind. San Francisco stood foursquare in the Union camp during the Civil War, so much so that when news of Lincoln's assassination arrived in the city in April 1865, Union supporters rioted, destroying anti-Unionist newspapers. Charles Duane was strongly pro-Union. One of his more recent arrests, during the election of 1864, had been for fighting with anti-Union Democrats.

Ross, on the other hand, was a southerner, a native of Virginia, and his southern sympathies were well known. In case the issue hadn't occurred to the jurors, the defense managed to get it before them in his summation. "Do not condemn Duane because he is a Union man," argued his attorney. "Do not acquit him because Ross was a Secessionist." All of which got the issue nicely before the jury.

Being tried for murder didn't mend Duane's violent ways. Two years later he was arrested in another land dispute, this time at the Potrero. And in 1871 Duane was again on trial, charged with perjury in yet another land case. Again he was found not guilty.

In the late 1870s, as he was approaching 50, an age when it could reasonably be expected that he should be settling down, Duane's membership in the Workingman's political party was revoked because propensity for violence—no mean feat given the activities of that group.

In May 1887, Duane's life finally came to an end—at home, in bed—while he was recuperating from a fall from a buggy. According to one obituary writer, "the deceased was a faithful friend and very bitter enemy and never lost an opportunity to display those characteristics." Another sympathetic memorialist commented that Duane "was somewhat prone to fight, and this was the worst that could be charged upon him."

Indeed.

Eighteen

THE HARBOR POLICE

The little settlement on Yerba Buena Cove, from which the city of San Francisco grew, was established in 1835 to service the needs of visiting merchant vessels. In those days, at high tide, the waters of the bay the came up to what is now the eastern side of Montgomery Street. During the Gold Rush years, a series of wharves were extended out over the shallows, and warehouses were erected on the adjoining piles. By the early 1850s, a large part of what is now San Francisco's financial district lay atop piles sunk into the Bay and, depending on the state of the tide, it was possible to make one's way by small boat or on foot for blocks under the city's waterfront and principal business district.

This provided an irresistible lure to ex-convict Australian boatmen, "Sydney Ducks." The thieves would approach warehouses by boat from under the wharves and attack them from below, out of sight of the authorities. In June 1851, the Vigilance committee established a water police to search out criminals about and under the wharves, and to check incoming and outgoing vessels for arriving criminals and escaping fugitives. After the committee adjourned in September, the idea of a harbor police fell by the wayside.

That's where the issue lay until 1859, when Police Chief Martin Burke asked the Board of Supervisors for four men and a boat to do something about the "crime committed, by means of boats, under and around the streets extending over the water." The ever frugal Board of Supervisors refused his request. Burke continued to ask for a harbor police, and each year the Board of Supervisors ignored him. In 1863, one supervisor joined the discussion, arguing that an "efficient harbor police would effectually break up 'shanghaeing' (sic) and abate the thefts now practiced on the wharves and on the vessels in the harbor."

The following year, the Supervisors authorized the hiring of nine additional officers and the acquisition of a whitehall boat to form the first regular harbor police in San Francisco. A Harbor Station was established at Davis and Pacific streets in the heart of the waterfront district, and a few years later a substation was opened South of Market at Steuart and Folsom streets. There was plenty to occupy the waterfront officers. Before the construction of the seawall to hold back the bay waters, the underside of the wharves offered a haven for pirates who issued out to prey on bay shipping. In the 1870s an intrepid news reporter entered a cave at Union and Front streets, and made his way at low tide under the piers to Commercial Street.

In January 1870, while searching for the murderer of six year old Maggie Ryan whose outraged body had been found under the Pacific Wharf, a block from Harbor Station, officers chased a man under the wharves for hours before capturing him by the India dock. The usual work of the Harbor Police was more mundane. Some officers were assigned to the Boarding Station at the foot of Powell Street from which they would embark on their open launch to check ships for arriving criminals and departing absconders, and to keep the peace among boarding house runners and boatmen. Others worked onshore, policing the Oakland, Sausalito, and Tiburon ferry docks, keeping order among pugnacious seamen and longshoremen, and controlling the "hack hawks" who preyed on arriving ships' passengers. In 1896 the Steuart Street Station burned and both sections of the Harbor Police were combined in a new station at Sacramento and Drumm, a block from the Ferry Building.

In 1893, Chief Patrick Crowley asked for a steam launch to patrol the harbor. In his request, the establishment position on labor relations at the port was made clear. The new boat, he said, would enable the police to protect non-union sailors on the bay. And for a suspiciously long time the police were incapable of putting an end to the boarding house keepers and runners who made a practice of shanghaiing unwary sailors and landsmen.

116

Finally, in 1908, San Francisco acquired its first motorized police boat, a 50-footer christened the *Patrol* and berthed at the Mission Wharf. Soon afterward the *Patrol* figured in a departmental mystery that still tantalizes. Just before midnight on November 30 of the same year, in the midst of one of the city's periodic civic cleansings, an embattled Police Chief William Biggy disappeared over the side of the launch while returning from a visit to the home of a police commissioner in Marin County. Two weeks later his body was found floating in the bay, and since then there has been unending speculation about the circumstances of his death.

In 1931 the department replaced the *Patrol* with a 66-foot, 42- ton, twin 175 horsepower engine motor launch, named the *D.A.White* after a former chief of police. The new police boat moved to a tonier address at the Yacht Harbor. The next few years were to witness the nadir of the relationship between the police and the workingmen along the front, culminating in the 1934 waterfront strike which resulted in the death by police bullets of two of the strikers. Thereafter, conditions on the waterfront stabilized, even as port business started into a decline from which it has yet to recover.

Gone were the "crimps" and the "hack hawks" who had done so much to enliven the old port, and in 1944, the Harbor Police Station was closed for want of business. The *D.A.White* continued in service for a few more years but its useful days had passed. "The 'White' and her crew appear to be in the category of most emergency equipment," commented a 1948 news account, "not very busy a lot of the time but vitally needed when they are needed." Not vital enough, however, to keep her afloat. She was unfunded in the 1949-50 fiscal year budget.

In 1994 the police commission reinstituted harbor patrols. Today the flagship of the maritime patrol is a 47 foot motor life boat, the *Komaki*, which maintains marine patrols from its berth at the Hyde Street Commercial Pier. It's not likely that the new harbor cops will find many "Sydney Ducks" prowling under the wharfs, and there is not much chance of being shanghaied these days, but perhaps the reestablishment of police marine patrols does signal, albeit in a small way, the renewal of interest by San Franciscans in their long tradition of involvement in maritime affairs.

Nineteen

LITTLE MAGGIE RYAN

These piers provided a covering for the poor, the criminal and the hunted. Around this waterfront, sent out by their parents, were many little children, ragged and shoeless, armed with baskets, ropes, and sacks, wandering among the sawmills and railroad tracks, sent out to gather anything loose enough to appropriate. . . ."

—POLICE CHIEF HENRY HIRAM ELLIS 1875-1876

It was chilly on the early afternoon of January 23, 1870, and Bridget Ryan sent her five-year -old daughter, Maggie, to find some woodchips to fuel the kitchen fire. Mrs. Ryan and her daughter lived on Davis Street between Jackson and Pacific in San Francisco's tough waterfront district. But it the middle of the day and the Harbor Police Station was just down the street at the corner of Pacific. Who would harm an innocent little girl anyway?

When Maggie had not returned by dusk, her mother became concerned, and when she still wasn't home by midnight Bridget Ryan visited the several police stations and asked officers to be on the lookout for the missing child. At 3:00 p.m. the following day, a man entered Harbor Station and reported that while walking beneath the Pacific Wharf at Drumm Street, he had come upon the body of a young girl under the Pacific Street sidewalk.

There, officers found the child's badly bruised body. "Her clothing was in disarray," reported a contemporary news account, "and it was plain to all that a fiendish deed had been perpetrated." The body had also been cut with a knife or some other sharp instrument. The coroner determined that Maggie's "death resulted from strangulation and that after death the person of the child was outraged."

The next morning, the police were on the waterfront in force, under the personal command of Chief Patrick Crowley and Captain of

Detectives Isaiah Lees. The investigation went well from the start. About 10:00 a.m., a boy named Richard O'Connor approached officers and told them he had seen a man wearing a red shirt go under the Pacific Wharf twice on Sunday. He had seen the man again that morning in a nearby saloon, he said, but the man left the saloon when he spotted O'Connor and went down under the wharf. Responding officers caught a glimpse of the man and the chase was on.

Captain Lees dispatched officers to cover the nearby wharves with orders to arrest anyone who came up from below. Other officers, accompanied by private citizens, went beneath the wharves to flush out their man. "The walking was by no means pleasant," recalled the author of a later account, "as it was over rough, wet rocks and

19-1 Author's collection.
View of Vallejo Wharf from Telegraph Hill. The Broadway (covered) Wharf is to the right. The outer portion of the Pacific Wharf, under which Maggie Ryan's body was found, can be seen at the far right. An opening out of which Quinn probably exited on his way to the Green Street Wharf can be seen on the Vallejo wharf, at mid-point on the left of the photo.

through slush and slime." Illumination was restricted to the "struggling rays of light that crept through openings in the wharf planks."

Equipped with lanterns and candles, the police first checked the immediate area, poking into the countless nooks created by the maze of piers and sewer lines. The man in the red shirt was not to be found. Thinking that he might have entered one of the sewers, some officers stripped and donned oilskins to search them. Still no luck. The entire area under the wharfs was sectioned off and groups were assigned to systematically cover the separate areas under the Davis Street Wharf between Broadway and Vallejo. At one point Officer John McDermott spotted the suspect and took a shot at him, but the man disappeared into the gloom. For several hours, search parties quartered back and forth under the wharves, sometimes knee-deep in mud, catching occasional glimpses of the wraithlike figure. After a time there were no more sightings, and the tired, muddy officers, thinking the suspect had eluded them, were about to give up.

Then, a man wearing a red shirt and black slouch hat was seen coming up from the Green Street dock. He ran along for a while, and then disappear again under a wharf. Officers surrounded the nearby wharves and a few minutes later the man entered the India Dock, north of Filbert Street between Battery and Front. Officer Jeremiah Dugan jumped down into the rising tidal basin, and after a fierce struggle, during which the suspect tried to drag the officer into deeper water, placed him under arrest.

When news of the police search had spread, large numbers of San Franciscans had made their way to the waterfront to watch and join in. At one time some 600 private citizens assisted the police with their search. As the suspect was taken up the stairs from the India Dock, thousands of people were on hand. It had been less than fifteen years since San Francisco's Vigilance committee had taken the law into its own hands, and the public's inclination to administer summary justice was still strong. As the officers walked their man toward the City Hall Jail, the angry crowd began to call for his immediate hanging. On Battery Street near Vallejo, according to one witnesses' later account, "a mob of women assembled," who called for the lynching of the terrified prisoner, and "even threw ropes among the crowd."

As the arrest party neared jail, the crowd redoubled its efforts, and judges, lawyers and other city officials rushed out of City Hall to support the police. At the last turn into the Dunbar Alley entrance to the jail, "a tall, well-formed man" forced his way through the crowd and seized the prisoner by the collar. Just as quickly, "Chief Crowley struck [the man] a stunning blow in the face, knocking him back in the crowd." The prisoner was spirited quickly into the jail.

After things quieted down a bit, police identified their terrified catch as Charles Quinn, 22, a slaughterhouse worker in Butchertown in the Potrero District. A native of New York, Quinn had come to San Francisco about 15 years earlier with his family. In the mid-1860s, his mother and one sister had been burned to death in a fire, leaving him with a brother and two younger sisters. His father, described by family members as "a dissolute and debauched character," later committed suicide. Quinn himself was a graduate of the Industrial School for wayward youths.

The only evidence against Quinn was that he resembled a man seen in the area on the day of the murder, and that he had run when approached by police. Not everyone was sure the police had the right man. Quinn's main concern, voiced many times during the proceedings that followed, was that the outraged mob shouting outside the jail would get in and hang him. Any official doubts about Quinn's guilt were erased later that night when police announced that he had confessed. He had been standing on the corner of Pacific and Davis streets about 3:00 p.m. on Sunday, he said, when he saw a young girl go under the wharf. He followed her, he admitted, then approached her and caught hold of her, placing his hand over her mouth so she could not scream. "I had hard work to accomplish my object," he said, but when he departed, he insisted, the girl was alive.

He went back to Butchertown and slept, he said, and when he returned to the scene on Monday he was surprised to find her body. He then almost went crazy, he continued, and wandered around for hours, thinking to kill himself. He returned again to the wharf on Tuesday morning and the first thing he knew, the crowd was after him. He later recanted that version of his confession and over the next several days gave several differing accounts of the event. Throughout, he insisted that he had not killed the girl.

Quinn's trial on a charge of first-degree murder began on Monday morning, August 1, 1870 in the 15th district courtroom at Montgomery and Washington streets. The heart of the prosecution's case was Quinn's confession. The most damning testimony was that of

19-2 Author's collection.
Another view of the Vallejo Street Wharf and the Green Street Dock which Quinn traversed during his escape attempt. Telegraph Hill is in the background.

Detective Henry Ellis who told how Quinn was familiar with the details of the crime that could only have been known to the perpetrator. (Or, we might add, to a subnormal wharf rat who was in the habit of prowling around in the gloomy half-world under the wharfs.)

The defense took the position—contrary to common logic, but well established in criminal defense practice—that Quinn didn't do the crime, but even if he did, he was not mentally competent to form the intent to commit first-degree murder. The defense questioned the circumstances of the confession, saying it was obtained after a heated chase and near-lynching without a bit of evidence against the defendant. While the mob outside hollered for his scalp, the attorney said, Quinn was visited in his cell by a man (now present in the courtroom) "who placed a pistol at his head and made him confess, telling him that he would die if he did not tell all that he had done." Whether that really happened is not known because neither the prosecution nor the court pursued the matter.

The main efforts of the defense were directed at showing that Quinn was not mentally competent. It was brought out that he had earned the sobriquet "Looney" Quinn during his Industrial School days because of his odd behavior. Two uncles testified that they had always considered him an idiot, and his brother said that the defendant had suffered several head injuries. A police officer testified that Quinn had thrown a fit on Third Street three weeks before the crime and the officer had thrown water on him to bring him around.

The main support to the assertion of the defendant's mental insufficiency, however, was testimony pertaining to his practice of what the press referred to, with characteristic Victorian delicacy, as "a certain vice." Several witnesses gave evidence that Quinn had been a practitioner of this "certain vice" for as long as twelve years. Dr. G.A. Shurtleff, Superintendent of the State Insane Asylum at Stockton, who claimed that 200 of the 1930 patients under his charge were insane "from the effects of a certain vice," testified that the practice "would tend to impair the mind, destroy the nervous system, and render the victim of this habit almost an idiot."

At first glance, the unnamed but universally deplored practice would seem to be masturbation. It was widely believed in 19th century medical circles that "self abuse" led to serious medical consequences. In 1848, the Superintendent of a Massachusetts asylum estimated that 32 percent of his patients had been driven insane by masturbation. Similar figures were reported by mental health "experts" well into the twentieth century. But there is a curiously intriguing contemporary comment which calls

PATRICK CROWLEY 1866 – 1873
1880 – 1897

19-3 Author's collection.
Patrick Crowley Chief of Police 1866-73 and 1879-97. The department's longest-serving chief. In earlier times, chiefs sometimes took a personal hand in the more physical aspect of police affairs.

that diagnosis into question for Quinn. The keeper of the County Jail who had charge of Quinn in jail mentioned in his testimony that he had been forced "to put a leather gag upon Quinn to prevent his practicing a vice." Several possibilities other than masturbation come to mind, none of which would have been welcome to the prevailing 19th century sensibility.

Throughout the week-long trial, angry spectators had been grumbling menacingly at the defendant. On Thursday, as the court was being cleared at the noon recess. Quinn became convinced that the spectators intended to seize him and he threw a public fit. His fears were not totally without merit. For the rest of the trial Chief Crowley detailed 30 officers to assist the sheriff with courtroom security.

After closing arguments on Saturday, the case was given to the jury and 40 minutes later they returned a verdict of second-degree murder. Quinn was visibly relieved, just as the courtroom crowd clearly was not. The defendant was ordered back to court on the August 10 for sentencing. The question became: how to get Quinn back to the county jail several blocks away through the angry crowd? The first plan was to take him over the rooftops for a block and then make a final rush to the jail. When that idea was seen as impractical, the police and sheriff's deputies formed a cordon around Quinn and forced their way by brute strength up Montgomery Street to Broadway and on up to the County Jail beyond Kearny. To avoid problems at the sentencing, the authorities pulled a fast one. Public notice was given that the sentencing was rescheduled for August 12, but on August 11 the defendant was quietly taken before the court and sentenced to a term of life imprisonment without the public knowing anything about it.

At his sentencing hearing, Quinn protested his innocence. "In less than three years (you) will know who did it." He declaimed. "God Almighty knows that I am innocent. God knows that I did not kill her, and God knows that I could go now and lay my hands on the very man." Quinn was quickly placed on board the steamer *Contra Costa* and taken to San Quentin prison. "The moment the depraved being found himself within the prison walls," reported one contemporary observer, "he expressed himself satisfied, for he was in constant fear that he would fall a victim to the mob."

Quinn was lodged in "Crazy Alley" at the prison where he remained for a decade and a half, isolated and alone. In keeping with the timeless code of prison conduct, other prisoners shunned him as a child sex murderer.

Did he do it? Certainly, the way his confession was obtained would be scrutinized in a later time. And his statement at the sentencing hearing suggests there may have been more to the case than came out at the time. But the same statement also admits to knowledge of the case beyond that of an innocent bystander. Quinn was no doubt somehow involved in Maggie's fate, either before, during or after the actual murder. Whatever the degree of his involvement, or the lack of it, given the public climate at the time, he no doubt continued to count himself fortunate that he hadn't been summarily hanged.

In the late 1880s, Quinn's physical health began to break down and on February 25, 1888, at age 39, he died in his cell in Crazy Alley, alone and unmourned.

Twenty
HOODLUM DAYS

On Sunday, August 6, 1876, Patrick McCarthy, David Condon, James Mugan and several other young members of the Hayes Valley Gang went "wilding" in the southern part of the city. They started at midday in a grocery/saloon at 24th and Mission streets, where McCarthy became embroiled in a dispute with a bartender over payment for his drinks. The group then moved on, in three rented buggies, to the Seven Mile House (at the present intersection of Bayshore and Geneva), harassing passers-by along the way.

Later in the evening they returned to the Mission District, to a saloon at 24th and Howard (South Van Ness), where they broke up the place and stole cigars and whiskey before making their way to another saloon at 14th and Valencia on their way back to Hayes Valley. Again they started a fight, which ended when McCarthy struck a man over the head with a whiskey bottle, injuring him fatally. At his trial the next year one of his fellows gave evidence against him and McCarthy was convicted of manslaughter.

As the young gang lords of present-day San Francisco neighborhoods swagger jealously over their claimed turf, they traverse many of the same streets claimed by hoodlum gangs of an earlier day. For it was in the San Francisco of more than a century ago that the word hoodlum was coined, to describe the young criminal gangs that then held sway. A number of origins of the word "hoodlum" have been advanced, but all trace its source to San Francisco in the early 1870s. It is most likely to have derived from the Bavarian German "hodalump," which means exactly the same thing. Southern Germans made up the largest foreign-language group in San Francisco in the 1870s, and many were small merchants, keepers of the combination grocery store/saloons that the hoodlums often graced with their presence.

The middle decades of the nineteenth century were a particularly violent period in American urban life, as the workshop gave way to the factory just as great waves of European immigrants arrived to compete for jobs with native-born Americans in the rapidly changing economy. Young urban white males, cast adrift from the societal anchors of small-town America, came together—in response to some primal impulse—on the street corners of the burgeoning cities and formed themselves into territorial or turf gangs. In adolescent San Francisco of 1870, by then a city of 150,000 people spreading to new neighborhoods to the west, east and north of the old core city, there arose a group of perhaps 500 young male hoodlums, ranging in age from 12 to 30 years.

Like their philosophical counterparts presently tormenting the city, the loosely confederated gangs organized themselves into groups of 30 to 40 members that jealously guarded their turf from interlopers from other neighborhoods. "In the days long gone by," wrote an old police officer in the 1920s, describing the hoodlums of 50 years earlier, "quite a number of young men would assemble every evening on different street corners in different sections of the city, and quite a number of amateur criminals sprang up among them from these associations."

The Kearny Street Gang hung around the cheap lodging houses at Kearny and Pacific streets. The Telegraph Hill Rockrollers roosted at the top of the hill at Montgomery and Alta streets. The Russian Hill Gang claimed the turf of the opposite heights across what is now Columbus Avenue, and the North Beach Gang held sway in that area from its headquarters on Francisco Street adjacent to Meiggs Wharf.

South of Market were the Folsom Street Gang and Tar Flat Gang, headquartered in a saloon at First and Mission. There were also the Brannan Street Gang (Sixth and Brannan) and the Brady Street Gang, which ruled the area near the San Jose Depot at 12th and Market, while the Old Mission Gang held the turf surrounding

16th and Mission streets. In the Western Addition flourished the Hayes Valley Gang and farther north the Sunrise Gangsters were the lords of the 1870s.

Also like their successors of a later age, the hoodlum gangs were given to distinctive dress. "The 'hoodlum' is remarkable for his clean-shaven face," wrote one contemporary journalist, "his wide baggy pantaloons, his high-heeled boots, and his low stiff-brimmed hat. His back hair is combed against the grain, made stiff and puffed out by the application [of a] profuse quantity of hair oil, the front hair being brought well down on the forehead and made to [lie] flat, with an occasional semi-quiver, resembling embroidery."

A favorite pastime of the hoodlum gangs was to fight with police officers walking isolated foot beats. Law enforcement institutions before the middle of the nineteenth century, dating from a rural and small-town America—a few constables and badly organized night watches—were totally inadequate to the task of con-

20-1 Author's collection.
Contemporary drawing of hoodlums depicting the distinctive attire of the group.

trolling the street gangs that plagued American cities. One institutional response to the urban violence of the period was the creation of municipal police departments similar to the modern ones. For the first time in the United States, large bodies of officers were organized along quasi-military lines to deal with unruly mobs.

Most of the time, though, officers walked their beats by themselves, out of contact with their stations or other officers where they were fair game for the hoodlum gangs. "Assaults on police officers are now of almost daily occurrence," wrote the editor of the *Bulletin* on September 15, 1873. "Yesterday morning, about half-past 2 o'clock, Officer Forner, while passing along Broadway Street above Dupont, was struck in the back with a brick, thrown by a hoodlum named Bill Harrington." The officer arrested his assailant but was then set upon by his hoodlum friends, members of the Hill Boys. An officer from an adjoining beat arrested one of the rescue party, but while he was transporting the arrestee to the station, another of the hoodlums knocked out Forner with a cobblestone, and Harrington escaped. He was later brought to justice.

The same day the Hayes Valley Gang rampaged through the Mission District in August 1876, Jack Rudolf and another hoodlum accosted an Officer Keuscher at Montgomery and Broadway streets, and without provocation Rudolf struck the officer in the head with a revolver, knocking him unconscious. The hoodlums then went to McVey's saloon at Green and Stockton, where they terrorized everyone on the premises at gunpoint. Two officers came on the scene, and after an off-and-on gunfight through the streets of North Beach, during which one officer received a bullet through the collar of his coat and Rudolf was shot through the hand, the hoodlum was finally captured, hiding in a tree in Washington Square.

It was a hoodlum member of the Hill Gang, James Runk, who contributed the name of the first officer killed in the line of duty to the plaque in the lobby of the Hall of Justice. Early on April 26, 1877,

131

20-2 Author's collection.
Hoodlums ridiculing police officer. Prior to the erection of fully staffed district police
stations in the 1880s the Police Department maintained little unmanned "telegraph"
stations connected to headquarters in the City Hall at Kearny and Washington streets.
Officers reported on duty by telegraph, and stored extra equipment in the little guard-
houses, which also served as temporary lockups for holding prisoners until they could
be transported downtown.

Officer Charles Coots arrested an ex-convict named Charles Wilson
who with 17-year-old John Runk, another member of the Hill Gang,
had been harassing the prostitutes on Pike Street (now Waverly
Place). As the officer walked Wilson down the few blocks to the jail
at Kearny and Washington, Runk walked up behind the officer at
Clay Street and Brenham Place and shot him in the head, wounding
him fatally. Runk was later tried, convicted and hanged.

The principal victims of the hoodlums, though, were the Chinese.
Relations between the Chinese and working-class whites had been
strained since the Gold Rush days. With the large increase in Chinese
immigration following the adoption of the Burlingame Treaty in 1868
which allowed for unrestricted immigration, things grew tense. But
conditions grew even worse in the economic depression that seized
California and the nation during the1870s. Just as the hard economic
times hit, thousands of Chinese laborers, released from work on the

recently completed transcontinental railroad, flooded into San Francisco looking for work. Unable to comprehend the complex reasons for the economic situation, working men in San Francisco focused on the Chinese as the sole reason for their problems.

It was from this group of disaffected workers that many hoodlums came, and in this economic environment that they rose to prominence. The Telegraph Hill Rockrollers were so called because of the practice of rolling large stones down their hill on any hapless Chinese person who might be crossing an intersection below. Other hoodlums south of Market would drop stones from the top of the bridge over the Second Street Cut at Rincon Hill onto wagonloads of Chinese immigrants being transported from the Pacific Mail Steamship dock to their new homes in Chinatown. Lone Chinese who wandered into areas claimed by the hoodlum gangs took their lives in their hands.

Things came to a head in July 1877. That month, a large group of working men met in the sandlots near the present Civic Center in support of striking railroad workers in Pennsylvania. Taking advantage of the confusion caused by the crowd, a number of hoodlums split off and began to attack Chinese wash houses. It was all the small 150 man police department could do to contain the mobs trying to invade Chinatown. In the following days the disturbances became general. Before they were brought to an end, the militia was called out and a "pickhandle brigade" of 5,000 citizens was formed to impose order on the city.

The forces of order were commended for their performance at the riots, but not everyone was satisfied with what the regular justice system was doing about the hoodlum problem. When a gang of young hoodlums, rioting at a circus at Seventh and Mission streets in 1874 killed a watchman with a thrown cobblestone, "there was a great outcry in the community at this crowning deed of hoodlum barbarity," reported the *Bulletin*, "and the police were compelled to

"HOODLUMS."

20-3 Author's collection.   Hoodlums harassing a Chinese man. A common sight in nineteenth-century San Francisco.

bestir themselves in the detention of the perpetrators." But when one of the two convicted defendants was sentenced, as a juvenile, to one year in the Industrial School "unless soon discharged according to law," the paper remarked, "That is what it costs to stone a citizen to death."

"Some didn't wait for the justice system to resolve the problems with the hoodlums. In January 1873, John McCormack, a conductor on the Bayview streetcar line, evicted John Coughlin for refusing to pay his fare and "ruffianly behavior generally." A week later the hoodlum again boarded the car and began to harass McCormack. The conductor tried to avoid trouble, but when the rowdy pulled a Colt revolver and fired at him, McCormack drew his own Smith & Wesson and shot Coughlin in the head three times, "resulting," according to a *Bulletin* reporter, "in the latter being permanently subdued."

One way or another, though, by the end of the following decade the hoodlum gangs had pretty much passed into history. Some would say it was because the understaffed police department was finally strengthened. In 1878, in the face of continuing depredations by the hoodlums, the state Legislature authorized an increase in the police department from 150 to 400 members. Thereafter the department was reorganized into two major districts, and police substations were established near the stamping grounds of the hoodlum gangs.

Others might point to the adoption of technological innovation that reduced the risk of hoodlum assaults on lone patrolmen and provided a ready response to riots and other emergencies. Officers still patrolled alone, but in 1889 a call box-patrol wagon system was established that placed telephones on beats connected with district stations, where patrol wagons staffed by two or more officers stood by to answer an officer's call for backup. No longer were officers completely isolated on their beats.

A change in police policy in dealing with hoodlum gang members was also offered as a reason for their decline. "Not until about 1890," comments Herbert Asbury in his classic *Barbary Coast*, "did the San Francisco police learn what the New York police had already known for more than 50 years—that the best cure for hoodlumism is the frequent application of the locust or hickory to the hoodlum's skull. Once the police had acquired this knowledge, the power of the rowdies rapidly declined." Or perhaps the demise of the gangs was assured by improving economic conditions in the decades following the 1870s, after which the previously unassimilated under-class was absorbed into the political and economic mainstream of the city.

Twenty-one

THE DAY THEY HANGED ST. PATRICK

Ethnic sensibilities, especially those of the Irish, were a bit tender in San Francisco in the 1850s and 1860s. According to one reading of history, the Second Committee of Vigilance was little more than a gang of nativist bully boys who illegally ran their Irish-Catholic political opponents out of town. Among those hanged by the vigilantes was James Casey, a member of the Board of Supervisors, who had fatally wounded newspaper editor James King of William.

There was more to it than that, to be sure, but the fact remains that those banished by the extralegal body were Irish and Catholic almost to a man. And in the post-vigilante period it became a St. Patrick's Day custom for anti-Irish pranksters to rile up the Irish community by displaying disrespectful effigies of Ireland's patron saint. The night before St. Patrick's Day in 1859, someone hung an image of the saint from the flagpole atop the Hall of Records. An alert officer found and removed it "before any offence was taken or a crowd collected." The next year the officers were not so prompt. They almost had a riot on their hands.

At 6 a.m. on Saturday, March 17, 1860, officers going off duty noticed an effigy of St. Patrick lashed two-thirds of the way up the 100-foot flag pole in Portsmouth Square, immediately across from the entrance to police headquarters in City Hall. The figure had a ring of potatoes strung around its neck, a whiskey bottle in one hand and a shillelagh in the other. Some of the crowd that began to gather thought the whole thing was rather humorous; the Irish among them did not. At 8 a.m., an indignant delegation of Irishmen called at police headquarters to demand that the offending figure be removed.

There was no one to hear their complaint, however, because the entire night watch had reported off duty two hours earlier. According to the work schedule then in effect the next shift didn't come on duty until 9 a.m. The complainants decided to take matters into their own hands. At 8:30, a newspaper reporter rushed into city jail and told the prison keeper, Officer Englander, the sole police officer on duty in the city at the time, that a group of angry men were preparing to cut down the flagpole with an ax. Englander gave the jail keys to the reporter, told him to keep an eye on things, and rushed out to stop the men.

Joined by two off-duty officers who responded to his whistled call for assistance, Englander approached the angry assemblage. He showed his star and commanded the ax wielder to desist, promising to get a sailor to climb the pole and take down the effigy. But by then events had gone too far and the officers were rudely shoved aside. In short order, the pole was down and the effigy was set afire.

21-1 Courtesy of Malcolm Barker.
Portsmouth Square in the mid 1850s showing the liberty pole from which the effigy of St. Patrick was suspended. The City Hall police station is shown at the right.

For the remainder of the day, large crowds remained in the square, but the destruction of the effigy seemed to have dissipated most of the anger. There were a few fist fights and some drinking; some arrests were made, but the police kept a low profile. A contemporary observer said of the strained situation, "with a little imprudence on the part of the police, [there] would have been a row."

Recriminations followed. The following Monday, Police Chief Burke brought charges of "culpable thoughtlessness" and neglect of duty against Officer Peter Quakenbush, the first officer to see the effigy, for failing to notify the chief. Quakenbush testified that he had tried unsuccessfully to get someone to climb the pole and only then had gone home. He also wondered why he was singled out. The fact of the matter was that the entire midnight watch had passed by the figure in going to City Hall to report off.

Nonetheless, Quakenbush was found guilty and sentenced to a 30-day suspension without pay, to take effect immediately. There is reason to suspect, however, that the trial had more to do with placating aggrieved community sentiment than with any strictly disciplinary purpose. For, as was noted by those following the case, Quakenbush returned to duty the next night and the sentence was never imposed. When asked why not, Chief Burke tersely commented that the minimally staffed department could not afford the loss of Quakenbush's service for a month.

Twenty-two
THE IRISH AND THE VIGILANTES

The fabled vigilantes of early San Francisco were not in fact the vigorous law'n'order citizens they have been made out in the history books, but rather a vicious, scheming anti-Irish mob.

—WARREN HINCKLE , NEWSPAPER COLUMNIST

In the summer of 1856, San Franciscans formed themselves into the largest vigilance committee in American history. According to one common interpretation of events, the vigilante movement was an attack by a nativist WASP merchant elite on Irish Catholic residents. Although Irish-Americans figured prominently among the targets of the committee, to characterize the movement as anti-Irish would be akin to those in our own time who label those opposed to crime committed by minorities as being anti-minority.

The great nineteenth-century immigration from Ireland—usually associated with the mid-century potato famine—actually began a couple of decades earlier. As early as 1820 the immigrant flow from Ireland already exceeded that from England, and by the late 1830s more than 30,000 Irish a year were arriving in the new world. During this period—one of the most turbulent in American urban history—the largely Roman Catholic newcomers came into conflict in American cities with lower-class Anglo-Protestant whites, contending for a share of an expanding though finite economic pie.

One of the battlefields where that conflict was played out was in the competition for political place. The natives did not give way willingly and the result was the decades of electoral violence that afflicted eastern American cities well into this century. The Irish immigrants—and more notably their American-born sons—did not invent the rules by which municipal elections degenerated into violence, but they took to the fray with a will.

When the California gold strike was made in the late 1840s and San Francisco grew to prominence as the main port of entry for California, some aspects of the conflict moved west. At first, most of the "better" people neglected politics and government in their quest for personal wealth. Many Irish-Americans, on the other hand, their hardball political skills honed in the fighting wards of eastern cities, gravitated toward local politics and joined David Broderick in his "Young Ireland" faction of the Democratic Party.

Politics was a volatile affair in San Francisco in the first half of the 1850s, attended by much of the violence that was learned in the East. Broderick's Young Irelanders were not the only ones who used violence at the polls—far from it—but they were certainly noticeable in its use. Tipperary-born, and New-York raised, Charlie Duane earned a reputation as a political thug as did New York-born Billy Mulligan. By the mid-1850s the better sort of people decided to stay in the West, and to do so they took over the politics. Unwilling to do the hard work of organizing at the polls, they took to more summary methods. In 1856 they reorganized the Committee of Vigilance, again bypassed the regular institutions of justice, and again hanged four and banished almost a hundred more.

It was the killing of nativist crusading editor James King of William by Irish-American County Supervisor James Casey in April 1856 that triggered the vigilante rising and resulted in Casey's hanging. Of the other three hanged, one was Italian, another English and the third a New Yorker with a distinctively non-Irish name.

On the face of it, however, there does seem to be something to the anti-Irish, anti-Catholic angle. Certainly, Irish Catholics were notably absent on the committee rolls, and among those punished, many had Irish names. Billy Carr, Billy Mulligan, Charles Duane, and Martin Gallagher were banished. And Irish-born Yankee Sullivan, former world heavyweight boxing champion, died in vigilante custody.

A close examination of the issues which brought on the committee suggests what bound the enemies of the Committee together was not so much their Irishness or their Catholicism but their participation in what was seen as a corrupt Democratic Party regime. No doubt there were anti-Catholic, anti-Irish, Know Nothing bigots among the Vigilance committee membership but the main thrust of their movement was to replace what they saw as a corrupt political establishment with one more suitable to the "natural" economic frontier elite who had by now decided to participate in the public business of the city. The conflict was more a contention between political parties and social and economic classes than between strictly ethnic or religious groupings.

Twenty-three
IRISH COPS

Whn Irish-surnamed Willis Casey was appointed San Francisco police Chief in 1990, he distanced himself a bit from his Irish heritage. "I'm one-quarter Irish," he was quick to point out to an interviewer. "My Irish grandfather died in 1901. But people jump to the conclusion that I'm an old Irish cop." Casey's need to downplay the Irish part of his heritage suggests that that being Irish can be a downright disadvantage for anyone seeking a career in American law enforcement in these days of the sometimes acrimonious debate about the merits of affirmative action.

Not so long ago the stereotypical image of the Irish cop was very much a part of the American conception of itself, from the caricatures of the police chiefs in "Batman" and "Dick Tracy" comic strips to the picture of the ham-fisted Irish beat cop of an earlier era, keeping order in horse-and-buggy American cities. As with other occupational stereotypes of years past—the Italian garbage collector or fisherman, the German brewer or baker, the Chinese laundryman or restaurant operator—that of the Irish cop has its roots in the real world.

There was once a time, however, when Irish police officers were a rarity on the American scene, kept out of the job by ethnic discrimination. Until the early decades of the nineteenth century, the United States was largely a rural society, peopled mainly by white Protestants (mostly of English extraction), blacks and Indians. Then began the great European immigration that would change the demographic face of American cities. Later years would see a massive immigration from southern and eastern Europe and more recently those from Asia and Latin America, but in the early decades of the nineteenth century, the Irish were among the first to come. By 1850

142

there were a million foreign-born Irish in the nation of 23 million. Like later unskilled arrivals, the Irish tended to huddle together for mutual support in the cities where they first arrived, working at low-paying manual jobs.

As American cities began to grow, to meet the demands of the rapidly industrializing economy, middle and upper-class native Protestants moved out of the inner cities—prefiguring the white flight to the suburbs of a century later—leaving behind lower-income Anglo-Americans to greet the hordes of arriving Irish immigrants. One view of the story of nineteenth-century urban America is that of one long, violent conflict between successive waves of immigrants and those who had been here before for a share of the economic pie. The first round of the fight was between native-born Protestant Americans—WASPs—and Irish-Catholic newcomers.

It was out of this strife, which turned the neighborhoods of nineteenth-century America into battlegrounds for warring ethnic gangs, that modern municipal police departments were developed. Beginning in the 1830s, large police departments, organized along military lines to do combat on an equal footing with the street gangs, first evolved in American cities. At first, the immigrant Irish were kept out of police jobs by earlier arrivals, who dominated the election machinery and thus controlled appointments to public employment. But as more and more Irish became naturalized American citizens, they began to make their weight felt at polls. Like many later immigrants, they looked to public employment as the way out of the dead-end jobs of the day. Their WASP adversaries did not give way easily. In Boston, that most Irish city of recent memory, the first Irish police officer to join the police in 1851, Barney McGinnity, did so only under court order, and when he showed up for work, the Chief of Police and the entire night watch resigned in protest.

From the start, the Irish had a better time of it in the West. When San Francisco exploded into cityhood during the Gold Rush years, immigrants came from everywhere, and in a town with no tradition of employment exclusion, at first almost anyone could go as far as talent allowed. Many Irish Americans, the sons of Irish immigrants of the preceding decades, who found life difficult in eastern cities, were among the first Gold Rush arrivals. Fired in the crucible of hardball eastern urban politics, the Irish made a place for themselves from the start in the wide-open political game in the boom town Rush city. David Broderick, son of an immigrant Irish stonemason, unable to advance himself in the then Protestant-controlled Tammany politics of New York City, came west to build a political career in the new country. As the head of the "New Ireland" faction of the Democratic Party, he was to have a leading role in California politics in the 1850s.

And when the San Francisco Police Department was formed in August 1849—two years before Barney McGinnity forced himself on the Boston Police Department with a court order—the man appointed as first chief of the new department was Malachi Fallon, a native of Athlone, Ireland, who had been raised, like Broderick, in New York City where he had served as a keeper of the Tombs Prison. It didn't hurt either that he was part of the Irish-American political faction then prominent in Democratic Party politics. Among the first 30 officers Fallon appointed to the department were men named Casserly, Cassidy, Claughley, Mullen, McGlaughin, McIntire, McRay, and Sweeney. There would be ups and downs but for the next 140 years the Irish were to play a major role in the police department of San Francisco. Most of the chiefs were Irish as were many of the officers who served under them.

The seemingly ubiquitous presence of the Irish in American policing is marked by the persistent efforts of others to get them into a different line of work. First, it was the WASPs. When native-born Protestants come to the realization in the mid-1850s that they were effectively losing control of municipal affairs in many cities with Irish victories in local elections, they moved the discussion to the statehouses which were then dominated by rural, largely Protestant and Republican votes. Laws were enacted placing city police departments under state control, thus diluting Irish Catholic Democratic influence over who got the jobs. New York City police were placed under a commission appointed by the state government in 1857, as were those in Baltimore in 1860, Chicago in 1861, Detroit in 1865, Cleveland in 1866 and Boston in 1885.

In San Francisco, the nativist counterparts of eastern WASPs were equally alarmed at the skill shown by the adherents of Broderick's "Young Ireland" faction to find their way into city jobs. But in California, where San Francisco, with its large Irish community, dominated the state legislature well into the present century, more direct methods were called for. In the summer of 1856, a group of public-spirited citizens in San Francisco, ostensibly outraged at crime and civic corruption, formed the famed Committee of Vigilance which hanged four of its adversaries and banished a number more, under pain of death should they return. Stripped of the accretions of legend which have attached themselves to the vigilante uprising, the true purpose of the famed committee is now known to have been rooted in local political conflicts of the day. The debate about the justification for taking the law into their own hands continues, but one thing is certain: Irish Catholic Democrats were as noticeable by their absence on the committee as they were well-represented among those hanged or banished.

For the next decade or so San Francisco was dominated by the Peoples Party, the political arm of the Vigilance committee, and while Irish names could still be found on the rolls of the police department, they were not present in their former numbers. It was only after the Civil War, during which many Irish were among those who swelled the population of California and San Francisco that the Irish again made their presence felt in local politics. By the mid-1870s more than a third of the department was Irish-born and the surnames of the rest indicate that many others could also look to roots in Ireland. Once entrenched, son followed father into the "business," as they will, down to the present time.

By the end of the nineteenth century, control of most urban police departments had reverted to local control but WASP concerns about immigrant (read Irish)-controlled city governments and police departments were not assuaged, giving rise to progressive "good government" movements around the country. The next several decades were to witness noisy investigations into civic graft and corruption in city after city, usually focusing on local police departments. One resulting reform which issued from this era was the introduction of civil service merit systems, with written entrance and promotional examinations, to replace political influence over hiring and promotions. San Francisco's 1900 "good government" charter provided for objective written testing in San Francisco to replace the old system whereby jobs could be purchased for a money stipend. In the 1930s New York Mayor Fiorello LaGuardia introduced written entrance and promotional examinations to the civil service system to give Jewish candidates, who tended to have better formal educations, a chance at city jobs. But the Irish began to "read the books" and soon mastered the new system. A generation later, their sons would be charged with using written examinations to exclude minority candidates.

In San Francisco in the 1940s, Chief of Police Michael Riordan, a native of County Kerry, allowed that 40 percent of the department was native-born Irish, another 40 percent was Irish-American and 20 percent were "other." Perhaps he overstated the case, but not by too much. Former Mayor Joseph Alioto remembered a time when "The Chief of Police in San Francisco not only had to be Irish, he had to be born in Ireland." A decade later, when a news reporter wondered at the number of so many Irish police chiefs in San Francisco's past, by then retired Chief Riordan ascribed the phenomenon to the English language skills the Irish brought with them, unlike other immigrants, and their innate sense of humor, a trait he thought essential to a police officer. Sonoma County Sheriff John Ellis, in answer to the same question, was perhaps closer to the knuckle. "In San Francisco," he said, "the force is Irish because in the early days San Francisco was Irish and if you weren't Irish you couldn't get a job in city government."

In our own time, more recent arrivals are knocking at the door, looking for jobs in the police, and many of them agree that it might be a good idea if the Irish looked elsewhere for employment. A new stereotypical police officer is emerging nationwide. Non-white police chiefs and large representations of non-white officers are appearing in major American cities, and not just those with minority voting majorities.

The ethnic shift in police representation is being accompanied by as much sound, if not as much fury, as that which attended the emergence of the Irish police officers in the nineteenth century. It is argued, on the one hand, that a disproportionate number of police jobs must go to non-whites to redress past grievances, or to provide role models for non-white youths. Others argue that a police department should reflect the composition of the community it serves if we are ever to see our way out of the urban disorder in which we are immersed. On the other hand, there are those who argue that the selection and promotion process should be based strictly on merit, the sins of the father should not be visited on the son, and that hard won standards of professional excellence should not be sacrificed by reverting to discredited political intervention in police affairs, no matter how worthy the object.

Inevitably, in the quest to change the complexion of the department's membership, the Irish have sometimes been singled out for special comment because of their previous prominence in police affairs. In some circles, Irish-bashing became the vogue and it became fashionable to dredge up real and fancied sins of the Irish past to justify any number of contrary practices. One observer talked about "troglodyte" pockets of "the old-guard, traditionally Irish-Catholic contingent in various stations" of the San Francisco Police Department, who resisted the changes that had to be made. Others cited what they call the "Irish affirmative action" of previous generations as justification for measures which would now exclude the Irish, among other white males, from an equal chance at entry and promotion in public jobs. Contemporary legal reasoning resulting in quotas (or goals) for previous under-represented classes in hiring and promotion is based on the conclusion that a group of white male police officers, often of Irish descent, had somehow manipulated the testing system—a process over which they had no control—to give themselves an advantage in written testing over such disparate groups as women, African-Americans, Asians and Hispanics.

Cast as it is in moral terms, the whole argument misses the important point. The simple fact is that the newcomers, like the immigrants of the past, want the jobs; they have the political horsepower to achieve their ends; and they will have them. It is not likely that the Irish bashing will end any time soon. White males of any type are one of the few groups it is politically acceptable to criticize with impunity in the hyper-sensitive age in which we find ourselves, and, prominent as the Irish are in the history of municipal policing, it is inevitable that they will come in for their share. It well may be that urban dwellers late in the next century will look back on our time and wonder what all the fuss was about. Who nowadays, after all, spends a lot of time thinking about nineteenth century urban conflicts?

Those who want to keep the ethnic composition of police departments suspended in amber should give a thought to what Barney McGinnity had to do to get a job on the Boston Police Department a century and a half ago. At the same time those who wish to bash the Irish, should remember their contribution to urban policing. It was largely Irish police departments that walked the beats of urban America in the long years before the development of radio communication and instant backup; that reunited lost children with their parents, settled neighborhood squabbles, fought the crooks, and did all the many order-keeping jobs in the long dangerous history of American cities.

The San Francisco Police Department, like many cities, has a Roll of Honor, on which are proudly inscribed the names of those who gave their lives in the line of duty. That roll attests to the sacrifices of the Irish police. From Galway-born Lieutenant William Burke of Mission Station who was shot to death on March 23, 1898 to Sergeant John Macaulay, of Irish/Scots heritage, who was murdered by a deranged killer in 1982, the Irish are disproportionately represented.

The world has turned a few times since the Irish police first trod the streets of America's cities and those cities have changed greatly. Demographic reality suggests that in the future Irish police officers will not dominate the nation's police forces as they did in the past. But it's safe to say that the sons and daughters of Ireland can be counted on to be on hand in the years to come, carrying a good part of the load of policing San Francisco and other American cities.

Twenty-four

THE LITTLE FROG CATCHER

O n Thursday, September 15, 1876, the evening quiet at San Miguel Railway Station was shattered by the report of a heavy shotgun blast. Pellets from the shot broke the window of a front bedroom of John McNamara's saloon/hotel, and struck 27-year-old Jeanne Bonnet lying in the bed beyond; she died instantly. Blanche Beunon, who was in the room with her, was not hit. Blanche, described in the contemporary press as "a French woman of bad character," and Jeanne were preparing for bed in a guest bedroom, which faced out on the building's small front porch, when the shotgun blast crashed through the window. Neither McNamara, who was tending bar in the adjoining room, nor anyone else in the nearby buildings heard any sounds of escape.

In 1876 the little hamlet at San Miguel, the last San Francisco stop on the San Jose Railroad, was located at what is now San Jose Avenue and Sickles Street in the Oceanview District. The settlement was then comprised of a dilapidated little railroad station, a country grocery store, and McNamara's four-room saloon/hotel. At first, the thinking was that the shooting was the deadly outcome of the dispute with a stable keeper the preceding day over late charges on a rented buggy, but on reconsideration it was thought highly unlikely that an established businessman would have resorted to such extreme measures to collect a small debt.

It was also evident that the killer had been familiar with the layout of the death room. The window through which the shot was fired had been covered with an opaque green shade, and examination showed that the shotgun had been rested on the sill and aimed accurately at the corner where the bed was located.

As police considered the victim's early life and recent activities, a more likely theory began to emerge. As a small child, Jeanne Bonnet was one of two daughters in a family of French theatrical performers quite popular in the post-Gold Rush city. She appeared to have a theatrical career ahead of her but the family began to go haywire. The family broke up, her mother died, and her 16-year-old sister was incarcerated in the State Insane Asylum at Stockton, where she also died. Her disabled father moved to Oakland seeking work, leaving Jeanne to her own devices. Jeanne had been a frequent inmate of the Industrial school. When not in trouble with the law, she supported herself by catching frogs in the ponds near Lake Merced and selling them to French restaurants in downtown San Francisco.

Jeanne Bonnet, the Frog-Catcher.

24-1. Author's collection.   The Little Frog Catcher decked out in male attire.

As an adult, Jeanne continued her trouble with the law, most frequently for refusing to wear female attire. She "bore a strikingly boyish appearance," according to one contemporary description. "She was of slight figure, below the medium height, rather good-looking, and always wore her jet-black hair cut short after the masculine fashion." Bonnet wore men's clothing, she said, because a dress would have inconvenienced her in her chosen line of work. Nonetheless, commented one editor, there were no frogs to be found on Kearny Street, where she spent a good part of her non-working time. It was Jeanne's oft-expressed opinion that the law prohibiting her from wearing male apparel was an infringement on the rights of women, and she said that she intended to continue, no matter what the consequences.

Hers was a turbulent life. "She made considerable money at her business," it was reported after her death, "but being addicted to drinking she made the acquaintance of bad women of her own nationality, and became embroiled in many fights, after each of which she found herself in prison . . ." "Frail and slight as Jennie [sic] was," remarked another, "she was courageous and reckless, and naturally a disturbing element in the peculiar society in which she mixed."

When interviewed by the police on the morning following the shooting, Blanche Beunon related that she had come to California from France about a year earlier with a man named Arthur Deneve, with whom she had a child. About a month before the shooting, she had broken up with Deneve, and in reprisal Deneve and his close friend, Ernest Gerard, had stolen her child.

As far as she knew, she continued, Deneve had departed for France a few weeks before the shooting. A week prior to the murder, however, while she and Jeanne were walking on Waverly Place, they had been accosted by his friend Gerard who accused Jeanne of luring Blanche away from her lover. He assaulted both women, Blanche said, and then called a police officer to have Jeanne arrested for wearing male apparel. Hearing later that Gerard had threatened to throw acid in her face, said Blanche, Jeanne arranged lodgings for her with a Frenchman named Pierre Louis and his wife Caroline at a farm (near the current intersection of Ocean and San Jose avenues.) Later she moved with Jeanne to McNamara's hotel. Blanche felt safe enough to go into town during the day, she told the investigators, but always returned to San Miguel at night.

On Wednesday evening, Blanche said, she was warned by Caroline Louis not to go about at night because there was talk in town "that the men of the class to which my lover belonged were making threats against us," particularly Jeanne, for having alienated Blanche from her pimp. Detectives picked up Gerard. He denied having made threats against anyone. He did admit, however, that he had indeed met Blanche in the street, along with Jeanne Bonnet, whom he said he didn't know, and who he at first assumed to be a man. When he upbraided Blanche for having abandoned her child, he said, Bonnet intervened and tried to pull a knife on him. He disarmed her, he claimed, and then called an officer to arrest her when he found out she was in fact a woman. Gerard offered witnesses to prove that he had been in his rooms downtown the night of the murder.

In hindsight, San Franciscans were not surprised at Jeanne's violent end. For all her vaunted independence and feistiness, it was evident that she was struggling with personal demons. When incarcerated in the Industrial School years before, it was said, she would gain entry to the boys' dormitory and there "attack the largest boy found in the room, just to show how she could whip him." As an adult, she was constantly getting into drunken scrapes which often resulted in her arrest. She had previous run-ins with pimps. "She was the cause, frequently," said one report, "of separation between the courtesans and their more degraded paramours, which of course excited the hostility of the wretches."

Two years earlier, she had attempted suicide by ingesting laudanum, but was saved by medical intervention. And a few months before her death she was hospitalized with a gunshot wound. (She told the city physician that the man who visited her in the hospital was the man who shot her. The physician identified that man as Ernest Gerard, putting the lie to his claim that he did not know her.) It was very much in character that Jeanne went to her death sporting two black eyes, sustained a few days earlier in a drunken fall from a horse.

With Deneve apparently out of the country and Gerard having a cast-iron alibi for the time of the crime, the case went nowhere. Then the police got a break. Captain of Detectives Isaiah Lees learned from an informant that a Pacific Street saloon keeper had been bragging that he knew who the killer was. When Captain Lees braced the man, he named Pierre Louis as the killer, the very man with whom Jeanne had sought shelter for Blanche two weeks before, and whose wife warned the women to be on their guard.

The deal had been cooked up in his saloon, the barkeeper said, by Arthur Deneve, who offered Louis $2,000 to kill Blanche as an example to the other "girls." According to the saloon keeper, Bonnet's death was a mistake. Lees and his detectives hastened to the farm near San Miguel but by then Louis and Caroline had flown the coop.

An 1879 summary of the case offered another explanation, one that the police detectives endorsed. It seems that Blanche had another lover, an otherwise respectable Market Street merchant of Italian ancestry. The merchant, who those acquainted with the triangle called L'Amant d'Blanche, was aware of Blanche's background but agreed to overlook it if she remained faithful only to him. The intensely jealous merchant nursed Blanche through her pregnancy, showered her with gifts and offered his hand in marriage. Friends warned him that she was playing him false but he was never able to catch her out. But it was when she took up with Jeanne Bonnet that he had enough. He went to Louis, really Louis Duffranant, and arranged to have Blanche killed. Louis went to San Miguel that night and shot through the window but killed Jeanne by mistake. The merchant reestablished his relationship with Blanche to divert suspicion and stayed with her until she died of throat cancer six months after the murder.

In mid-July 1880 Duffranant was arrested near Montreal for assault on Caroline. Caroline came forward and said that he had indeed killed Jeanne Bonnet. She confirmed that Blanche, not Jeanne, was the intended victim, and said she was in fear of her own life, having left Louis when he threatened to kill her if she told what she knew. Captain Lees rushed to Canada but found out that he was again too late. Louis had hanged himself the day before his arrival. Not all agreed with the idea that Blanche was the intended victim. One police detective argued that Jeanne had been the intended victim because she interfered with the pimps' operation by freeing prostitutes. This detective said that after her death the pimps assembled and had a big party in Alameda.

In the end it all came to nothing. All were dead or gone and the merchant apparently went on his merry way.

Twenty-five
THE GREAT RIOT OF 1877

T imes were bad in California in the summer of 1877. The nation was in an economic slump, the rich Comstock silver lode that had fueled the coastal economy for more than a decade was playing out, and the worst drought in a decade reduced wheat production, throwing thousands out of work. In San Francisco, conditions were aggravated by the continued arrival of thousands of Chinese laborers to compete with white working men in the shrinking job market.

At 7 p.m. on Monday, July 23, 1877, several thousand working men gathered in the sand lots to the south of the new City Hall (on Market Street between 7th and 9th) to voice their support for eastern railroad strikers. At 8 p.m., a drunk fired into the crowd from a nearby rooming house, striking three of the demonstrators. The man was promptly arrested, but tensions were running high and when the crowd broke up an hour later, its more volatile members split off and started to attack Chinese washhouses.

Officer Charles Blakelee fended off the mob at pistol point on Leavenworth Street, and Mounted Officer John Sneider did the same thing at Pacific and Taylor. But the officers guarding a washhouse on Hyde Street were overpowered, and the Chinese inside just managed to scoot out the back door before the building was torched. The main part of the mob headed for Chinatown, where they were met by a double police line across Dupont Street at California under the command of Captain William Douglass. The police charged, driving the crowd to Kearny. A similar police line at Broadway prevented another mob from entering the Chinese quarter from the north.

But while the beleaguered police were so occupied, splinter ele-

25-1 Courtesy of Robert Chandler.   The "sandlots" in front of City Hall (between 7th and 9th streets at Market). This was the scene of many anti-Chinese demonstrations. It was from a demonstration at this location that the great riot of 1877 erupted.

157

ments of the mob destroyed isolated washhouses in the North Beach and Tenderloin areas. The fight continued the next day, this time South of Market with police officers under Douglass and Captain Isaiah Lees fighting running battles with gangs of hoodlums, who ranged through the sector bent on destroying Chinese laundries. Two hundred prominent merchants and property owners met that day at the Chamber of Commerce and formed a Committee of Public Safety to assist the police in keeping order. Police Chief Henry Ellis was thankful for any help he could get. The regular force of 150 officers was hardly sufficient to police the city of 200,000 in normal times.

On Wednesday, as thousands of San Franciscans enrolled in the Committee of Safety, dubbed the "Pickhandle Brigade" for the weapons issued to its members, dissident interests called an "anti-coolie" meeting for 8 p.m. at City Hall. The signs were ominous. The more activist members among the radical group didn't show up for work that day. And the rumor spread that the Pacific Mail Steamer *City of Tokio* (sic) was due in port with a full load of Chinese immigrants; the word was that efforts would be made to stop them from landing.

During the day, members of the Pickhandle Brigade were organized into military units, police were issued longer batons, and large furniture wagons were fitted out with benches to transport police officers and committee men quickly to trouble spots. Naval and Marine forces were positioned off South Beach in the *USS Pensacola* to lend a hand if needed. At 7 p.m., a load of lumber, on the Beale Street Wharf, a block from the Pacific Mail Wharf, was set afire. As firefighters fought the blaze, about 1,500 hoodlums ensconced on Rincon Hill above rained stones down on them. A joint force of police and committeemen charged the hill, and when police were fired upon from the crowd, they returned fire, killing four and wounding 18.

In the meantime, a mob from the Market Street rally, many of them 12 to 16 years old, moved through the South of Market sector with a battering ram, destroying Chinese washhouses. On Thursday, the rioters had worn themselves out. By then, too, the Committee of Public Safety was fully organized, and 4,000 of its members were patrolling the streets, their pickhandles at the ready. By July 30, conditions had returned enough to normal that the body could be disbanded.

But the root problems did not disappear overnight. Following the riot, unemployed workers, and others disaffected with the economic situation, formed the political Workingmen's Party, under the leadership of Dennis Kearny, the owner of a small drayage firm who had been a member of the Pickhandle Bridge, radicalized, he said later, by the brutality of his fellow committee men.

Over the next several years, the Workingmen's Party, which gained control over the municipal government in the next election, supplanted the pro-business ethos in City Hall with its own, more radical agenda. In the immediate aftermath of the riot, the police department was more than doubled in size to 400 officers and, because of the fear that it might come under the control of the "communistic" Workingmen's movement, was placed by an act of the Legislature under the control of a state-appointed commission, where it remained for the rest of the century.

Twenty-six

LEST WE FORGET

On a little-noticed wall in the lobby of San Francisco's Hall of Justice on Bryant Street, where modern-day hoodlums pass by on the way to their frequent court appearances, are engraved the names of those officers of the San Francisco Police Department who gave their lives over the years in the line of duty. The first name on the list is that of "Substitute" Officer John Coots, listed as killed in 1878.

For all the supposed lawlessness of early San Francisco, it was more than a quarter century after the department's 1849 founding before the first officer's name was place on the roll of honor. That is not to say, however, that the criminals weren't trying. In the early morning hours of February 7, 1850, shortly after the department was organized, Officer Blackman had occasion to arrest an off-duty bartender named Oliver Dewey for assaulting a man with a billy club on Pacific Street.

In those days, long before the introduction of patrol wagons, it was up to an arresting officer to get his prisoner to the station the best way he could. If far from the station, he might commandeer an express wagon to transport his prisoner to jail; if the prisoner was a helpless drunk, the officer might use a nearby wheelbarrow to trundle him in; or, as was most often the case, officers would walk their prisoners to the station, sometimes fighting all the way.

As Officer Blackman escorted Dewey toward the station house, then on the southwest corner of Portsmouth Square at Clay Street and Brenham Place, the prisoner wrenched himself free (handcuffs were not yet a regular item of police equipment) and darted into a saloon at Kearny and Washington streets with officer Blackman hot on his tail. Once inside, Dewey armed himself with a pistol and shot the approaching officer point-blank in the face. Blackman was

160

able to retreat to the station house diagonally across Portsmouth Square, where he summoned help from his fellow officers. The officers responded immediately across the square where they found that saloon patrons sympathetic to Dewey had closed and locked the doors. By the time the officers forced entry, they found that their bird had flown the coop. Later that day "on information received," officers went to a rooming house on Washington Street and arrested Dewey. He was later released by the court, though, and in a pattern familiar to police officers of any age, was again arrested on an assault charge a couple of months later.

One explanation for the low number of police fatalities in the early days was the undependability of firearms of the time. As often as not, before the development of self-contained cartridges, cap and ball pistols were prone to misfire. That's what happened in Blackman's case. Dewey's pistol was improperly charged and his shot merely blackened the officer's face. And that's why nineteenth-century officers almost invariably equipped themselves with long bowie knives or daggers which they carried in scabbards under their uniform coats, as a backup weapon should their pistols fail to fire. On more than one occasion, the lives of officers were saved by their backup knives.

Down through the years, there were many other attempts on the lives of officers, and by the 1870s things really began to go downhill. Economic conditions were bad, giving rise to a decade of anti-Chinese agitation and violence by angry white workingmen. In the increasingly hostile social environment, the tiny police department of the time was not up to the tasks demanded of it. Experience has shown that the universal and never ending demands of police officials for more staff should be viewed with a healthy skepticism. That said, San Francisco in the 1870s was seriously under policed with a ratio of police officers to citizens that would be comparable to 525 officers to police the city of today. (Current department is about 2000 officers.)

One consequence of the economic dislocation and the enforcement vacuum created by a personnel-starved department was the growth of a large group of alienated young men who banded together in the "hoodlum" gangs which terrorized San Francisco all through the decade and beyond. Among their favorite targets were police officers, afoot and often out of immediate contact with other officers. "[The hoodlums] particularly enjoyed a conflict with a policeman," recalled an *Examiner* reporter in later years, "and the officer who attempted to arrest one of the gang was lucky if he escaped being pounced upon and beaten by a crowd of the prisoner's associates."

26-1 Courtesy of John Boessenecker.
John Runk, the murderer of Officer Charles Coots.

Sometimes it went beyond a simple trouncing. At 11 p.m. on New Year's Eve, 1876, Officer William Hensley went into the Racine House on Kearny near Pacific to break up a fight involving a group of hoodlums. The officer seized one of the principal participants, a young man named Frank

Doran, the son of police officer William Doran. Frank's brother, William Jr., intervened, and others of the hoodlum gang locked the barroom door. They then began to beat Officer Hensley, who broke away momentarily and smashed out a window with his pistol to attract attention. William Doran was able to disarm the officer and shoot him in the face with his own pistol, whereupon Hensley drew his backup knife and plunged it into his assailant's heart, killing him instantly. Other officers, drawn from nearby beats by the sound of the gunshot, took charge of the scene, and Officer Hensley walked to the nearby Receiving Hospital where he was diagnosed as having a fractured skull. He later returned to duty and retired for service in 1890. "Substitute" Officer Coots was not to be so lucky.

For most of the nineteenth century, police officers didn't have paid days off. They were responsible for covering their beats every day of the month, and the only way an officer could get a day off was by hiring a substitute to take his place. To provide a pool of replacement officers, the police

26-2 Courtesy of John Boessenecker.
James Wilson, Runk's companion when he killed Officer Coots.

commission periodically appointed a group of "substitute officers," who received no pay from the city but had all the "authority to act as regular policemen whenever regular officers wished to absent themselves from their beat."

On the midnight watch of April 26, 1877 (it wasn't 1878, as is engraved on the Wall of Honor), regular Officer Charles Coleman took the night off and hired Substitute Officer Coots (his first name was actually Charles, not John, as is inscribed on the wall), to replace him on the beat. At about 1:30 that morning, two young members of the Hill Boys, 17-year-old John Runk and a young graduate of San Quentin named James Wilson (aka Charles Johnson, aka Frank Keyes) were seen on Washington Street "quarreling with the women in front of the houses." As the young hoodlums turned into Waverly Place where they began to harass the Chinese prostitutes sitting at their windows, a French woman who lived on the corner blew her police whistle, summoning Officer Coots to the scene.

Officer Coots sent the young miscreants on their way and followed them down Waverly Place to Sacramento Street where they continued to abuse him verbally. Finally, his patience at an end, the officer placed Wilson under arrest and marched him toward jail, down the center of the Clay Street railway tracks, gripping him by the coat collar at arm's length from the rear. Runk followed along behind. At Clay and Dupont streets, the party came upon Officer Joseph Kelly, who, according to his later statement, said that he offered to accompany Coots but that the officer declined.

As Officer Kelly watched from above, Coots and his prisoner continued down Clay, headed for the City Hall prison at Kearny and Washington streets. Just as they reached Brenham Place, from where the station house could be seen, impressing the finality and inevitability of the arrest on the young hoodlums, Wilson began to struggle and Runk walked up behind officer Coots, placed a large-bore Colt six-shot revolver to his head, just behind the right ear, and fired, killing him instantly.

Both hoodlums then ran up Brenham Place, with Officer Kelly in pursuit blowing his whistle to attract attention. They ran across the top of Portsmouth Square to Washington Street, where they were seen running through Washington Place [now Wentworth Alley], to Jackson Street and on through Bartlett Alley [now Beckett Street] to Pacific, where they ran into officers Charles Eaton and Thomas Price, who, according to a contemporary news account, "after a somewhat exciting struggle, succeeded in handcuffing the two, and bringing them down to the City Prison. . . . "

Wilson was eventually freed by the courts the following month as not having been directly responsible for the shooting, but Runk was placed on trial on a charge of first degree murder. With more than one witness testifying that they saw him shoot the officer, there was no way that Runk could claim that he hadn't done it. Instead, the defense offered his dysfunctional family background in mitigation of the offense. His attorney characterized Runk, in the parlance of the time, as "a boy, little above the age of childhood . . . who had been reared in the most inauspicious circumstances."

His family, the attorney claimed, was "distracted by discord," resulting in his parents' eventual divorce. Thereafter, his father—out of spite the attorney said—procured the boy's commitment to the Industrial School (the nineteenth-century equivalent of the Youth Guidance Center). Since then the young boy had been allowed to run wild, the defense claimed, and at 15 he was sentenced to the County Jail where "the associations of the jail further tended to vitiate his moral sensibilities."

The prosecution showed that Runk had first been sent to the Industrial School in 1872 at the age of 12 for larceny, well before the breakup of his family. After three months there, he was sent to a reform school in Weaverville for two years and then returned to the city, where he lived with his mother when not in jail. At 14 he was sent again to the Industrial School for a theft, and a year later he was convicted of larceny and assault and battery, and sentenced to 375 days, this time in the county jail. Runk broke out before his term was completed, was recaptured and sentenced to an additional 125 days for the escape. He subsequently committed an assault on a cell mate for which he was sentenced to an additional 50 days. He was last arrested on February 9, 1877, for vagrancy and disturbing the peace and was returned to the County Jail for 40 days. He had been released just two weeks prior to the shooting of Officer Coots.

One editor seized on the Coots killing as a metaphor for the deteriorating condition of city life. "It is evident that the lawless element of our population is rapidly increasing," wrote *The San Francisco Chronicle* on the occasion of Runk's trial, "not only in numerical force but also in reckless audacity."

"The most alarming feature of this business is that [Runk and Wilson] are representatives of a large class of audacious criminals by which this community is infested. For months past the suburbs of the city have been made dangerous after nightfall by gangs of full-grown hoodlums ready for the perpetration of crimes of violence. They prowl during the hours of darkness . . . and may be frequently found during the day sunning themselves or sleeping in sequestered nooks in the neighborhood of North Beach or among the sand dunes between Black Point and the Presidio." To the editor's thinking, "the police must hunt them down with inexorable pertinacity" and "the courts must visit them with the extremist [sic] penalties of the law..." Runk was found guilty of first-degree murder and his sentencing was set for July 27, 1877.

Among his other problems, John Runk was guilty of fatally bad timing. In July 1877, the festering issue of anti-Chinese sentiment exploded into a week-long riot which threatened to bring the city to its knees. In the several days prior to Runk's sentencing hearing, gangs of rioters rampaged through the city, burning and looting, un-

166

til brought to a halt by the beleaguered police department, assisted by the "pickhandle brigade" of citizen volunteers. At his sentencing hearing on July 27, Runk's defense attorney asked for leniency, again citing his client's harassment by the police and his generally troubled past. But with portions of the city still smoldering from the effects of recent activities of hoodlum gangs, the court was of no mind to be merciful. Runk was sentenced to be hanged.

As the execution date approached, attempts were made to obtain a gubernatorial commutation of the death sentence. The *Bulletin* editor pointed out that the root of the problem of the hoodlum gangs was the unemployment faced by the city's youth. They wanted to work but there was no work for them. According to the *Chronicle*, however, "It has become absolutely necessary to check [the hoodlum gangs]," and, "as a means of doing that, nothing can be more effective than to make an example of one so prominently associated with them and so clearly guilty of murder."

The Governor declined to intervene, and on April 26, 1878, one year to the day after he murdered Officer Coots, Runk was taken from his cell to an improvised gallows in a corridor of the Broadway County Jail, and hanged by the neck until he was dead. He was 18 years old. That same month the State Legislature approved of an increase for the police department.

The day after Runk's hanging, the *Chronicle* editor summed up the lessons of the execution from his point of view. "An officer of a city like San Francisco," he wrote, "is frequently called upon to risk his life . . . . His only protection [in case he is disabled or killed] is the knowledge that the law will surely punish anyone who attacks an officer. . ." Otherwise, the editor added, "without such protection, no officer who has a wife and family could be blamed for keeping out of the way of danger." The execution was necessary, he continued, "as a powerful warning to the reckless class of youths to which [Runk] belonged, and as a pledge to officers that their lives are held sacred by the authorities."

Twenty-seven
DANIEL "RED MIKE" SULLIVAN

Police response time was 11 hours in a long-ago murder case in San Francisco. When Ann Barry's brutally murdered body was discovered at Parker and Fulton streets at 10 a.m. on November 7, 1878, it took an hour for the neighbors to locate the nearest police officer, John Maloney, who rode to police headquarters where he reported the crime about noon. Not until 9 p.m. did an investigation get under way.

The inner Richmond District in those days comprised the thinly settled western outskirts of the city, a neighborhood inhabited mostly by the families of gardeners and other laborers who worked in Golden Gate Park and in the nearby cemeteries. At 7 a.m. that day, Richard Barry left home for his job in the park. His 12-year old son left for school an hour later, leaving his mother at home alone. About 9:30 a.m., a gardener in the Masonic Cemetery across the street (now the site of the University of San Francisco) heard screams in the house. Thinking the woman was whipping her son, he paid them no mind.

Shortly thereafter a family friend arrived and discovered the murder scene. The floor, walls and stove near the body were splattered with blood. The victim's clothing was in disarray. Her throat was cut. The side of her head had been caved in with a hatchet found nearby. The house had been ransacked. Clothing belonging to the victim's husband had been stolen.

Neighbors summoned Officer Maloney, who lived on Eddy Street between Pierce and Scott. He conducted a cursory preliminary investigation, then mounted his horse and trotted four miles to police headquarters at Kearny and Washington streets. He reported the crime to the detective on duty at 12:30 p.m. but for some reason, the message wasn't passed along immediately, and the investigation didn't get under way until later that night.

Once involved, the investigators "were galvanized into action" by the excitement of the nearby residents. Their efforts were "fanned to fever heat when it became known that the murderer had another object in addition to that of robbery . . ." reported the *Alta*. A huge manhunt was mounted by the entire detective force and supplemented by a detachment of mounted soldiers from the Presidio who quartered the sparsely inhabited area in search of a suspect.

27-1 Courtesy of Bill Secrest.   Daniel "Red Mike" Sullivan, the murderer of Ann Barry.

On Friday morning investigators found some bloody clothes near the murder house, which were identified by workers at the nearby Calvary Cemetery (now the site of the old Sears' store and Kaiser Hospital), as belonging to a co-worker, Daniel "Red Mike" Sullivan, "a man inordinately fond of the opposite sex." Figuring correctly that Sullivan would head to his haunts on the Barbary Coast, police brought cemetery workers who knew the suspect downtown on Saturday night. The workers were teamed up with police officers to search for him.

At about 9 p.m., a cemetery man named John O'Connor, who had somehow become separated from the officer with whom he had been paired, came upon Sullivan in the Chinese section of Dupont Street, soon to be renamed Grant Avenue. With the help of a bystand-er, O'Connor managed to arrest Sullivan after a struggle. Sullivan vehemently protested his innocence but detectives searched second-hand stores until they found where he had sold the stolen clothing.

At trial it was revealed that the defendant had murdered a man in New Orleans years earlier, and deserted his wife and 12 children. Sullivan then came to California, where he served a term in San Quentin for theft. He had twice been incarcerated in the state in-sane asylum at Stockton and was an escapee from there at the time of the Barry murder. Sullivan was found guilty of first-degree mur-der, but because of his history of mental illness, escaped the hang-man and was sentenced to life in San Quentin Prison.

The 11-hour response time on the day of the murder led to newspaper criticism of the police. In their defense, the detectives to whom Maloney reported the crime said later that he had told them merely that it had been a case of sudden death, and hence they had referred him to the coroner. Nonsense, said the *Alta's* editor. "It is absurd to suppose that Officer Maloney, having seen a woman ly-ing dead on her kitchen floor, mangled with a hatchet, would go to the Police Office and report a woman found dead in bed."

Twenty-eight
FONG CHING aka "LITTLE PETE"

Things were tense in Chinatown in 1897 as its residents prepared for the Year of the Ram. On the eve of the festivities, at 9:00 p.m. on Saturday January 23, two Sze Yup gunmen entered the barber shop at 819 Washington Street and fatally shot Fong Ching, leader of the Sam Yups and Chinatown vice lord. Police quickly arrested two men found in an upstairs room of the building next door, but the smart money in Chinatown knew right away that they had the wrong guys.

Fong Ching, or "Little Pete" as he was more commonly known, was born in China in 1864 and came to San Francisco as a young boy. His fluency in English, learned in a mission school, made him useful as an interpreter around the courts, where he picked up a working knowledge of the American justice system. The Chinese Exclusion Act, passed in 1882 when Pete was 18, to restrict the importation of Chinese laborers, had the unintended consequence of ushering in two decades of bloody "tong wars." The act also reduced the supply of females for the brothels of Chinatown, and the "Highbinder" tongs, which had run Chinese vice operations in Chinatown for decades, competed murderously for the reduced stock.

In this climate, Little Pete, who fit comfortably in both the white and Chinese worlds, rose to the top in the Gee Sin Seer fighting tong. The Six District Companies, which had lost face by counseling their members not to oppose the exclusion laws, in hope of a favorable court decision, were supplanted by the fighting tongs for a time as the dominant element in Chinatown. In this way, Little Pete also rose to the leadership of the Sam Yup District Company. During the 1880s and 1890s, Little Pete was one of the leading forces in Chinatown vice. With the help of compliant police officials, he would have Sze Yup Company gambling houses closed and then

171

promptly reopen them under his own management. He had one temporary setback late in the decade when he served a short prison sentence for trying to bribe a police officer, but he returned and resumed his old ways.

On one occasion he was caught fixing races at the Bay District Race track and was barred from the track. On another, he hired a group of race track hangers-on to disguise themselves as police officers and break up Sze Yup headquarters. The Sze Yups saw through the ruse and identified Pete as the instigator. By late 1896, the word on the street was that Little Pete was a marked man. Some thought it was because he was a bit too cozy with the authorities. Others said it was because he had rejected the efforts of a well- respected peace commissioner from China to settle the difficulties between the Sam Yups and Sze Yups. Some thought he had carried his oppression and harassment of the more numerous Sze Yups too far.

Pete got the word and outfitted himself with a chain-mail vest, armed himself with two pistols, and went about with two German shepherds and a white bodyguard, on the theory that tong gunmen would not want to bring down the wrath of the white community by harming a white man. On the night of January 23, Pete left his third-floor apartment in the building at Washington Street and Waverly Place, and descended the interior stairway that led to the ground-floor barbershop. Feeling secure within his own building, he left his guard dogs upstairs and sent his bodyguard out to get a newspaper. It was then that his assailants struck.

The immediate reaction was fear of a widespread war. Nobody believed that the men arrested for the crime had anything to do with it. Pete's widow posted a reward a few days later offering $2,000 for the arrest of the real culprits, and the two men arrested were eventually released. The real killers are supposed to have made it to China. With thousands of Chinese from the interior heading for San Francisco to join in the New Year festivities, tong gunmen from both sides

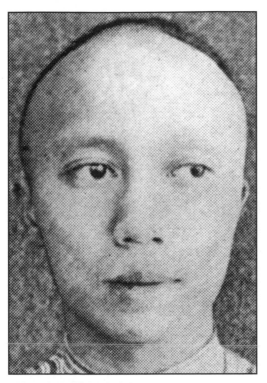

28-1 Courtesy of San Francisco History Center.
Fong Ching aka "Little Pete."

among them, one contemporary editor feared that Pete's killing was "only the signal for a war of extermination of Sze Yup against Sam Yup, which will make the gutters of Chinatown run with blood."

The police reacted promptly. The night after the murder, the Chinatown squad—adopting tactics employed several years before but rejected in the face of lawsuits—broke up several tong meetings. And Chief Patrick Crowley beefed up the six-man squad to 20, and divided it into a day and night shift. With the constitutional gloves off, the police forced their way into the dens of the highbinder tongs and effectively drove them out of town. Whether it was the police raids or, as some have suggested, a few selective assassinations of Pete's most ardent supporters, the Chinese New Year celebration that year was peaceable—if somewhat subdued—and shortly thereafter, the Sam Yups and Sze Yups patched things up—for a time, anyway.

Twenty-nine
THE MURDER OF MAMIE KELLY

It was sweet to love

But oh! how bitter,

To love my sweetheart.

And then to kill her.

— ALEXANDER GOLDENSON

A t 3:00 p.m. on Wednesday, November 10, 1886, 14-year-old Elizabeth "Mamie" Kelly left John Swett Grammar School at McAllister and Franklin streets with two of her school chums. The group walked down McAllister to Polk Street where they turned south toward Maggie's residence at 22 Hayes Street, two blocks farther on. As the girls approached the corner of Polk and Ash streets (at about the present location of the Polk street steps of City Hall), a young man came out of Loderhose's Grocery across the street and beckoned to Mamie. She separated from her friends, telling them that she would soon rejoin them and went to the young man.

The two were seen to exchange a few words and then, with no warning, the young man drew a pistol, said "Damn you, take that!" and shot Mamie in the face point-blank, killing her instantly. The killer then ran to the nearby "New City Hall" police station at Larkin and McAllister streets, where he turned himself in to Sergeant John Ayers. "I've shot my girl," he said, "I've done it. Lock me up at once; lock me up—they want to lynch me." A laundry truck driver who had followed the murderer from the scene confirmed what he said and showed police where the man had thrown a .32-caliber pearl-handled revolver into the bushes in front of the police station.

Police identified the shooter as 18-year-old Alexander Golden-son, a self-described artist, who lived with his parents next door to the Kellys on Hayes Street. News of the killing spread rapidly and angry crowds began to gather. Police Chief Patrick Crowley immediately sent detectives to bring Goldenson to the more secure prison at the "Old City Hall" at Kearny and Washington streets. That evening, Goldenson made a voluntary written statement to the police in which he claimed that he and Mamie had been lovers. He said that her grandmother, who supervised her during the day while her mother worked as a domestic, disapproved of the rela-tionship and ordered Mamie to stay away from him.

The young lovers continued to see each other on the sly, he wrote, but recently the romance had paled, at least on his part. Ma-mie wanted him to marry her, he continued, and had threatened to commit suicide. Goldenson gave a note to the police, ostensibly written by Mamie the day before her death, in which she chided him for his neglect. Mamie's unwanted attentions, he claimed, had cost him his place in art school. Prior to the shooting, he said fur-ther, he had been awake for 48 hours and drinking steadily. The next day, when police escorted Goldenson from the basement pris-on across Dunbar Alley to the coroner's inquest, they had to fight their way through an angry crowd. At the inquest, friends of the victim testified that Mamie's conduct was above reproach and that she had steered far clear of Goldenson because of his reputation for misconduct in the neighborhood. The note found in his possession was declared to be a forgery by Mamie's teacher and fellow stu-dents familiar with her handwriting.

Autopsy results showed that Mamie had died of a gunshot wound to the brain. "The other organs of the body were found to be in a healthful condition," reported the autopsy surgeon, "and the charges made by Goldenson against the virtue of his poor victim were ascertained to have emanated from his filthy brain." Witness-es went directly from the coroner's inquest to the Grand Jury, which came back that afternoon with a murder indictment. As Goldenson was returned to City Prison following the inquest, police again had to force their way through the angry crowd on Dunbar Alley. Instead of taking him down to the prison, however, they continued on through the building and out the Kearny Street entrance.

There, Goldenson was hustled into a buggy for transport to the still more secure County Jail a few blocks away, on the north side of Broadway, between Kearny and Montgomery (Columbus) Avenue. When members of the Merchant Street crowd became aware of the ploy, they raced up to Kearny and chased the buggy in its flight to the jail, but the officers arrived first and got their prisoner safely inside. Public anger continued to build. San Francisco in the mid-1880s was only 30 years removed from the second Committee of Vigilance. In living memory, angry vigilantes had rolled a cannon up in front of the same County Jail, removed two killers, and hanged them without benefit of a legal trial. More recently, in 1870, the police had all they could handle to prevent the seizure and execution of Charles Quinn who had ravished and murdered 5-year-old Maggie Ryan under the Pacific Wharf.

To the public mind, not only had Goldenson, an adult, murdered a female child, but before she was even laid to rest, he had defamed her memory with an attack on her virtue. There was also an ethnic subtext to the case which just about assured that matters would not proceed peaceably. The area where Mamie lived, and was killed, and that around the County Jail where Goldenson was held, were heavily populated by working class Irish Catholics. Alexander Goldenson was a Jew. In case anyone hadn't gotten the implication, a reporter for the *Chronicle* described Goldenson at the time of his arrest as "a passably good looking man with marked Hebrew features." Goldenson complicated matters for himself by introducing the "ethnic card" in his own behalf. He claimed that what set him off just before the shooting was Mamie calling him a "damned Jew."

In response to rumors that the "Hebrew" community was contributing to a defense fund for Goldenson, a group of prominent Jewish leaders promptly issued a statement saying that if necessary they would contribute $100,000 to prosecute Goldenson but would not provide a dollar for his defense. San Francisco never did experience anything like the level of ethnic and racial strife which visited other nineteenth-century American cities, but ethnic distinctions were still clearly understood by all.

The morning papers on November 12 announced a monster rally for that night at the Metropolitan Hall (at the present site of the 5th and Mission Garage) to express public outrage at the offense. By 6:30 p.m. the street in front of the hall was crowded with humanity, and when the doors were opened, thousands poured in. At 8:00 p.m., the meeting was called to order and when its sponsors tried to counsel moderation they were shouted down. One group walked

29-1 Courtesy of the San Francisco History Center.
The Broadway Jail. Erected in 1851, it served as the principal detention center in San Francisco until damaged in the 1906 Earthquake. It was from here that citizens tried to rescue Goldenson so they could hang him.

up the aisle with a noose attached to a long pole, to the cheers of the assemblage. The crowd then spilled outside.

There they joined a large crowd gathered in front of the Mint, and proceeded toward the County Jail. One large group led by shouting, hooting hoodlums moved up Kearny Street; another, proceeded up Dupont Street. Still another crowd had begun to gather in front of the County Jail at sunset, and by 7:00 p.m. there were several hundred assembled. An enterprising street peddler set up a patent medicine stand to take advantage of the potential customers.

The authorities were prepared. Having received intelligence reports that an attempt would he made to incite the crowd at Metropolitan Hall, Sheriff Peter Hopkins ordered all deputies to duty in the County Jail. The building was barricaded from the inside, rifles were positioned in the prison office and each deputy was equipped with a .45- caliber revolver. Coiled hoses were in position to turn water on the crowd should that become necessary. The prisoners were secured in their cells before nightfall; tension ruled the jail. The inmates had as much reason to know as anyone that when vigilantes came for their man in 1856, they took along another unsentenced murderer and hanged him as well. Goldenson is said to have asked his jailers that night if the crowd outside the jail had a cannon with them.

Police officials summoned reserve officers from district stations and equipped them with riot batons. Patrol Captain William Douglass took the precaution of moving the department rifles into the locked cells at the rear of the station in case a mob should attack while officers were on outside duty. Sergeant George Birdsall was stationed with a company of officers in and about the County Jail in the early evening, and at 8:30 Chief Crowley, accompanied by Captain Douglass and another company of fifty men, marched from police headquarters to the Broadway Jail to join them.

When the crowd from Metropolitan Hall arrived at the jail, Sergeant Birdsall formed a double rank of officers in front of the jail with clubs drawn. The crowd soon filled the street on Broadway from Kearny to Dupont, and spilled on up into side streets. The first trouble began at 9:00 p.m. when a hack containing the Sheriff's son came up Kearny to Broadway. The cry went up that Goldenson was in the vehicle and a rush was made to grab him; the sheriff's son scooted into the jail, the crowd hot on his heels. The police made a charge and cleared the immediate area.

At that point, a man named McCann climbed up onto the balcony of a fandango house opposite the jail and incited the crowd to make another rush on the jail. Officers from Sergeant Birdsall's command made a sortie across the street, knocked the struts out from under the balcony, and dragged McCann into the jail. A hail of rocks and bricks rained down from nearby roofs on the police lines. Captain Douglass ordered his men into a double wheel formation and sent them both ways on Broadway. Sergeant Birdsall's group drove the crowd east toward Kearny Street, clubbing as they went. Captain Douglass' unit fought their way west toward Montgomery Avenue (Columbus Street).

The police then established lines across Broadway at Kearny Street and Montgomery Avenue, and at Hinckley Alley above the jail to keep the crowds back. Some in the rear of the crowd continued to pelt officers with rocks, however, and another charge was ordered. This time the officers clubbed their way down Kearny Street and Montgomery Avenue to where the two streets joined, and then up as far as Stockton away from the jail. On the return trip, officers entered saloons where rioters had sought refuge and "clubs beat a lively tattoo on the heads of those present." The rioters were driven out into the street where they were greeted by more police clubs. One saloonkeeper on Broadway near Montgomery Avenue refused police orders to close up but "four or five raps on his cranium changed his mind."

The police then returned to clear the front of the jail with repeated charges until the entire street was again clear. "It was the greatest clubbing exhibition the police force ever gave," reported one paper admiringly. "Eighty-nine heads were patched up in the hospitals that night." The police reestablished their lines on Broadway at Kearny and Dupont. By 11 p.m. there was nothing more to see and most of the crowd had dispersed. By midnight only the regular habitués of the neighborhood were seen around and Douglass marched his men down to Kearny and Washington, where he dismissed them.

Following Maggie's funeral at St. Joseph's Church at 10th and Howard streets the next morning, the funeral procession wended its way past the Hayes Street address where the Goldenson's were in the process of moving out. A young man named James Conlan detached himself from the procession and began to destroy the family's furniture on the sidewalk. Police officers intervened and arrested him for being drunk. That same morning, Goldenson was taken from the County Jail to the Superior Court in City Hall for arraignment on a charge of murder. While he was being escorted on foot down Kearny by two deputy sheriffs, a crowd began to gather. On the return trip, he was guarded by a police sergeant and a squad of officers. Thereafter he was transported to court and back in a hack.

Urged on by the court, which was eager to have the matter done with, the case proceeded despite defense maneuvering to obtain a change of venue. In early March 1887, the trial commenced in Superior Court, Judge Daniel Murphy presiding. District Attorney John Wilson appeared for the state. Carroll Cook was the lead defense attorney. The prosecution's case was simple enough. Several witnesses to the crime, including the wagon driver who followed Goldenson from the scene to police station, testified, as did Sergeant Ayers about the defendant's spontaneous statement when he entered the station. Detective John Meagher testified about the contents of Goldenson's written confession, and other detectives testified as to its voluntary nature.

The defense did not dispute the fact that Goldenson had killed Mamie, but offered as a defense that he was mentally unbalanced. Immediately after the shooting there had been published reports of Goldenson's bizarre behavior in the neighborhood. He was reported to have been in the habit of insulting young women in the street and attacking old men and smaller boys without provocation. There was testimony that on at least one occasion he had struck his mother and once run his father out of the house.

Goldenson's mother said that she had questioned his sanity since a bout of typhoid fever, after which he was subject to monthly spells. He would paint pictures with elaborate detail for long periods, she said, then be seized by a headache and not work for a week. When he came out of a spell he would remember nothing and cry without reason. She traced the insanity back to his paternal grandfather in Russia who had to be watched closely to prevent him from doing violence. "It is apparent," commented one paper when the issue first arose, "that the murderer will endeavor to save his life by advancing the time-worn plea of insanity."

On rebuttal, the district attorney introduced several witnesses who testified that except for often being drunk and troublesome, there was nothing unusual about his behavior. The jury did not buy the insanity defense. After considering the matter for 41 minutes, they returned with a verdict of guilty of murder in the first degree. The sentence was death by hanging. Over the next year and a half, as the case worked its way through the appeals process, Goldenson managed to keep himself in the news with his antics in the County Jail. His supporters saw his behavior as proof that he was insane. His jailers said it was all an act.

In July 1888, as his execution date approached, Goldenson retracted his earlier comments about Mamie. They were lovers, he said, but only in the purest sense. He regretted what he had done, he added, and accepted responsibility. On September 14, 1888, Alexander Goldenson was hanged in the County Jail. He died with a picture of Mamie in one hand and an American flag in the other. His remains were turned over to his parents for burial but even in death, Goldenson caused his parents distress. Around his neck when he died was a crucifix and Catholic medal. In his last hours Goldenson converted to the Catholic faith under the tutelage of the jail's Catholic chaplain. Jewish religious leaders denied him burial in the Jewish cemetery because of his last-minute religious conversion, and his parents forbade his internment at Holy Cross Cemetery. He was eventually buried at the non-denominational Odd Fellows Cemetery out by Point Lobos Road.

Thirty

CELEBRITY HOMICIDE

Some circumstantial evidence is very strong,

as when one finds a trout in the milk.

-- HENRY DAVID THOREAU

A s rich and celebrated murder suspects dance their way through the justice system today, we might be inclined to look back nostalgically to an imagined time when justice was swifter or at least more certain. Criminal cases a century ago might have moved through the system faster, but the outcome was not necessarily any more predictable, particularly if defendants had the means to muddy up the legal waters. Even cop killers.

Shortly after midnight on Friday, September 11, 1891, the neighborhood around Southern Police Station, then located at 829 Folsom Street, was startled awake by the sound of gunshots. Officers rushed outside to find a fellow officer, Alexander Grant, dying on the sidewalk. Officer John Allen took off after a man seen running from the scene toward 5th Street, overhauling him around the corner at the intersection with Shipley.

The gravely wounded officer, shot through the forehead, was bundled into the patrol wagon in front of the station and rushed to the Receiving Hospital but it was too late. A forty-year-old native of Nova Scotia, Grant had come to California in 1874 and gone to Bodie, where he worked for seven years as a carpenter. He had joined the police department in 1886 and at the time of his death was about to be married.

The arrested subject was immediately recognized as a most unlikely candidate to be involved in a police killing: Maurice B. Curtis, a well-known theatrical personality about town who also went by the name of "Samuel of Posen," after a character he had popular-ized on the stage in New York and San Francisco, making a fortune in the process. Curtis had retired to private life a few years earli-er to manage his extensive real estate holdings. "He was generally looked upon as a talkative, rather good natured fellow," comment-ed one contemporary news account, "and about the last person in the world to commit an act of viciousness."

Nonetheless, as the evidence piled up, it appeared that the police had an airtight case. There was plenty of direct evidence. There was little street traffic at that time of the morning and those few who were up and about had an unimpeded view of what transpired. Horace P. Badgley was walking down 5th Street to Folsom, he said, and had just turned the corner on to Folsom Street from where he witnessed two men struggling. Then he heard a gunshot followed by a pause and then two more shots. One of the men fell to the ground; the other ran away.

James Creighton, a former police patrol wagon driver, who was closing his father's saloon at the southwest corner of 5th and Folsom at the time, heard the shots and saw a man running to 5th Street and down toward Shipley, where he was arrested. Thomas Mullens and E. Toomey, residents of the neighborhood, were walking on Folsom Street toward 5th on the opposite side of the street from the shoot-ing when they were attracted by the voice of Officer Grant saying, "Come along now." At almost the same moment, they heard shots and saw the shooter running toward 5th Street.

They followed him and when Mullens passed the building un-der construction at 5th and Folsom he saw something glistening in the darkened site. He recovered a hammerless Smith & Wesson re-volver with three expended rounds and turned it over to officers at the scene. Most telling of all, from an evidentiary point of view, was that at the time of his arrest, Curtis was found to have a pair of po-lice "nippers" (a claw-like steel come along device), later identified as belonging to Officer Grant, firmly affixed to his right wrist.

At the point of his arrest, Curtis spontaneously exclaimed, "My God! I'd give the world to get back the last four hours." According to witness Horace Badgley, Curtis said something to the effect of "Yes, yes, I did it," as officers brought him back past the scene of the shooting. Others reported that when brought to the station, Curtis said, "I haven't done anything. O, my poor wife." By general agreement he appeared to be intoxicated. .

In initial interviews with the police, Curtis said that he had been at the Grand Opera House (on Mission between 3rd and 4th) with his wife and that he had left her there at about 10 p.m. to go have a drink with a friend at the Tivoli Opera House (on Eddy Street just off Market). As he was returning to the Grand, he said, he was tumbled into the gutter at 3rd Street. The next thing he remembered, he said, was being hand-cuffed and placed in the wagon. He never carried a revolver, he claimed, and did not have one that night. By the next day, a "dream team" defense of three of the most high-powered attorneys in town had been engaged, and Curtis wasn't talking anymore. As the story unfolded in the press, however, it was revealed that he wasn't such a "good-natured fellow" as earlier reported, but a philandering braggart who

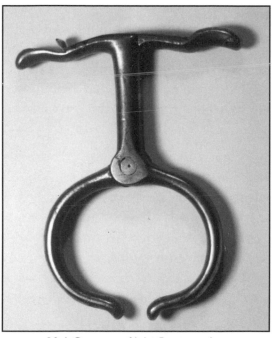

30-1 Courtesy of John Boessenecker.
"Nippers" like those used to restrain Curtis and found still attached to the perpetrator's left arm when he was apprehended by the police.

boasted about his sexual conquests and fighting prowess, and tyrannized those under his power.

By the September 14, the police had firmed up their case. Mrs. Anna Johnston who was sitting up with a sick grandchild at the front window of her home at 816 Folsom street came forward to relate that she had observed two men—one tall, one short—angling across Folsom Street from the north to the south side opposite her house when she saw the brief struggle and heard one of the men say, "Come along now" several times, followed by three gunshots. Her two daughters confirmed her account. Mrs. John Holden, who lived at 858 Folsom, directly across from shooting, didn't see the struggle but did hear the first shot, and was drawn to the front window where she witnessed the second and third shots and saw the man run away with the officer in pursuit.

When these accounts were put together with those of other witnesses who viewed the incident from various vantage points along the route from the point of the shooting to the place of arrest, it was established to a certainty that the man seized was the man who had done the shooting and that there was no one else nearby who could have been involved.

Other witnesses placed Curtis at the Manhattan Saloon at 6th and Market after he left the Tivoli — in the opposite direction from where he claimed to have been mugged. The point of original arrest was established to have been at 6th and Howard, and a tamale vendor located at 6th and Folsom observed the officer and his arrestee walking peacefully along Folsom from 6th toward Southern Station and watched as they crossed the street diagonally at the corner to the south side of the Folsom, 160 feet short of murder spot.

The defense team tried to "paper" the prosecution with a number of motions to delay the case, but the court brushed them aside and the trial, characterized by one of Curtis' attorneys "as an unholy persecution of an innocent man by the police," began on January

25, 1892. At trial, Curtis had to change his story. Given testimony placing him several blocks in the opposite direction from where he said he had been mugged, his statement that he had been attacked at 3rd and Mission was no longer operative. He now testified that he had noticed a strange man following him on Mission Street, so he continued to Howard Street when he was struck on the back of the head and fell to the ground. An officer then appeared, he said, and placed both him and his assailant under arrest. The nippers were placed on his wrist and the party had gone a short distance when he heard three shots and ran for his life.

In his 1910 account of the case, Police Captain Thomas Duke said that Curtis "could give no satisfactory explanations to why he did not continue to the theater which was close at hand on Mission Street if he feared an assault, instead of going out of his way to walk down a comparatively dark street, thus inviting attack."

Still, by the time of the trial, Curtis' resourceful defense team had turned up some previously unrecorded "eyewitnesses" who confused the issue by suggesting that there may have been a third man on the scene. The police were never able to tie the murder weapon to Curtis but as to his claim that he never carried a pistol, Henry Faust, whom he formerly employed as a gardener, testified that he had seen his employer carrying a pistol on numerous occasions.

If Curtis had done the shooting, the question remained unanswered about why such an ostensibly respectable citizen would be involved in such a case in the first place. Some speculated that it was the fear of being caught with the lottery tickets found in his possession at the time of his arrest that prompted him to try to escape. Illegal gambling was almost an open business in San Francisco at the time so that explanation doesn't hold much water.

In his 1910 account, Captain Duke offers an explanation of why the otherwise respectable Curtis might have acted so violently in such a minor matter. "Captain of Detectives [Isaiah] Lees who handled the case, stated that he had reliable information that Curtis was a degenerate," Duke reports, "and it was Lees' theory that Grant had caught him in a compromising position and Curtis, becoming frantic when he realized that exposure would follow his arrest, decided to forever seal the lips of the officer and then escape."

Veterans of the old "degenerate" section of the Sex Crimes detail will tell you that working the public toilets and theater balconies in the old days was one of the best jobs in the department in which to find a fight. People who resort to chance encounters in public places to act out their sexual fantasies are frequently conventionally respectable individuals, often with responsible jobs and families. While the danger of being caught might add flavor to encounters, the reality of actual capture is met with dread. Arrestees would fight with the desperation of madmen to avoid arrest and exposure.

If Lees' assertion is correct, that would help to explain Curtis' sudden eruption when the station came into view and the inevitability of his exposure was assured. And also if true, there may have indeed been another man involved in the incident at some point, but if so, he would have been long gone by the time of the shooting. In any event, the defense witnesses had created enough doubt that when the trial ended in late February, the jury could not agree. At the second trial, Curtis was acquitted and set free.

Shortly afterward, however, William J. Hurley, a juror who had held out for acquittal in the first trial was arrested and convicted of hanging a jury in another trial. He admitted his guilt and also stated that he had been promised $5,000 to hang the Curtis jury but complained that he had received nothing in the end.

And a few years later, Horace Badgley, the first witness to come forward on the night of the shooting, who had unaccountably been absent at the time of the trial, turned up in Stockton. He alone among the other witnesses had recognized the arrestee as Curtis and had overheard the spontaneous admission made at the time of his arrest. Badgely claimed that he was approached by a "richly dressed, decidedly pretty woman" who professed to have fallen in love with him at first sight and tried to get him to accompany her to Chicago. Badgley wasn't buying any of that, he said, and declined.

He was next approached by a man who offered to pay him $15,000 to say that he had seen a third man there that night. Badgley was not ready to perjure himself but he did agree to accept $3,000 for a cheap picture on the wall of his home and to move east for the good of his health.

In the end, Curtis' only punishment was financial. After his second trial he was financially ruined. He was forced to return to the vaudeville stage as a low-grade producer where he eked out a meager living.

Thirty-one
OFFICER JOHN H. GILLEN

On Saturday, November 7, 1891 at about noon, dairy workers for a "milk ranch" in the Richmond District picked up a load of grain at the San Francisco Stock Brewery at Powell and Francisco to feed their stock, and started back to the dairy. As the wagon passed Lombard and Powell, one of three young men riding in the rear of the wagon threw a handful of grain at Chew Sin Cheong, who was standing on the corner. The young hoodlum picked the wrong man to harass.

The wagon drove on and turned onto Montgomery Avenue. Unbeknownst to its riders, Cheong was following it. He caught up with the wagon as it neared Green Street and fired one round from a .38-caliber revolver. Special Officer John Henry Gillen, 33, came upon the scene in time to see the shooting and approached the shooter, calling to him that he was under arrest. Cheong turned and, without a word, fired on the officer, striking him in the breast. Gillen drew his own revolver and returned fire as he fell dying to the ground. His shots missed.

Seeing Gillen fall, Joseph Corwell, the driver of the grain wagon, jumped off and chased Cheong south on Stockton Street, accosting him as he neared Vallejo Street. Again Cheong turned and fired, striking Corwell in the chest, wounding him seriously. As Cheong made his way toward Broadway, followed by a cautious crowd, two young men, Edward Carosio and Antonio Bacciagalupi, jumped him. Carosio threw his overcoat over the wildly struggling shooter, who got off another round which struck a nearby restaurant owner.

Officer Sam Alden showed up from his nearby beat and kicked the gun out of the perpetrator's hand and, with the assistance of Officer Edward Wren, placed him under arrest. The enraged crowd

SAN RANCISCO'S LATEST FAD—THE MURDER EPIDEMIC.

31-2 Author's collection.   *The Wasp* in its November 21, 1891 issue, commented that if the murder of police officers didn't come to an end the city was going to need a new force. The murder of Officer Grant is depicted in the middle. Officer Gillen's killing is shown at the left, and the woman at the right is May Cotter, who killed her husband, Officer Jeremiah Cotter, on November 10, 1891.

began to call for a summary hanging, and it was all the officers could do to get the arrestee to the station house several blocks away at Kearny and Washington.

On December 2, 1891 an information was filed in Superior Court charging Cheong with murder in the first degree. There was some question about the shooter's sanity for on March 11, 1892, he was tried by a jury as to his sanity and found to have been sane at the time of the hearing. At the first trial on his guilt a few days later the jury could not agree. At his second trial in May, Cheong was convicted of murder in the first degree and sentenced to a term of life in prison at San Quentin. He was later moved to the State Insane Asylum in Stockton, where he remained for the rest of his life.

Thirty-two
LIEUTENANT WILLIAM BURKE

At 9:30 on the morning of Wednesday March 23, 1898, Alfred Hopkinson telephoned the 17th Street Police Station from the grocery at 24th and Alabama streets. He reported to the corporal on duty that his neighbor, Theodore Haynes, had just taken a shot at him and then killed his dog. Two mounted officers, Thomas Kennedy and James Wilkinson of the Outer Mission Mounted Force, were dispatched to the scene at Montcalm and Peralta. When the officers approached Haynes at the rear of his shack at 300 Montcalm, he confronted them with pistol in hand and ordered them off his property. Not wanting to shoot a man over such a trivial matter, Officer Wilkinson later said, they retreated and called in on a box phone to the station for directions.

Residents of Bernal Heights steered clear of the reclusive Haynes, or the "Irish Tinker" as he was known, except for the neighborhood boys who threw rocks at his shanty in hopes he would chase them. Haynes' principal human contacts, outside of the customers to his tinsmith business, were his neighbors with whom he engaged in countless disputes. One ongoing conflict was with the legal owner of the property to which Haynes held "squatters title." Another was with Hopkinson, who lived down the street at 304 Montcalm, regarding a strip of land between the two lots. What prompted Haynes' attack on Hopkinson on March 23 was the latter's attempt to erect a fence enclosing the disputed property.

Six months earlier, sheriff's deputies, acting on behalf of the legal owner of the property, had gone to Haynes' shack to dispossess him. Haynes was not at home when they arrived so the officers put his property outside and barricaded the door. When he returned home, the outraged tinker broke the Sheriff's seal and replaced his property, claiming he would have killed the officers if he had been present. And he had the means to do so: deputies found two shot-guns, two revolvers, a dagger and hundreds of rounds of ammunition on the premises.

On receipt of the call from the officers on the scene on March 23, the station keeper sent the patrol wagon, driven by Patrol Driver George Cashel, to notify Lieutenant William Burke at his home at 238 Shotwell Street a few blocks away. Burke, 46, a native of County Galway, Ireland, had been appointed to the department in 1878, and later assigned with his good friend, Officer Bill Price, a County Leitrim man, to patrol the Mission. The Mission District at that time extended from its borders with the Southern and Potrero districts, along the line of Market Street all the way out to Ocean beach and the county line. Prior to Burke's appointment, the entire police complement of the district consisted of two men equipped with a wagon to patrol a 20-square-mile area.

Pockets of hoodlum gangsters had taken advantage of the enforcement vacuum to terrorize the residents of the sparsely populated area. Officers Burke and Price cleaned up the district, and for their good work both were promoted to sergeant. In 1895, when the rank of lieutenant was created, Burke was among the first to be promoted to that rank. Lieutenant Burke instructed Cashel to take him to the scene of the shooting. Enroute, they picked up Officer Timothy Marlowe on his 26th Street beat. Rookie Officer Christopher Merchant also responded to the scene on his own. Lieutenant Burke stopped the wagon on Montcalm, at the middle of the hill between Alabama and Peralta, and conferred with his officers.

Brushing aside warnings of neighbors and other officers about Haynes' predisposition to violence—he had faced down a lot worse than this in his long career in the Mission—Lieutenant Burke, who was in civilian dress, approached the shanty along the alley to its east side. He did take the precaution, however, of removing his revolver from his hip pocket and placing it in his outside right coat pocket. Burke knew Haynes from previous encounters and was confident that he could bring him in. In this case, however, he seriously misjudged the situation and his man. As Lieutenant Burke made his way along the side of the shanty, Officers Wilkinson and Marlowe were at his right and left rear and Kennedy and Merchant were on the rise to the east at what is now the little garden patch called Peralta Park. Haynes met him at the northeast corner of the shanty, pistol in hand.

Lieutenant Burke counseled the armed man to surrender and assured him that things had not gone so far they could not be worked out. But Haynes wasn't hearing any of that. He pointed his revolver at Burke, as he had at the original responding officers, and ordered him off the property. Burke began to retreat down the alley, according to witness accounts, and when he was back about eight

32-1 Jesse Cook Collection.
Depiction of scene on Bernal Heights when Lieutenant Burke was murdered.

feet, Haynes fired, striking him in the abdomen. Some witnesses said that the lieutenant had his weapon in hand at the time; others said no. In any event, Lieutenant Burke returned fire as he fell but missed his mark.

After the lieutenant was shot, the other officers scattered for cover, firing as they went. And what followed next was cause for much later recrimination. While the officers repositioned themselves, Haynes was somehow able to leave the cover of his shack, walk along the alley to the supine lieutenant, wrench the gun out of his hand and shoot him again with his own weapon. The assailant then made his way back into the safety of his shack without any interference from the nearby officers. As Burke lay wounded in the alley, Patrol Driver Cashel, at the bottom of the hill with the wagon, learned that his lieutenant had been shot. He asked a bystander to hold his horses and made his way up the hill. Passing by the officers who remained under cover, Cashel went directly to the lieutenant. Unable to carry the much larger man by himself, Cashel dragged him by the wrist down the alley, past windows from which he was vulnerable to gunfire from the shack, around the corner and down Montcalm, out of the line of fire.

The call went out immediately that Lieutenant Burke had been shot, and while Cashel raced in the wagon with the mortally wounded officer to the County Hospital on Potrero Street where he died a few hours later, the department mobilized a response. At the Hall of Justice, Chief of Police Isaiah Lees equipped a squad of detectives with Winchester rifles and dispatched them to the scene in a patrol wagon. Sergeant Henry Colby put together another rifle squad at Central Station and headed for the scene. Before long there were 30 officers surrounding the shack engaged in furious gunfight with its well-armed occupant.

Despite hundreds of rifle rounds poured into the little shack, Haynes—who would pop up at windows and doors, and once from a hole in the roof, to return fire—remained unscathed. On one occasion, he offered to surrender, but when he started to come out, a "thoughtless" officer, according to police historian Peter Fanning, fired from the hill and the battle was on again. Eventually, Officer Merchant, who, after running out of ammunition for his revolver, had equipped himself with a rifle borrowed from a neighbor, crawled within a few feet of the shack and fired through the door. When Haynes edged the door open to fire back, Officer Kennedy, who had also crept close to the cabin armed with a borrowed over-and-under rifle/shotgun, let fly with a round of birdshot, striking the tinker in the face, chest and left shoulder. Blinded by his own blood, Haynes again offered to surrender and was pounced upon by several officers.

Haynes was placed in a patrol wagon and taken to the County Hospital. More angry than hurt, he insisted that he be allowed to retrieve $1,000 he had buried under the floor boards of his cabin, fearing it might be stolen in his absence. Officers accompanied him back to the shack where, sure enough, they found three buried cans containing $930. An additional $130 was found sewed into the lining of the arrestee's coat. No doubt, fear of the loss of his hoard contributed to Haynes' reluctance to submit to arrest in the first place.

Haynes' attempts to protect his stash came to nothing, however. Despite efforts to create the impression that he was insane, Haynes was convicted of murder in June and sent to Folsom Prison on a life sentence. In the aftermath of the shooting, questions were raised about the adequacy of the police response. One question centered on the inability of all the weaponry arrayed against him to hit a man inside such a flimsy shack. In July, the police department replaced its 100 Winchesters with 400 Colt repeating rifles. They also acquired a dummy in the likeness of Theodore Haynes for target practice.

And then there was the question of the failure of the officers on the scene to prevent Lieutenant Burke's second shooting, and their reluctance to assist Patrol Driver Cashel in his efforts to rescue the wounded officer. The day after the shooting, the Police Commission rewarded Patrol Driver Cashel by appointing him to a regular position in the department. Charges of cowardice were filed against officers Merchant, Wilkinson, Kennedy and Marlowe. Their trial before the Police Commission commenced on August 11, 1898. Conflicting testimony was given at the hearing, some of it self-serving and some from witnesses with agendas of their own. But the sum of it was that there were lapses on the part of many, including Lieutenant Burke himself. Nobody wanted to say anything immediately after his death, but at the hearing in August, Chief Lees, through the questions he posed to officers, brought out the suggestion that Lieutenant Burke, through his own foolhardiness, was in part responsible for his demise.

When Burke was first shot, it was established, all four officers on the scene scattered and took cover. No real problem there. What was not so easy to explain, however, was how Haynes was able to approach the downed lieutenant and shoot him again with his own weapon without interference from the other officers. What apparently happened was that the officers became rattled at the point of Burke's shooting and emptied their weapons in the first volley of return fire. And at the time Haynes approached Burke, the officers looked on with empty weapons.

Throughout the gun battle, the officers had a difficult time keeping their weapons loaded. Twice Officer Kennedy exchanged empty weapons for loaded ones from citizens and returned to the fray. Officer Merchant exchanged his empty revolver for the rifle he used in the final assault, and Officer Marlowe gave a neighborhood boy named Conroy fifty cents to go and buy him ammunition.

Cashel's actions to save the lieutenant were truly heroic, but whether the other officers' choice to avoid exposing themselves to direct gunfire constitutes cowardice is subject to debate. Whatever the case, in its October decision, the Police Commission found Officers Wilkinson and Marlowe guilty of cowardice and dismissed them from the department. Officers Kennedy and Merchant were restored to duty.

What saved Officers Merchant and Kennedy from dismissal was their heroics at the point of the final capture. The commission concluded that they too had fallen back when Burke was shot, but disengaged only to obtain suitable weaponry, and returned immediately to the fight. Office Marlowe, on the other hand, wasn't much involved in the later phases of the gunfight. And Wilkinson chose to accompany the mortally wounded lieutenant to the hospital, at the lieutenant's request, he said.

The bloody events of March 1898 were to have a tragic epilogue ten months later. On January 13, 1899, Officer Kennedy became engaged in a dispute with his common-law wife. In the exchange of unpleasantries, she accused him of cowardice in the Burke affair. Enraged, he armed himself with his pistol, she later said, and attacked her, but the weapon was turned back on him during the struggle and discharged, wounding him in the head fatally. She was released without charge.

Other effects of the tragic incident still resonated in the department a generation later. The city charter, which went into effect two years after Burke was killed, provided, for the first time, for civil service appointments to the police department on the basis of written tests. Apparently some of the older officers, who had been brought into the department by direct Police Commission appointment, felt that officers selected on the basis of written testing couldn't measure up to the rigorous physical demands of the job. A quarter of a century after the Burke killing, Captain of Detectives Duncan Matheson, a member of the first group of civil service recruits in 1900, commented on the careers of the fellow members of his class. For the benefit of any oldtimers who still might be around, he made sure to point out that none of those who had been selected on the basis of written testing had ever been charged with cowardice.

Thirty-three

POST-QUAKE CRIME WAVE

F ollowing the great geological upheaval of April 1906 which devastated physical San Francisco, the city was visited with a corresponding social aftershock. Immediately after the earthquake and fire, the city was plunged into a major political scandal which, before it ran its course a couple of years later, saw the entire Board of Supervisors resign in the face of bribery charges.

Mayor Eugene Schmitz was convicted of accepting police graft for awarding liquor licenses to "French Restaurants" and escaped prison by the most tenuous of legal technicalities. Chief of Police Jeremiah Dinan retired from office facing a charge of perjury. During this period, and perhaps in part because of all the political disruption, the city was visited by a wave of crime. Thousands of San Franciscans, their homes destroyed and jobs gone up in smoke, left town. In a stroke, the population was reduced by half, from 350,000 to 175,000 and, with no tax base to pay them, 20 percent of the city's police officers were forced to take leaves of absence.

During the disaster itself, saloons had been ordered closed to reduce the potential for drunken disturbances, and the thin police lines were augmented by National Guard forces and self-appointed citizen police who executed several people summarily. In the immediate aftermath of the disaster, order was reasonably maintained. By summer, the militia was withdrawn and the saloons reopened, and with the infusion of ready money in the form of insurance payments, an "eat, drink and make merry" attitude seized the town. The ferries which had transported San Francisco families to Oakland a few months earlier returned with a less savory passenger list.

"[R]umors of a thieves' paradise," says chronicler Walton Bean "had increased the number of criminals by attracting newcomers from all over the country." Human scavengers prowled the un-lighted downtown ruins, looking for targets of opportunity. The St. Francis Hotel warned its guests not to venture more than a block from the building after dark, for fear they would be robbed. The fears were not unfounded. On August 20, 1906, Johannes Pfitzner was bludgeoned to death with a window sash weight during a rob-bery at his shoe store at 964 McAllister Street. On September 14, William Friede was found dying, his head crushed, in his clothing store at 1386 Market Street.

On October 3, a customer entered the Japanese bank at 1588 O'Farrell Street to find the bank's president, M. Munekato, dying of a brutal head wound. His seriously injured clerk, A. Sasaki, lay next to him. A 14-inch length of gas pipe covered with blood was found nearby. "That this city has become a refuge for desperate criminals is evident," bristled a contemporary editorial. "The city is infested with people who do not work and are well supplied with money. Brutal robberies occur in broad daylight and in crowded streets." While deploring the idea of vigilante justice, the editor reminded his readers that earlier San Franciscans had been unwilling to "pa-tiently stand still and be murdered."

"Hardware dealers sold an estimated twenty thousand pistols in one month," says writer Lately Thomas, "and women walked the streets clutching long hatpins." The governor offered a $1,500 reward for the arrest and conviction of the "gaspipe" murderers. In response to the crisis, officers placed on leave were returned to duty and at a special meeting of the Police Commission on October 10, Chief of Police Jeremiah Dinan was given his marching orders. "His tenure of office will be short," said the Commission, "unless he proves himself able to cope with the present situation." For his part, Dinan gave orders to his men to take their guns and clubs to "idlers and criminals around the refugee camps." Every man or youth who could not give a satisfactory explanation of his activi-ties, the chief said, was to be put on a ferry to Oakland.

On November 3, three men entered the jewelry store of Henry Behrend at 1323 Steiner Street. In Behernd, the "gaspipe gang" met their match. The intended victim resisted and in the resulting struggle one of the robbers accidentally injured one of his crime partners with an iron bar. Two of the robbers fled but the injured Behrend managed to hold one assailant until the police arrived. Under police questioning, the man admitted that he was Louis Dabner, the son of a respectable Petaluma family, and identified one of the other robbers as his roommate, John Seimsen. Dabner confessed to the three murders as well as a number of unsolved robberies that had fueled public concern about crime. On April 27, 1908 Dabner and Seimsen were hanged from the same scaffold at San Quentin.

It was also one of the most dangerous periods in the city's history for police officers. In the two years following the disaster, four police officers gave their lives in the line of duty. First was Officer James S. Cook. After the fire, officers were assigned to guard the banks in the burned district. Officer Cook, who had been guarding a bank at 7th and Market, reported off duty at midnight August 29, 1906, and proceeded down 7th Street to the Southern Pacific Railroad yard where he hoped to catch a freight train to his home in the Ocean View. At Brannan Street, the officer came on four men stealing some telephone cable from a large spool. When Officer Cook approached the men, one of them pulled a pistol and shot him in the stomach three times. As he fell, Cook returned fire but did not hit his assailant. Before he died on September 5, Officer Cook identified a man named John Dunnigan as his assailant, but the identification did not hold up and charges against Dunnigan were eventually dismissed.

Less than two months later, on the evening of November 16, retired officer George P. O'Connell, 55, was chatting with friends at the bar in a saloon at the northeast corner of 6th and Brannan streets—a block from where Cook had been killed in September—when the front and side doors were suddenly thrust open by two armed men wearing blue handkerchief masks. The robbers ordered the patrons to "throw up their hands," but O'Connell drew his own pistol and fired on the man at the front door. Both robbers returned fire, killing O'Connell and another patron. But O'Connell got one of them; responding officers found a dead bandit, still wearing his handkerchief mask, a few feet from the front door. The man was identified as Frank Burke, an ex-con who was known to frequent Sullivan's saloon, "a rendezvous for thieves and cutthroats," on 6th Street just south of Brannan. Officers went there and arrested an ex-con named John Byrne who fit the description of the escaped robber and who had a similar handkerchief in his pocket. A pistol was found under the back stairs of the saloon. Byrne was found guilty at trial and sentenced to be executed. Before his date with the hangman, his sentence was commuted to a term in prison. He was paroled in April 1921 and died six months later.

In the midst of all the other trouble, the city was visited with a major labor disturbance as the embryonic Carmen's Union struck against the United Railway Company, which was in the process of consolidating rail lines in the city into what would become the Market Street railway. When strikebreakers were imported to replace the union men, violence and hard feelings resulted. At 3:00 a.m. on September 2, 1907, Labor Day, Officers Peter Mitchell and Edward McCartney came upon a boisterous crowd leaving Crowley's saloon at 24th and Howard Street. (South Van Ness.) The officers accosted two of the men at 24th and Shotwell streets.

The officers ordered the men to be quiet and to go home. The larger of the two men commented that he was under the impression that the "streets were free." At that point, according to Police Captain Thomas Duke's account, "the officers then shoved both men violently and told them to move on or be locked up." The men disappeared down 24th Street and the officers crossed over to get a cup of coffee when they saw men coming back up their side of the street. Officer Mitchell, according to his later account, seized the smaller of the two men and Officer McCartney advanced toward the larger man. As McCartney approached the man, his adversary drew a pistol and fired twice on the officer striking him fatally in the neck.

Mitchell disengaged from his combatant and by the time he lowered his mortally wounded partner to the pavement, both men had disappeared into the dark. On the basis of Mitchell's description, officers suspected that the killer was in some way connected with the street railway company. They were informed at the car barn at 24th and Utah that the larger man could have been one of two men, one of whom was John Tansey, a striking carman. Police arrested Tansey in his bed at 1025 Vermont Street. He denied any involvement but Officer Mitchell positively identified him as the shooter. The next day, a man named Bell was identified as his accomplice. Bell quickly admitted that he had been with Tansey and identified him as shooter. By the time Tansey was brought to trial, Bell had disappeared; Tansey admitted that he was present but tried to lay the shooting off on Bell. Tansey was convicted of manslaughter and sentenced to ten years in prison.

The next police shooting occurred on the night of June 4, 1908. Officer William H. Heins was filling in for vacationing Officer Jack Cameron on the Barbary Coast beat (Pacific Street from Battery to Stockton). About 1:15 am, two identical twin brothers, James and Thomas Young, 22 (sons of United Railway Inspector Beauregard Young who had shot a union carman during the recent labor troubles) were drinking with some sailors in the OK dancehall on Pacific just east of Kearny Street. Thomas argued with a waiter named Robert Pacheco over the cost of a beer and pulled a pistol. As he fired, a waitress, Lucile Sharp, pulled down his arm and the weapon discharged harmlessly into the floor. The powder flash caught his trousers on fire, however, and he made for the door. Some nearby sailors disarmed him but as he fled, his brother handed him another pistol. Officer Heins, who had been on the corner of Pacific and Kearny when the shot was fired, took off after him. As Thomas neared Montgomery Street, Heins ordered him to stop and fired a warning shot into a vacant building. Thomas fell, feigning injury, and when the officer grabbed him by the scruff of his neck, the young man turned and fired on him, striking him in the chest and wounding him fatally. The brothers ran around to Montgomery Street, where Thomas passed the pistol back to James.

Police Chief William Biggy, who had replaced Chief Dinan the year before, was on the street nearby that night and took charge of the investigation. Thomas was seen running into a dark vacant lot on Montgomery near Jackson and James proceeded up Jackson to Kearny, where he entered the International Saloon. Officers surrounded the lot and sent for lanterns to make a search. Shortly thereafter, Officers John B. O'Connor and John Evatt entered the lot and arrested the killer. They also recovered a distinctive red tie he had secreted near his hiding place. Detective Angelo Rocca arrested James Young in the International saloon and recovered the murder weapon.

Six horse-drawn patrol wagons filled with officers responded from other stations to the original call. The first word was that Heins had been shot by a sailor, and a general fight ensued between the responding officers and navy sailors visiting the "Coast." When the officers got the story sorted out correctly and it became apparent that Young had done the shooting, there was talk of dealing with the situation summarily, but cooler heads prevailed and the matter was left to the courts.

Officer Heins was given a hero's funeral at St. Bridget's Church at Van Ness and Broadway. His entire company from Central Station attended, as did Chief Biggy and the Commission. Mounted officers stopped all traffic down Van Ness following the funeral as the cortege made its way to Market Street, where it was placed on the car to Holy Cross Cemetery.

In the aftermath of Heins' shooting, Chief Biggy ordered double details of uniformed and plain-clothes officers to the Barbary Coast area "with specific instructions to wage relentless war on the men who make it their refuge. . . ." And department officials "expressed the determination that the murderer of Policeman Heins should pay the full penalty of the law and as quickly as the machinery of the courts could be made to work." But the intended result was not to be. The Barbary Coast dives were to flourish for another decade before being shuttered during the First World War, and Young was to escape "the full penalty of the law." At the first trial for the two Youngs, the jury could not agree. At the second trial, James tried to save his brother by claiming that he was the actual shooter. That story didn't fly, and Thomas Young was convicted and sentenced to a term of life imprisonment. James received a ten-year sentence. Thomas was paroled in 1932.

By the end of 1908, Chief Biggy was under fire himself, accused by his political enemies of treating the vice operators in the Barbary Coast with kid gloves. In late November, Chief Biggy disappeared off the police launch in the bay and was later found drowned. Questions remain about the circumstances of his death.

Six months after Officer Heins was killed, Sergeant Antone Nolting, also assigned to Central Station, was patrolling a few blocks from where Heins had been killed, at Clay and Montgomery, when he was shot and killed by an AWOL soldier named Thomas Jordan who he was trying to arrest for discharging a firearm. It was truly a crazy time in a town with a very full history of crazy times.

Thirty-four

WHAT REALLY HAPPENED TO POLICE CHIEF BIGGY?

J ust before midnight November 30, 1908, while returning to the
city from Belvedere, San Francisco police chief William J. Biggy
disappeared over the side of the police launch "Patrol." Two
weeks later his drowned body was found in the bay off Yerba Buena
Island. The official verdict was that he had accidentally fallen from
the boat and drowned. But there was evidence pointing to suicide,
and some even thought he might have been done away with. In the
circumstances surrounding his last few months in office, anything
was believable.

The first decade of the century was a turbulent time in San Francisco, politically as well as geologically. When a group of moneyed
reformers, charging corruption in the highest places, went after the
city's governmental and business leaders, the town was turned on
its ear. The trouble all started with a bitter teamsters strike in 1901,
which was broken with the help of police who rode on dray wagons to protect strikebreaking drivers. Vowing never to have the police used against them again, the labor unions formed their own
political party and elected their own mayor in the November election, "Handsome" Eugene Schmitz. At Schmitz's side, throughout
his mayoral career, was his political mentor, Abraham Ruef, North
Beach attorney and political fixer, who had done much to ensure
Schmitz's electoral victory.

From the start of the Schmitz regime, there were rumors of officially condoned police graft—not an uncommon reality in American cities at the time—and by mid-decade, many of the "better"
element were also convinced that Ruef-controlled city officials had
entered into a corrupt arrangement with public utility companies
to control the award of valuable city franchises to a select few.

In December 1905, Fremont Older, the reform editor of *The San*

206

Francisco Bulletin, went to Washington to see President Theodore Roosevelt and extracted from him the loan of Assistant U.S. Attorney Francis Heney and Secret Service operative William Burns to assist with a graft investigation/prosecution in San Francisco. Funded by former Mayor James Phelan and prominent citizen Rudolph Spreckles, and supported by an honest district attorney who had somehow slipped into office at the November 1905 election, the graft hunters set about cleaning up the town.

Their project was put on hold for a time when San Francisco was leveled by the great fire and earthquake in April 1906, but later in the year, at a specially convened grand jury, the mayor, his political mentor, and the chief of police were indicted on felony graft charges, but not before Ruef audaciously tried to have the District Attorney removed from office and himself installed in his place. In March 1907, just as his trial was about to begin, Abe Ruef suddenly made himself unavailable, and when regular law enforcement officials, all of whom owed their jobs to him, couldn't locate the lawyer, the court appointed William J. Biggy as elisor, a temporary court official, to arrest and detain the missing political boss.

Biggy was an old, if eccentric, hand at local and state politics and had previously filled a number of offices. In 1892 he had been elected to the state legislature, where he gained a reputation for uncompromising honesty. Later he served as Registrar of Voters in San Francisco and for a short time as a member of the Board of Supervisors. In 1900, Mayor Phelan appointed him to the police commission and when the chief of police retired, Biggy made himself temporary chief. A rigid moralist who followed the dictates of his own conscience without paying much attention to the opinions of others, Biggy was soon in the soup. He began his term by raiding Chinese gambling houses and charging police officers with accepting petty graft. Within a month, Phelan, the self same who was to lead the reform movement a few years later, removed Biggy from office on the grounds that he had appointed himself chief of police without authority and because he wouldn't work cooperatively with the other commissioners. (Shortly after Biggy's departure from office the mayor's office was implicated in an investigation by the State legislature into Chinatown graft.)

In August 1907, upon Mayor Schmitz's conviction, the entire city government, including the Board of Supervisors and the chief of police were swept out of office. The police commission appointed by the new mayor, Edward Robeson Taylor, appointed William J. Biggy chief of police. Big-gy brought his reputation for inflexible honesty with him to the office. And given the political climate of the time, it is difficult to see how anyone could have succeeded in the job, Biggy least of all.

WM. J. BIGGY 1907-1908

34-1 Author's collection. Police Chief Biggy

The graft prosecutions notwithstanding, turn-of-the century San Franciscans were very much divided about the issues of vice and petty graft. Despite laws making the practices illegal, gambling and prostitution had persisted more or less openly since Gold Rush times and, as in many late Victorian American cities, it was the considered opinion of leading law enforcement officials that vice was inevitable and it was best to keep it contained in restricted districts. There were exposés from time to time, followed by the arrest of a few officials, usually resulting in no convictions, after which conditions returned to normal. (Officially and popularly sanctioned vice would not be effectively ended in San Francisco until the mid-1950s administration of Mayor George Christopher.)

It was in such a moral stew that Biggy tried to enforce the vice laws. Along the way he made enemies of just about everyone. The first to line up against him were the Fillmore District merchants who, fearing a loss of business, opposed his efforts to move brothels out of the residential district and confine them to Chinatown. A few months later the Chinese Six Companies and Chinese Chamber of Commerce charged the chief with oppression when police officers enforced orders against playing dominoes in Chinatown. Shortly thereafter, on the other side of the ledger, the pastor of St. Francis Church in North Beach publicly accused Biggy of extending the limits of the Barbary Coast by issuing a permit to allow women in saloons on the 700 block of Pacific Street. By that time, it seems, the chief of police had a hard time pleasing anyone.

In April 1908, while examining potential jurors in preparation for trial, prosecutor Heney had exposed one potential juror, Morris Haas, as having served a prison term for embezzlement in the 1880s. Haas, who had since mended his life, left the jury box in disgrace. For months he brooded, and on Friday morning, November 13, as court was about to convene, he entered the courtroom, walked to the prosecutor's table and shot Heney in the head. Haas was seized by Burns and nearby police officers and placed in custody in the county jail. The suspicion immediately arose that Haas was part of a conspiracy to destroy the prosecution which was by then closing in on the wealthy owners of the transportation and telephone utilities who had participated in the boodling. That suspicion was lent credence when Haas, under close police guard, was found shot to death the next day in the county jail, a derringer in his hand.

The wrath of the prosecution immediately focused on Chief of Police Biggy. Investigator Burns accused the chief of being responsible for Haas' death for letting him obtain a gun in the jail. Biggy countered that Haas had brought the pistol in with him and that Burns himself was responsible for not searching the prisoner more carefully at the point of arrest.

In the spate of press accounts which followed, there was a steady drumbeat of calls for Biggy's dismissal. The flavor of those articles is best captured in the closing sentence of the November 18 editorial in *The San Francisco Call* : "Biggy is unfit to be chief of any public department. Biggy is a blowhard. Biggy is chicken hearted and chicken witted. Biggy has no shame. Biggy has no honor, either in his public or his private relations. Nobody respects him—NOT EVEN BIGGY." By November 26, it was reported that the Citizen's League of Justice, comprised of former supporters of Biggy, was about to ask the mayor for his ouster.

Beset from all sides, on the evening of November 30, Biggy took the police launch to Belvedere to submit his written resignation to Police Commissioner Hugo Keil. According to Keil's later account,

34-2 Courtesy of San Francisco History Center.
The police launch *Patrol* from which Biggy fell, jumped or was pushed.

210

he convinced Biggy that his retirement would play into the hands of his adversaries, and the chief withdrew his resignation before re-embarking on the launch for the return trip to San Francisco. It was during this brief voyage that Biggy disappeared over the side.

Against the background of these events, there was immediate speculation about what had happened to the chief, but the autopsy showed no signs of foul play and the verdict of the coroner's jury was that he had fallen over the side and drowned accidentally. Many were not satisfied with that finding.

One theory—one that persists to this day in the lore of the police department—is that the chief might have been killed. It is apparent from a reading of the contemporary accounts of the tragedy that in the aftermath of Biggy's demise public officials evaded or gave ambiguous answers to questions of the press. There was talk of a letter Biggy supposedly left in his office before departing on the launch. And Commissioner Keil reported that he had submitted a memorandum to the mayor of his last conversation with Biggy along with Biggy's letter of resignation. These documents were suppressed. And then there is the curious statement of William Murphy, the engineer who piloted the boat the night Biggy disappeared. Two years later Murphy was picked up wandering about in a downtown hotel muttering to himself. As he was being taken away to Agnews State Mental Hospital, he is reported to have screamed, "I don't know who did it, but I swear I didn't do it."

It would take more than the ravings of a madman to support a finding of murder and there are other explanations for the actions of officials after Biggy's disappearance. The most reasonable explanation is that Biggy took his own life—unless one considers it murder to drive a man to his death.

Part of the explanation of what happened to Biggy lies in his own temperament. He had a rigid, uncompromising personality. "Biggy was almost fanatic in his desire to satisfactorily police San

34-3 Jesse Cook Collection: Tessie Wall, the city's most prominent early twentieth-century madam. (second from left) with Officer John Hightower left..

Francisco," remembered Mayor Taylor after the chief's disappearance. And he had no ability to shrug off criticism. "He is too nervous and sensitive," reported his estranged wife at one point, "and he gets worked up too much over his trouble and newspaper attacks." His was a personality that, when confronted with real adversity, was almost sure to break rather than bend.

As was indicated by his previous experience as chief of police in 1900, he was not much given to compromise. The tendency to play it close to the vest might be interpreted as good sense in a law enforcement environment where every time a vice raid is to be conducted the object of the raid knows in advance of the planned operation. But the suddenness of Biggy's departure suggests that he was out of step with the prevailing institutional ethos of that period.

When he was reappointed chief in 1907, he was not well supported by the officers. As an outsider in a department, the large part of which opposed the graft investigation, he could have expected a certain amount of resistance. His efforts to clean up gambling in the Fillmore District came to nothing, and throughout his tenure, despite his best efforts, a highly organized syndicate of gamblers continued in operation with the quite obvious connivance of his subordinates and the courts. In enforcing his orders about gambling in Chinatown, his subordinates aroused the ire of merchant leaders by harassing innocent businesses while nearby gambling joints ran in full swing. The officers were careful to mention that they were acting on the orders of the chief. His captain of detectives, a man he had placed in office, was heard running him down in saloons around the Hall of Justice.

By the end of the November, it was evident that the chief was beginning to crack. On the early morning hours of Sunday, November 29, in a pathetic and perhaps alcohol-induced effort to do finally do something about the goals of his administration, Biggy took it upon himself to personally raid the notorious brothel of Tessie Wall at Larkin and Ellis streets, which he had been trying to close unsuccessfully for months. Without informing his subordinates of his intentions, the chief stormed through the hallways of the whorehouse, ordering the inmates out into the street. (Thirty years later when Tessie Wall died, the principal beneficiary in her will was Biggy's chief deputy at whose home the chief had his last Sunday dinner and where he spent the last night of his life. Wall's biographer points out that the officer had never been assigned to a district in which Tessie had a resort. No, but . . .)

One newspaper played the story of the raid mock seriously as the work of a drunken, bumbling imposter. All this must have severely distressed the rigidly moralistic chief of police; it must have seemed as though his world was coming apart.

By the final night of his life, Biggy's actions suggested a man having a mental breakdown. For some reason he left his pistol in the lavatory of the Ferry restaurant where he dined before leaving for Belvedere. And as he got on the police launch he pointed out two men on the pier as spies sent by Burns to watch him. He instructed the engineer to leave the dock as "quietly as possible" and not to blow the whistle if it could be helped. A witness to his departure later said that the two men on the pier were longshoremen known to frequent the area. In the end, the object of ridicule, almost friendless and alone, feeling betrayed and misunderstood, and deluded into believing that he was being spied upon, Biggy may well have taken his own life.

As to the evasive behavior of public officials and the suppressed documents, that can perhaps best be understood as a belated attempt to salvage Biggy's name. The immediate and almost general belief was that he had taken his own life. It was only later, as the implication sunk in that, as a suicide, he would be denied burial by his church, that officials started equivocating in their statements to the press. Perhaps they felt some responsibility for his death and that now he deserved some consideration; he certainly hadn't gotten much in the last days of his life. Finally, after a funeral with full police honors at St. Mary's Cathedral, he was buried in the hallowed ground of Holy Cross Cemetery.

After Biggy was put to rest, a search was made for a replacement chief of police. One leading contender turned the job down with the statement, "I would not take the place if it was the last job on earth. . . . No man can fill that position without sacrificing his reputation. He might be an angel, but if he took that office he would retire with the reputation of being a crook and I don't want that to happen to me."

If Biggy had more insight into his own nature and the environment in which he would have to operate, perhaps he would have come to the same conclusion himself. As things were, he just wasn't flexible enough to function in the extreme ethical ambiguity of the world in which he found himself. He was the wrong man in the wrong job at the wrong time, and that cost him his life.

Thirty-five

CALL THE WAGON

*The Police Patrol [Wagon] system is responsible for another general im-
provement in the Department. . . . Antecedently to the adoption of this
system, street officers were compelled, and frequently with much trouble
and many struggles, to convey their prisoners along the public streets to
the nearest police station.*

— CHIEF OF POLICE ISAIAH LEES, 1897.

O ne of the basic differences between the work of nineteenth-
century police officers and that of officers today is the
extent to which the old-timers were forced to work alone.
Before the development of motorized patrol response—and more
recently, instantaneous radio communication—officers were
isolated on their individual beats most of the time, cut off from
their headquarters and other officers. Those with beats in the more
densely populated downtown districts might double up for mutual
protection, but in the outlying districts a lone officer had only his
whistle for summoning help—assuming there was someone within
earshot to come to his aid. It was partially out of this condition that
the culture of police force as a preferred method of social control
evolved.

Knowing that an officer was on his own hook, neighborhood
hoodlums were more than willing to test his authority. Beating up
lone policemen came to be almost a rite of passage for urban toughs,
and police officers often responded with preemptive force—swift
and brutal—to assert their authority over those with whom they
had to contend. As Chief Lees pointed out in 1897, it was frequently difficult to get an arrested subject from the point of arrest to the
lockup. An officer had to walk his suspect in, often struggling all
the way and fending off the arrestee's friends who were bent on

setting him free. If a man was particularly obstreperous or hard to handle, the officer might hail a passing cart or express wagon to haul him to jail. (A fund was maintained at the stations to pay the commandeered teamster for his time and the court would assess cart hire as part of the penalty for the defendant at trial).

When an officer had a particularly messy drunk, he might grab a nearby wheelbarrow and trundle his man to jail. If transport was needed to move large numbers of officers to a distant riot or other emergency, improvisation was the order of the day. In 1859, when Chief Martin Burke transported a group of officers from downtown to put a stop to the Broderick/Terry duel out by Lake Merced, he

35-1 Courtesy of San Francisco Police Museum. "New York"-style patrol wagon in front of Mission Station on 17th Street, adopted over the objections of Chief Patrick Crowley, who feared that the confinement would cause officers to become ill.

used the coroner's "dead wagon." During the anti-Chinese riots in 1877, large furniture wagons were fitted out with benches to transport police officers and citizen members of the Public Safety Committee to trouble spots.

As the department began to decentralize into district stations in the 1870s to serve the needs of the ever-expanding population, a horse-drawn van was provided to carry prisoners downtown from the outlying stations. The officer assigned to the Mission District was given a horse and wagon to patrol his 20-square-mile beat and a couple of officers were mounted on horses to patrol the western reaches of the city. But for the most part, officers did all their work as individuals alone and on foot, separated from their fellow officers and headquarters.

Another cultural byproduct of the officers' occupational solitude was the reluctance—now declining—of officers to call for help. In living memory, it would be an occasion for mild ridicule from his fellows for an officer—"unable to handle his own beefs"—to call for help except in the most extreme circumstances. What finally started to put an end to the officers' isolation was the development of patrol/wagon call box systems. The first such comprehensive system, which for the first time connected beat officers with their headquarters and provided for a two-way exchange of information and transportation, was organized in Chicago in 1880. (At least one local writer contends that such a system was pioneered in San Francisco in the 1860s. He is probably thinking of the telegraph system of the 1860s which did connect the various stations, but was a very different type of operation.)

The Chicago system consisted of two or more telegraph boxes on each patrol beat, connected to precinct stations and containing several coded messages by means of which officers could report riots or other crimes to headquarters, or call for prisoner transportation. On the other end of the line, a four-man wagon team stood by in the station to promptly answer calls for assistance. The telegraph system was soon replaced by a net of telephones. Other cities quickly followed suit.

In 1886, Police Chief Patrick Crowley began asking for a patrol wagon/call box system for San Francisco. He was turned down at first but each year he continued to ask. In 1887 he appealed to civic pride by pointing out that even Oakland had a patrol system while San Francisco went without. Finally, in 1889, the Board of Supervisors appropriated $20,000 to get started on a patrol wagon/call box system for San Francisco.

The following year, a sample wagon was acquired from Chicago at a cost of $800 from which two more were made in city shops. The open wagons, which were also intended for use as public ambulances, were designed to hold nine men on benches in the wagon bed. In emergency, two more men could join the driver on the seat and, with two additional officers on the rear step, the department could deliver a squad of 13 men quickly to the scene of a disturbance. A tarp was provided to protect injured passengers from the elements. The first wagon was placed in service at the Old City Hall Police Station at Kearny and Washington streets on September 13, 1890. By the end of the year there were three more, assigned to the Folsom Street Station, the New City Hall Station (at McAllister and Hyde) and at the 17th and Howard streets station. On November 7, the first street call boxes went into operation, making the service complete. Later that month, a local news reporter was treated to a tour of the new system and immediately recognized the officers' safety implications of the new device. "The thief or hoodlum thug gets the wholesome conviction," he wrote, "that in any part of the city he is thus likely to have to encounter a heavy detail of picked officers within three or four minutes after an alarm has been turned in. It will be no longer be a question for a conscientious officer whether he shall risk his life in breaking up a hoodlum row in Brannantown, Tar Flat, or out in the Mission. He will not be alone long."

By mid-1891, the city had 81 telephone call boxes hooked up with district stations and by the following year there were 166. As the population and police stations moved farther out into the outlying districts, the number of call boxes was increased accordingly. Oddly enough, despite the obvious benefits of the new system, it was at first resisted by the officers it was designed to help. Some of the real old-timers saw the wagon as a needless and expensive frill. If the existence of the system meant that help was only a phone call away, it also increased managerial control. (Or perhaps it's not so odd. The same sort of thing occurred with the introduction of hand held radios not too long ago. But in both instances the innovation was soon seen as indispensable and all the resistance was dissipated.)

As currently organized, the patrol wagon is used for the most part to transport prisoners or, on occasion, to transport groups of officers from one place to another. But in the beginning, there was more to it than that. From the start of American municipal policing, the concept of "called for services" was seen as an implicit part of the job. Most officers were assigned to beats but even in the very early days a number were held on reserve in stations to respond to complaints received from citizens who stopped by. For a long time, until the introduction of the automobile to police work, the idea of police responding from the station to complaints at remote locations was a largely unrealized ideal. An officer might be dispatched to a problem within walking distance of the station but other than that problems were mostly left for the beat man to handle when he happened by.

With the introduction of telephone call boxes, an officer could be given an assignment when he called in. What's more, a citizen no longer had to walk all the way to the station to make a complaint. As originally envisioned, telephone boxes could be placed in private homes so that when a call was made, said one advocate of the system, "of burglars, for instance, the occupants of the house can remain snugly in bed, with their heads covered up, while the policemen answering the call [in the wagon] . . . step quietly in at the front door, to the surprise and confusion of the enterprising burglars."

In practice, direct telephone calls by citizens for police service had to wait the general installation of telephones in private homes, and the introduction of large numbers of patrol vehicles. But the system introduced in 1890 did permit limited use of street boxes by private citizens. The street boxes contained telephones for the exclusive use of officers but were also equipped with levers which, when pulled by a private citizen, would presumably bring the officers running. At first, there was little inclination for citizens to use the system to call for help. After fifteen years in service, the patrol wagon service reported only 19,100 annual runs, or slightly more than fifty a day. And most of those were for prisoner transportation, although 564 fire calls were logged, as were 114 calls to take persons home and 131 lost children united with parents.

In the beginning, no provision was made to provide cover for the wagon crews and teams. They were forced to stand in the street in front of the stations day and night, in all kinds of weather, awaiting calls. Finally, in 1892, facilities were acquired near the station-houses where men and horses could wait for assignments out of the weather. The same year, the press began to agitate for covered wagons. "It is considered proper," said one editor, "that men and women, whether criminals or drunkards, or sick or maimed or dead, should not be driven through the streets exposed to the weather or the public gaze."

On March 29, 1895, the ambulance service was separated from the patrol wagon function with the introduction of a medical ambulance service. In practice, however, most medical emergencies were still handled by police patrol wagons. Finally, in January 1896, the Police Commission entertained the idea of acquiring covered "New York"-style wagons. "The great objection raised to the wagons of the local department," commented one editor, "is that they are uncovered, thus exposing to the gaze of everyone those who are unfortunate to be forced to ride in them." Also, he said, the open wagons provided no protection from the elements.

There was the usual institutional resistance to the new idea. According to Police Commissioner Moses Gunst, Chief Crowley was opposed to the idea of covered wagons on the grounds that officers would become sick if forced to sit in the enclosed wagon beds. Whatever the case, on November 1, 1896, the department accepted delivery of the first "New York" wagon at Central Station. At first, the patrol wagons were driven by civilian teamsters. Eventually, they were phased out and replaced by officers who could handle teams. In 1902, when Police Chief George Wittman was refused a fifty-man addition to the force, he removed the officers from the wagons and placed them on patrol, which forced the Board of Supervisors to replace them again with the civilian drivers. In 1907, the wagon drivers were placed under civil service and they continued to serve in that capacity until recent decades.

In 1912, with the assignment of the first motorized wagon to the recently completed Richmond Station, the old horse-drawn wagons began to give way to the motor age. Since then, and until recently, except for model year changes, the function remained pretty much the same. Indeed, the very name patrol "wagon" evokes the image of horse-drawn vehicles.

Until recently, patrol wagons stood by in stations, under the supervision of station keepers and exempt from regular patrol assignments. One man was assigned as driver, and the other was designated as "back of the wagon." When transporting prisoners, the second man mounted the rear outside step, in the same manner as his horse-equipped predecessors, to prevent prisoners from escaping through the open rear door. In the 1950s, officers, concerned about their safety when fighting off prisoners attempting to escape through the open rear door of the wagon while bouncing through city streets hanging from the back of the vehicle, suggested that the department acquire wagons with locking rear doors like those used by military police. After due deliberation, the answer came back from downtown: "Put bigger men on the back of the wagon." Since then, in this case at least, reality has become congruent with reasonableness and wagons with locking rear doors have been acquired.

Thirty-six

CORPORAL FREDERICK COOK AND THE AUTO BANDITS

If modern mechanics can so improve the bicycle until it becomes the piece of exquisite workmanship which we see every day, there can be no doubt that in the near future the automobile will be so far improved, both as to its mechanism and as to its cost, that it will effect the supersession of the more expensive patrol wagon.

— Chief of Police Isaiah Lees, 1899

The introduction of the automobile to municipal policing in the early decades of this century did indeed "effect the supersession of the more expensive patrol wagon" as envisioned by Chief Lees. It also changed the police job in ways that the far-seeing chief had no way to predict. Prior to the introduction of the automobile, police officers worked almost exclusively on foot. (There were a few mounted patrols in the more thinly settled portions of the city.)

In the absence of any way to receive complaints and to dispatch officers quickly, most of the work of the department was done by officers on their beats. Reserve forces were maintained in the stations to respond to riot calls and important calls for service, much like the response model used by the fire service. Then as now, crime was largely a local matter. Most thieves and burglars lived in the neighborhoods where they operated. Officers, restricted as they were by the lack of transport, came to know the people intimately in the business and residential areas they patrolled every day.

In neighborhoods where the police had the residents' confidence, the people provided moral and sometimes physical support to the officers in controlling local miscreants. Police departments today are trying to recapture that aspect of the police/public relationship with a number of programs under the general heading

223

of "Community Policing." In neighborhoods where there was less agreement with police goals, an officer's lot was not a very happy one. Young hoodlums would commonly gang up on lone officers making an arrest, and without a ready backup, officers had to work things out for themselves.

The introduction of the patrol wagon/call box system helped the situation somewhat. With the introduction and proliferation of the automobile, however, the face of crime, and eventually the way the department dealt with it, changed fundamentally. The criminals were the first to see the possibilities. While officers continued to patrol their foot beats in the more densely populated business and residential districts, gangs of "auto bandits," equipped with automobiles for fast getaways, would attack businesses in the more isolated sections of the city. The bandits could be on their way, often before the police knew of the crime. Even if a foot officer happened on the scene, he would be helpless to pursue a fast-moving automobile. In 1914, as an organizational accommodation to the changing situation, each police district was equipped with a Ford sedan. In the beginning, the vehicles were not used for regular patrols. Like the patrol wagons that preceded them, they were held at the station ready to respond to calls about in-progress crimes and other serious incidents.

At 1:30 a.m. on November 24, 1915 four gunmen wearing handkerchief masks alighted from a stolen five-passenger Ford automobile and entered the barroom of the Claremont Roadhouse at 36th and Fulton in the then sparsely populated outer Richmond District. (The building still stands, now converted into an apartment house.)

The bandits pistol-whipped one of the proprietors, emptied his pockets and took $200 from the cash register. They then lined up the employees, entertainers and patrons in the adjoining dance hall and robbed them of $500 in all. When an automobile full of revelers pulled up to the roadhouse, the robbers were distracted and one of the entertainers slipped out to make a telephone call to Rich-mond Station. Noticing that one of their victims had disappeared, the bandits hurried to their auto and sped off, eastbound on Fulton. At the station, Lieutenant Dan Sylvester, Corporal Frederick Cook, and officers Bob Lean and Frank Starrett piled into the station's Ford and took off for the scene. A young motorcycle officer named Charles Dullea (who would go on to be chief of police) joined the responding party.

The officers showed up on the scene just as the robbers were de-parting. As the chase proceeded down Fulton, the officers fired on the getaway car to puncture its tires. Two of the bandits hunched down in the tonneau of the car returned fire. At 6th Avenue the bandit car made a sharp left. The gun duel continued as the ban-dit car careered north on 6th Avenue, past Richmond Station, and then on past Lake Street, where it crashed into the Presidio wall. (Throughout, the bandits displayed a singular lack of familiarity with the layout of the streets in the Richmond District.)

Two of the bandits scampered over the wall and into the dense-ly forested Presidio. Two remained on the city side and fired on the approaching officers, striking Corporal Cook in the abdomen. The officers returned fire, hitting one of the bandits twice in the chest. The uninjured bandit managed to get over the wall and disap-peared into the trees. The wounded officer and bandit were trans-ported to the Park Hospital, and Presidio authorities were notified to commence a search.

Police officers were posted along the Presidio wall and residents of the upscale neighborhood, aroused by all the commotion, joined the search for the criminals. (This was a neighborhood where the people supported the police, and a time when that support took concrete form.) The wounded bandit first gave his name as Joseph Ross, then changed it to Henry Miller. A fingerprint check proved that he was really Harry Wilson, a small-time crook from the East

36-2 Author's collection.
Armored police vehicle. 1932 Captain (and future Chief) Michael Riordan is at the left (holding the shotgun). Police Chief William Quinn (on the running board) is at the right.

Bay. (Fingerprint identification had been introduced to the department in 1909.) Wilson died the next morning without giving up his accomplices. Two days after he was shot, at 2:20 a.m. on November 26, 1915, Corporal Frederick Cook, 42, died at the Central Emergency Hospital with his wife at his side.

At first the case went nowhere. The identification of the dead bandit suggested that the robbers were from out of town. And since the crooks had an automobile, the traditional investigative methods of watching the ferry and train stations didn't turn up anything. The break in the case came a few months later, in early February 1916, when a man identifying himself as Howard Dunnigan, 23, showed up at the Methodist Hospital in Los Angeles seeking treatment for a gunshot wound in his shoulder. Los Angeles police placed Dunnigan under arrest along with three of his companions, two of whom, Harry Green and Clifford Conway, as events revealed, had been involved with him in the Claremont robbery.

San Francisco detectives brought the wounded Dunnigan back to the city and placed him under guard at the County Hospital. Dunnigan, it turned out, was the son of a prominent Baltimore family who retained a leading San Francisco law firm to defend him. Several society women visited the prisoner at the hospital, one of whom asked that he be released into her custody so that she could "make a man out of him." Dunnigan remained in custody, however, and several weeks later, according to press accounts of the time, he "broke down under the third degree" and laid out for detectives the details of a multi-state crime spree.

Dunnigan had met Wilson in Los Angeles in early November, he said, and then hooked up with other gang members, with whom he went to Sacramento, where they stole a car and robbed a roadhouse. The gang then moved to San Francisco, where on November 20 they robbed the "Sloat House" in the then sparsely populated Parkside District. Four days later they committed the Claremont Roadhouse robbery, which resulted in the death of Corporal Cook. With the heat on, the gang went to Seattle, where they recruited another crook to take Wilson's place and they committed a robbery at a gambling house, during which their new confederate was shot.

On December 12, to get morphine for their wounded companion, the gang robbed a Seattle drug store, but when they returned to their stolen auto several blocks away, they encountered rookie Seattle Police Officer Lawrence Kost, 24. While Kost struggled with one of the bandits, another shot him in the back, wounding him fatally. The gang then returned to San Francisco where they took an apartment South of Market, at 272 Ninth Street. The holdup spree continued. On December 23 they held up a saloon run by Henry Doelger (of later Westlake fame) at 7th Avenue and Hugo Street. The same night, just before midnight, the gang robbed the High Gear Saloon at Ellis and Leavenworth.

The next night, Christmas Eve, they robbed a house at 2385 Howard Street where James Schade, a private citizen, was shot to death. Then the gang drove to Howard at Fourth streets where they robbed the Niagara saloon. As the bandits departed, two patrons followed them outside and sent them on their way with a fusillade of gunfire. (It was here that Dunnigan received his wound). Again the gang left town for Los Angeles, where Dunnigan was captured and the crime spree came to an end.. At the trial that followed, Harry Green and Clifford Conway were convicted and sentenced to life imprisonment at San Quentin. For his help to the prosecution in putting his fellow bandits away, Dunnigan was placed on probation for seven years.

After Corporal Cook's murder, the department organized the first pro-active motorized anti-crime patrols. "Shotgun squads" of detectives equipped with automobiles were organized in the Detective Bureau. Teams of detectives were placed on patrol to look for trouble, with orders to keep in contact with their headquarters by telephone for information on breaking crimes. Among the first members of the elite group was Detective Charles Dullea.

Later, uniformed vehicular patrols were established, first working out of the Chief's Office and then under district command. They too were required to call the stations regularly. Although the patrol wagon/call box system and vehicular patrol capability was a decided improvement over the bad old days of lone patrol officers, problems remained. Depending as it did on someone calling the station to inform the officers of complaints, and with no way to dispatch officers already in the field, the system required that reserve officers be positioned in stations so that they could respond promptly. The comic image of the Keystone Kops rushing out of the station house in a large group, entering a touring car and racing off in all directions is an accurate, if distorted picture of the patrol system of the time. It was an extremely inefficient process that tied large numbers of officers in station houses, making them unavailable to perform other police services.

By the mid 1920s, radio technology had advanced to the point that in theory a police officer could be summoned to a reported crime instantaneously. In 1926, during the murder spree by the Buck Kelly Gang (the Terror Bandits), the idea of using radio to summon the police was given its first practical test. Regular programming on a commercial broadcast was interrupted one night in October with a message calling all San Francisco police officers to duty.

According to a later account by Police Chief William Quinn, the announcer also stated "Neighbors and friends hearing this broadcast will confer a great favor on the police department by notifying all police officers of this message." Within a few moments, Quinn reported, "the streets near the various police headquarters were thronged with reporting officers and with volunteer civilians." Everyone thought it was great.

In following years, the radio communication system was refined. With receivers installed in patrol cars, dispatches about crimes in progress could be made to officers on patrol. At first the officers listened to a commercial radio station—which interrupted its regular programming and called attention to police calls by sounding a gong. Only later was a radio channel dedicated to police communications. Broadcasts were sent out from a room adjoining the chief's office.

By 1940 the idea of citizens telephoning for police help was beginning to catch on. That year the Bureau of Criminal Information logged in 217,258 "complaints made and services rendered." Among them were 30,421 disturbances, 3,556 bank alarms, and 15, 445 reports of suspicious activities involving autos or persons. But the most numerous category was the 108,305 requests to return books to libraries and schools.

By the 1960s, calls for police service increased. The idea of the police as an around-the-clock all-purpose social agency was taking hold. In 1969, the department received about 4,000 emergency and non-emergency telephone calls a day. More recently, improvements in the computer-aided dispatch capability and 911 phone management systems have contributed to the public belief that immediate police service is a reasonable expectation. And now the department is flooded with more than 1 million calls a year to 911, everything from homicides to requests that an officer be sent to the store to pick up baby formula.

From foot patrol, to emergency wagon response to regular motorized patrols back to foot patrols the circle now promises to complete itself. "Community Policing" concepts have re-emphasized the value of the police officer as part of the neighborhood being policed, and there is a return to increased interaction between foot officers and the people who live in the areas they serve.

Thirty-seven
ROUGH JUSTICE

In the early morning hours of Friday, December 10, 1920, a group of rough talking masked men gained entry to the Santa Rosa Jail. There they seized three men being held for the shooting deaths a few days before of the Sonoma County Sheriff and two San Francisco police detectives. The mob took the men to a nearby cemetery where they hanged them. For decades, it has been rumored that the men were hanged by San Francisco police officers avenging the deaths of their murdered comrades.

The tragic events began in San Francisco a couple of weeks earlier when a group of men cozened two young women into a small cottage on Howard Street, where they raped and otherwise sexually abused them. When her assailants fell asleep, one of the young women, Jean Stanley, managed to escape and returned with the police, who rescued her friend and arrested the men in the house. Several others involved in the case were quickly arrested but three more remained at large.

In early December, police got word that the three wanted men had been seen in Santa Rosa. On December 6, San Francisco police Detective Sergeant Miles Jackson, Detective Lester Dorman and Policewoman Katherine O'Connor (to take charge of the woman believed to be with the fugitives) went to Santa Rosa where they met Sonoma County Sheriff James Petray and began to scour the west side of town where the suspects were supposedly holed up. About 3 p.m. they found their quarry at a little bungalow at 28 West Seventh Street, next to the Toscano Hotel.

The sheriff and the two San Francisco detectives entered while Sonoma County deputy sheriffs watched the exits. In the following burst of gunfire, all three lawmen in the house were shot fatally. Four days later the three men arrested at the scene were lynched.

The rumor arose immediately that San Francisco officers had done the hanging. Chief of Police Daniel O'Brien swiftly denied it. There were hints that there was more to it than was revealed but there the story sat until 1985 when an elderly rancher from the Healdsburg area approached *Santa Rosa Press Democrat* columnist Gaye LeBaron after she had published an account of the lynching, and admitted that as a very young man he had participated in the incident.

It was a group of men from Healdsburg that did the hanging, he said. "There was no one from San Francisco there that night." His statement might be expected to put to rest suspicions of police involvement. But still, the claims persist. Old men sidle up at places where old men congregate and mention that so-and-so, who they knew at the time, once told them such-and-such. When informed of the Healdsburg angle, they just nod and smile knowingly. Their comments are all hearsay, of course, but other indicators suggest that there is more to the story than has yet been revealed.

On the evening of Thursday, December 9, the day of the San Francisco officers' funeral, according to the later account of a ferry boat operator, and just hours before the hanging, he transported a number of San Francisco police officers wearing plain clothes to Marin County. Harry Coleman, a San Francisco press photographer, in his memoirs published in 1943, told of what happened next in his 1943 memoir. "I was sitting at home one night in Sausalito," he writes, "when a contingent of boys [police officers] from San Francisco drove off the ferry and skidded into my driveway."

At their invitation, he joined them on their trip north on the promise of an exclusive picture. "Somewhere at a crossroad beyond Petaluma," he wrote, "we joined a convoy of other cars. . . ." Coleman described the subsequent hanging and the photograph he obtained. It's evident from Coleman's account, if he is to be believed, that there was some prior knowledge on the part of the police officers that a hanging was to take place. Contemporary ob-

37-1 Jesse Cook Collection. Jean Stanley. One of the victims of the Howard Street gang.

servers counted 24 automobiles in the caravan from the jail to the place of hanging. The Healdsburg vigilante says that there were 12 to 15 cars from Healdsburg. They went to and from Santa Rosa separately, he said, not in caravan. Sonoma County Coroner Frank Phillips reported seeing a convoy of a dozen autos headed toward San Francisco about the same time that the Healdsburg contingent would have been arriving back in Healdsburg.

When the two groups of automobiles are added together, they just about match the number counted at the hanging. It could well be that as a young member of the necktie party, the Healdsburg witness was not familiar with all aspects of the plan and did not know of the meeting Coleman reported as taking place in the roadway north of Petaluma. Perhaps some survivor of the San Francisco contingent will shed light on that part of it—but don't count on it.

Every few months a bunch of old cops and their friends meet for lunch in Santa Rosa. Ironically, the restaurant where they meet is on the site of the old Toscano Hotel, right next to the little bungalow where the officers were shot down more than 80 years ago. Most of those who attend are retired from the San Francisco Police Department or members of Sonoma county law enforcement agencies.

37-2 Author's collection.
George Boyd, Terry Fitts and Charles Valento, lynched for the murder of Detective Sergeant Miles Jackson, Detective Lester Dohrman and Sheriff James Petray.

Thirty-eight

AL CAPONE'S TAILOR

W hat's old is new again. Consider the arrest of Al Capone's tailor in light of the San Francisco Police Department's recent troubles. A *Chronicle* series in 2002 focused attention on the department's miserable record in solving violent crimes—an average of only 28 percent between 1996 and 2000. The SFPD fails to solve homicide cases 50 percent of the time. In response, the chief of police pledged reforms and the Board of Supervisors formed a special committee to investigate. Seventy years ago, the solution was different.

After unfavorable publicity followed a spate of unsolved homicides in early 1932, San Francisco police rounded up more than 1,000 criminal "suspects"—among them Al Capone's tailor. Louis Dinato, recently arrived in San Francisco, was able to convince officers that his involvement with Capone was restricted to the gang lord's wardrobe, and he was released the next day on $250 bail.

The 1932 dragnet came after a series of unsolved Prohibition-era gang killings. The first was the shooting death of Genaro Ferri in his Lombard Street home on November 24, 1928. Police said the killing was the result of a dispute over control of the liquor rackets and named Alfredo Scarisi as the killer. Before the authorities had a chance to talk to Scarisi, however, his body was found with that of Vito Pileggi, a fellow gangster, on a road near Sacramento. A week after those killings, Mario Filippi was shot to death in the basement of his restaurant at 18 Sacramento Street.

A few months later, in April 1929, the body of Rene Fabri, an immigrant French pimp, was found with his throat slit and a back full of bullets at Rockaway Beach on the San Mateo County coast. Informed opinion had it that he was "taken for a ride" after getting into an argument in a Romolo Place gambling dive. In July 1929,

Joe Bocca, known as "the Sicilian Strong Man" and believed to be a member of the gang that killed Scarisi, was found shot and stabbed to death in his car, its motor running and lights on, in the sparsely settled sand dunes at 39th Avenue and Noriega Street.

In our own time, a disproportionate number of unsolved homicides involve young, gang-affiliated people of color competing for turf, drugs and respect. Similarly, most of the unsolved cases in the 1920s and 1930s involved gangsters with Italian surnames. (Twenty years earlier, Chinese names would have been disproportionately represented; 30 years before that, most of the names would have been Irish.)

Another constant is that the circumstances of unsolved killings often point to disputes over vices operations. In the 1920s and 1930s, the popular vices were illegal alcohol, prostitution and gambling. After Bocca's killing, Italian gang-related killings declined for a while, but there were other sensational cases to stir the juices of the press. Taken together, the cases evoke a city far different from that of our nostalgic imaginings.

On April 29, 1930, Officer John Malcolm was killed by payroll robbers at Pier 26. In September, Louis Frost was shot and killed by "persons unknown" while making an illegal liquor delivery on Hoffman Avenue. On December 8, Rosetta Baker, a wealthy widow with a taste for much younger men, was found strangled in her California Street apartment. The same month, Virgil Turner, the father of soon-to-be screen goddess Lana Turner, was found murdered on Minnesota Street after he won big in a card game.

In January 1931, Henry Schmidt was found bound, gagged and strangled in his Fulton Street store, the apparent victim of robbers. And the following month, Albina Voohries was murdered and her 48th Avenue store set afire to cover up a robbery. In 1932, the pace picked up. On March 3, George Gordon was found slain in a Utah Street factory. Twenty days later, Paul Hanson was killed by three thugs at a lovers lane at Lake Merced as he tried to defend his date from a gang rape.

Jessie Scott Hughes was killed near her home on Lakeview Street in April in a faked automobile accident. The case shook the foundations of the city's justice system when it was revealed that Frank Egan, the county public defender, had engineered the killing. The same day, Louis Zanardi was beaten to death by three unknown men after a baseball game at Rolph Playground, and on May 5, O'Bryan Bemis, who had had a good day at the track, was found dead at the California Rod and Gun Club range at Fort Funston.

On May 15, William McCann, a cousin of Municipal Court Judge Frank Dunne, was found shot dead at Marin and Kansas streets after telling a girlfriend that he was "going for a ride." If there was any remaining police or public apathy about these unsolved homicides, it ended abruptly three days later. On May 18, Luigi Malvese, another bootleg gangster, was ambushed and shot to death in broad daylight in his automobile in front of the Del Monte Barbershop at 720 Columbus Avenue. Genaro Campanello (a.k.a. Onorino Caprano) was immediately named as the suspect.

Unable to find Campanello, the police brass did the next best thing. They bounced Inspector Allen McGinn as the head of the "Death Squad" and set out, in the words immortalized by Claude Rains' Captain Renault in "Casablanca," to "round up the usual suspects." Captain Arthur Layne, commanding the Central Police District (and now chiefly remembered as the straight-arrow maternal grandfather of Oakland Mayor Jerry Brown) led the raids. Officers under Layne's command swept through the Tenderloin, according to one press account, picking up "gangsters, crooks, known and suspected, and undesirables generally."

Six patrol wagons full of suspects were sent to the Hall of Justice in the first haul and in the next several days, they were joined by 1,000 more. The criminal justice processing mechanism became clogged. Those rounded up had about as much to do with the Malvese killing as did Al Capone's tailor. But that wasn't really the point of the exercise. It was considered a legitimate police tactic to put so much pressure on the underworld that economic dislocation would force wiser criminal heads to rein in the wild men.

In light of a number of court decisions since then and shifting public attitudes about what police practices are acceptable, we can criticize the methods used in the 1930s to deal with perceived crime waves. Supporters of the police of 1932 would point to a homicide rate less than half that of the current rate, lower than any time in the city's history, and a clearance rate—for all the shouting at the time about unpunished murderers—of more than 80 percent.

In 1932, there was an often-expressed fear, stoked by periodic killings by Italian gangsters that San Francisco was in danger of going the way of Chicago, which still provides a picturesque metaphor for Prohibition-era urban crime. In hindsight, San Franciscans really had little to fear. The number of gangland killings here, more than could be counted on the fingers of one hand, did not begin to compare with the 400 or more in Chicago.

In his doctoral dissertation, "The Meaning of Community: A History of the Italians of San Francisco," Dr. Sebastian Fichera explained why. In Chicago, the large population of recent immigrants overwhelmed the stabler population of earlier arrivals and the gangster element prospered in the confusion. In San Francisco, the established Italian community dominated Italian civic life and cooperated with the authorities to keep the criminal element in check.

In the world as it has evolved since 1932, massive roundups of "undesirables" are out of the question, of course. But there is still a lesson to be learned from that earlier time. In the end, perhaps the best long term hope for reduced homicide rates—and an improved solution rate—is the creation and nurturing of a set of societal relationships similar to those found by Fichera in the San Francisco of two generations ago. For all their other differences, other groups of San Franciscans, like the Italians of an earlier day, may come together to bring the killing to an end.

Thirty-nine

THE TERROR BANDITS

F or all the contemporary concern about random attacks from heartless criminals, one of the most deadly periods in the city's history came during the October 1926 rampage of the "Terror Bandits." The first police contact with the drive-by killers—who in their two-night crime spree would leave four men dead and more than a dozen injured—was by Chief of Police Dan O'Brien, personally.

Shortly before midnight on Saturday October 9, 1926, as Chief O'Brien and his wife were leaving the home of friends on Clay Street, he heard the sound of gunshots around the corner on Powell. The chief sent his wife back into the house and ran to the scene with his driver, Detective Sergeant James Neely. There they found Mario Pagano dying in the street. Just then, a closed sedan raced down Powell from Washington, and when the officers signaled it to stop, gunfire erupted from within. The officers returned fire as the car sped past them toward California Street.

The murderous crime spree of the Terror Bandits had actually begun a few hours earlier with the theft of an automobile from in front of 1350 Vallejo Street. Shortly thereafter, two men in an automobile robbed cab driver Harry Giannini at gunpoint at Sutter and Steiner. A few minutes later, Lester Irish, another cabbie, was robbed at Webster and Washington. Both victims reported the license plate of the stolen car.

Next the robbers accosted Dr. Nicholas Jacobs as he was about to enter his home at 2441 Webster. Then they got John Copren at 1344 Pine. Station and Detective Bureau shotgun squads began to scour the area north of Market. Realizing the heat was on there, the bandits moved their operations across the line. At 8th and Bryant streets, the robbers accosted George Karinsky, who was stroll-

39-1 Author's collection.   Police Chief Daniel O'Brien. He engaged in a gun duel with the bandits at the beginning of their reign of terror.

ing with Mrs. Emma Bird, her 13-year old daughter, and a female friend. They robbed the group at gunpoint, dragged Mrs. Bird into the car and drove off. Two blocks farther on, after flashing a light in her face and deciding, "She ain't young enough," the thugs unceremoniously threw her from the automobile on 10th Street.

The auto bandits then doubled back down to Fifth Street and Harrison, where they accosted, pistol-whipped and robbed Anthony Gonzales on the street. A few moments later, and a block away on Sixth Street, they again leaped out of their car and robbed Manuel Salazar. When police responded to the calls South of Market, the bandits headed back across Market. At the poolroom run by Constantino Guillen on Lombard between Buchanan and Webster, they pistol-whipped Guillen, then shot him twice when he fell. They also shot Clarence Schivo, striking him in the arm, and robbed the other patrons.

The bandits then drove to Powell and Washington, where they killed Pagano and dueled with Chief O'Brien and Sergeant Neely. After the Pagano killing the bandits drove to a poolroom at 2112 Market Street, where they gained entry under a ruse, knocked the janitor down, tied him up, and cleaned out the cash register. At 2:30 a.m. on Sunday, they robbed Jack Storey and Henry Berthiaume as they entered their house at 1225 Clay street. Those were the last crimes in that particular spree. In all, the robbers made about $400 and assorted pieces of jewelry from the dozen robberies they committed that night.

At noon on Sunday, Officers Henry Kiernan and John Ross of the Bush Street Station recovered the stolen auto at Haight and Laguna streets. There were blood stains on the upholstery, suggesting that one of the robbers may have been hit in the exchange with the chief. At that point, detectives had little to go on other than a description of two young white males. Two days later, at 6:00 p.m. on Monday, it all started up again. Two men hired Yellow Cab driver Walter Swanson at a stand at 29th and Mission and drove with him to 16th and Third street where they shot him fatally, took his cabbie's uniform, and threw his body under the viaduct there.

They then drove in his cab, one of them outfitted as a cab driver, to San Bruno and Mariposa, where Michael Petrovich was enjoying an after-dinner walk and cigar. According to witnesses who watched from across the street, one of the bandits asked him for the time. When Petrovich pulled out his watch, the man shot him fatally. After shooting Petrovich, the bandits drove to 100 Mississippi Street, where they robbed two pedestrians. Next the bandits went to a restaurant at 798 Brannan Street, where they robbed the cook, Louis Fernando, and two patrons. They shot Fernando when he did not comply with their commands quickly enough.

They then walked across the street to the Associated filling station, where Jack Duane, a night watchman for the American Can Company, was talking with Carl Johnson, the attendant, and a man named Rex Hayden. Seeing the gun, Duane tried to run, but was shot in the back of the head and fatally wounded. Johnson and Hayden resisted and both were shot. From there the bandits went to Pier 36, where they robbed and pistol-whipped Alvin Anderson, a marine engineer. Next, the killers drove to the filling station at 17th and Missouri streets, where they were assaulting and robbing patron Steve Walker when Potrero Station Officer Dorsey Henderson drove by. The bandits sped off with Officer Henderson in pursuit.

A running gunbattle ensued which ended at 16th and Mississippi, where the killers drove the cab into the curb, wrecking it. As Officer Henderson stopped to reload, the bandits ran from the car and escaped on foot across a lumber yard. Shortly afterward, Officer Harry Doyle, who was waiting for the morgue wagon with Swanson's body at 16th and Third streets, saw an auto speeding toward him on 16th Street with its lights out. When he signaled the car to stop, it sped by him, its occupants firing as they went.

The officer returned fire as the vehicle disappeared down the viaduct toward the Bayshore highway. Peninsula authorities were notified and the Great Highway and other roads to the Peninsula were blockaded. The entire rampage that evening, which left three dead and a number wounded, was over in less than an hour. When reports of the shootings and robberies came in, Chief O'Brien ordered the mobilization of the entire police department. To facilitate the call up, the chief enlisted the aid of commercial radio stations. Just before 8:00 p.m.—by which time the crime spree had ended—radio station KPO put out a message for all police officers to report to their headquarters. Within minutes, the streets around the various stations and headquarters were jammed with the cars of officers and volunteer citizens. The entire department was organized into shotgun squads and placed in vehicles, many of them the officers' personal autos.

Supplemented by fire department volunteers and equipped with more than 1,000 rifles borrowed from the National Guard, a force of 2,000 men was soon patrolling the streets with orders to "shoot to kill." Shortly after midnight, a wrecked touring car was found at 11th and Harrison streets. There were no further incidents that night.

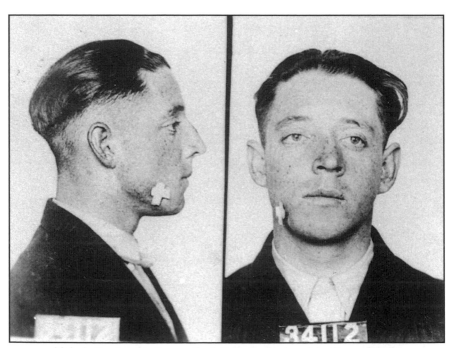

39-2 Author's collection.   Buck Kelly, the leader of the Terror Bandits.

For the next week, as patrol officers continued intensive patrols, detectives worked around the clock. They shook the underworld tree and rounded up vagrants and other "undesirables" for intensive grilling; it was not a good week for men "known to the police." Detective George "Paddy" Wafer and Detective Sergeant Louis De Mattei broke the case. The detectives got word from an underworld source that a man had been talking it up at a Waller Street bootleg joint run by a city fireman.

The detectives did not advertise their methods but reports were that either the proprietor volunteered the information or someone else gave information about him. In any event, goods taken in the robberies were found in the bootleg joint and in the home of one of the owners. Later one of the owners of the bootleg saloon was arrested for burning some houses in San Mateo belonging to Detective Wafer in reprisal for his work on the case.

On October 18, the detectives picked up Lawrence Weeks, 22, from his job as a laborer on the Duboce Tunnel, then under construction. Under police questioning, Weeks quickly confessed to twelve holdups on Saturday night. He also admitted to having shot at Pagano but denied he was involved in the Monday-night spree. Weeks gave up Clarence "Buck" Kelly, 22, as ringleader of the group. Kelly, a sometimes cabdriver and club boxer with fifteen amateur fights, was a well-known South of Market thug. He had been arrested at age 16 for grand theft, and later on other minor charges. In April 1926, he was apprehended for criminally assaulting a woman. His case was pending at the time of the murder rampage.

Kelly lived with his parents and several siblings at 47 South Park, a six-unit, three-story walkup. With Weeks' information in hand, a posse of detectives under Lieutenant Bernard McDonald went to the South Park location armed with rifles and shotguns. As the officers surrounded the building, Kelly realized that something was up. He ran down the back stairs, where he met detectives coming up, and he scooted into a second-story apartment with the officers in pursuit. The officers let fly and Kelly was hit twice by rifle fire.

The badly wounded arrestee was taken to San Francisco General Hospital. He denied everything—a posture he was to retain until the very end. When Homicide Squad Lieutenant Charles Dullea produced Weeks in his hospital room, Kelly admitted knowing the man but said he had nothing to do with any crimes. Weeks was a hophead, he loudly proclaimed, not to be trusted in anything; it was all a police frame. But a search of the South Park premises turned up the dead cab driver's puttees and other incriminating evidence. Surviving victims of the robbery/shootings positively identified Kelly as the principal shooter.

Police were at first puzzled by Weeks' continued insistence that he had nothing to do with the Monday night rampage. He was willing to admit to the robberies on Saturday night and even of having shot at Mario Pagano but he emphatically denied being involved Monday evening. As part of the larger investigation, Detectives Allen McGinn and Charles Iredale questioned the patrons of a pool room at 3rd and Harrison streets, where Kelly was known to hang out. There they learned that Michael Papadaches, 17, a friend of Kelly and frequent visitor to the pool room since his release from Whittier Reformatory a month previous, had dropped out of sight.

On Monday, October 21, officers went to his mother's house at 665 10th Avenue and arrested him as he lay in bed. Under grilling, Papadaches confessed to the robberies on Monday but denied doing any of the shooting. Police received word from several sources that cabdrivers, outraged at the brutal and unprovoked killing of one of their own, planned to go to the hospital and lynch Kelly. Officers were dispatched throughout the city to warn cabdrivers to stay away from the hospital. Mission Station Captain Frederick Lemon assigned 25 men to guard the hospital with orders to "shoot to kill" if anyone tried to seize the prisoner. Kelly's trial for the first-degree

246

murders of Swanson, Petrovich and Duane began on December 7, 1926. The star witness was Michael Papadaches. Kelly had the only gun, he testified, and no one — except perhaps Swanson — was more surprised than he was when Kelly began shooting.

Papadaches described the murder/robbery spree and characterized himself as a virtual prisoner of his crime partner. He separated from Kelly, he insisted, at his first opportunity, after they fled through the lumber yard. The defense argued that Kelly had not done the murders, but if involved in the crimes at all, he did not fully appreciate their seriousness because of head injuries he received as a child. Kelly's mother took the stand and testified about several such injuries.

Kelly testified that he had been suffering from alcoholic blackouts recently and remembered nothing of the events of the night of October 11. The jury of five men and three women was not swayed, and after 22 minutes deliberation returned three guilty verdicts of first-degree murder. On May 11, 1927, after an unsuccessful appeal, Buck Kelly had his date with the hangman at San Quentin.

His mother and his sister Jean were with him to the end. His father, John, was serving time in San Quentin himself, on a burglary conviction, but neither father nor son asked to see the other. As Kelly ascended the gallows stairs, his defiance collapsed and he had to be carried the last few steps.

As he was about to go to trial in March 1927, Lawrence Weeks pled guilty to the murder of Mario Pagano and the robberies on the night of October 9, and was sentenced to seven consecutive life terms. Mike Papadaches, who had cooperated with the prosecution, was sent to Preston School of Industry. He was released early, and in October 1929, was arrested for violating his parole by getting drunk. For that infraction he was sentenced to a five-year term in San Quentin.

Forty
OFFICIAL MISCONDUCT

Warren and Verna Louw took in "The Champ" starring Wallace Berry and Jackie Coogan at the El Rey Theater on Ocean Avenue on Friday evening, April 29, 1932. Afterwards, as they walked toward their Kenwood Way home, about 9:45 p.m., the couple noticed a suspicious-looking automobile slowly circling the area. Thinking the occupants might be robbers, the Louws stepped into a recessed doorway and watched as the auto appeared and reappeared several times before racing off with its lights out. The couple continued up Kenwood, where they came upon the crumpled body of a woman lying on the pavement near the curb in front of 150 Kenwood.

At first, official thought was that the victim had been struck by a hit-and-run driver, but responding detectives soon noticed that, though the night was chilly, the woman wore no coat. Neither had she been carrying a purse and contrary to the custom of the time, she wore no hat. On Saturday morning, a Westwood Park neighbor identified the victim as Jessie Scott Hughes, a 59-year-old widow who lived alone at 41 Lakewood Street. Public Defender Frank Egan could tell them more, the man said, for he was a close friend of Mrs. Hughes and managed her financial affairs.

The 50-year-old Egan was a well-respected figure in San Francisco's political and criminal justice circles. A former city police officer who had passed the bar and established a private law practice in 1914, he had been appointed the city's first Public Defender in 1918 after the office was established by the State Legislature. Egan was elected to the post in his own right at the next election and re-elected continuously thereafter.

Later that Saturday morning, Egan himself showed up at the coroner's office. In answer to routine questioning he acknowledged

40-1 Author's collection.   Chief Charles Dullea. Dullea had a very active police career.
In 1918 he was a founding member of the Shotgun Squad. In 1923, as a lieutenant, he
formed the first Homicide Squad in the department. Thereafter he was appointed
Captain of Detectives, during which time he prosecuted the Egan case. In 1940, notwithstanding the dire predictions attending that case, he was appointed Chief of Police, in
which capacity he served until 1947.

that he was in charge of Mrs. Hughes' affairs, and mentioned that she
had an insurance policy listing him as the beneficiary. Egan added
that his client had been in the habit of going on night hikes without a

hat or coat, a practice he had warned her about repeatedly. As to his whereabouts at the time of Mrs. Hughes' death, Egan volunteered that he had attended the fights that night at Dreamland Auditorium with Dr. Nathan Houseman, his physician and friend.

Police detectives under Captain of Detectives Charles Dullea went to the Lakewood address, where they were forced to break a window to gain entry and, once in the house, found that all exterior windows and doors were locked and bolted from the inside. The house and garage keys were found in Mrs. Hughes' purse, neatly stowed in the dining room sideboard. The woman could only have left the building through the garage door, which had a self-engaging spring lock. Suspicious-looking stains were found on the garage floor. By Monday morning, police located the death car in a private garage at Turk and Masonic streets.

The blue 1925 Lincoln phaeton belonged to Fire Lieutenant Oscar Postel, who said he had loaned it on the morning of the killing to a man called Verne Doran, who claimed he wanted to use it to take Frank Egan for a ride. Doran, 23, a convicted burglar, indebted to Frank Egan for his release on parole, worked for the Public Defender as a chauffeur. Detectives went to the home of Doran's sister, where they were told that Doran had left a half-hour earlier after receiving a telephone call from a man she thought was Frank Egan. The sister thought Doran might be in the company of a recently acquired friend, Albert Tinnin. The 37-year-old Tinnin was also an ex-convict, having spent nine years in Folsom Prison on a conviction for attempted murder of a woman in Tehama County. He had been paroled the preceding February, in part through the intercession of San Francisco Public Defender Frank Egan. Tinnin was not to be found either.

The case smelled, and the taint kept leading back to Public Defender Frank Egan. On Monday night, it took an odd turn. At 9:00 p.m. Captain Dullea received a telephone call from Egan, who said that he had been kidnapped. Yet an hour later a hotel clerk and a police officer saw the Public Defender at Powell and Geary streets in no obvious distress. Egan then dropped from sight as well.

From the start, the case commanded front-page attention as enterprising reporters dug into every aspect of Egan's past and police scurried around the state in response to reports of sightings of the fugitives. As in other celebrated cases, once the story broke, witnesses to unusual behavior came forward. For one thing, it soon became evident that despite outward trappings of affluence, Egan's finances were in a sorry state. A bank had started foreclosure proceedings on the Egan home at 225 Urbano Drive to recover a $9,000 mortgage that had gone unpaid.

And Dr. Alexander Keenan, who had treated Mrs. Hughes several months earlier, said that when he had presented her bill to Egan for payment as the patient suggested, the Public Defender told him that her funds had been exhausted. Dr. Keenan said Mrs. Hughes seemed surprised when that comment was relayed to her. Mrs. Hughes was not the only older woman of means connected to Egan. A decade earlier, about the time Egan and his wife, Lorraine Kipp were married, she came into a sizeable inheritance from Margaritha Busch, an heiress of the Busch brewing fortune, for whom she had served as a companion and nurse. Within 48 hours of Miss Busch's death, a deed of gift was filed with the county recorder transferring a row of apartment houses on O'Farrell Street to Egan's bride. When Chicago relatives sued, Mrs. Egan settled out of court for one-third of the $200,000 on the advice of her attorney/husband.

After Mrs. Catherine Craven died in 1929, supposedly from the effects of alcohol, her nieces examined her estate, which they estimated to be worth about $25,000, and found it to consist of an empty safe deposit box and real estate plastered with mortgages. When they contacted Egan, who had been in charge of her affairs, he ordered them out of his office.

Another case was that of Mrs. Katie Weber, who died in No-

40-2 Public Defender Frank Egan on the day of his arrest for murder. He is flanked by his attorney, Vincent Hallinan, and Police Chief William Quinn (in hat holding cigar).

vember 1930, leaving an estate of some $8,000 which had dwindled to $4 under management of her friend and counselor, Frank Egan. The executor of Weber's estate said that he had been pressing Egan for repayment of a loan from the estate at the time of Mrs. Hughes' death. More recently, in February 1932, another of Egan's clients, Mrs. Florence Cook, had been found dead in her home, also apparently from the effects of alcohol. According to neighbors, Egan visited her frequently, sometimes in the company of Dr. Houseman. Cook's divorced husband said he had given his ex-wife $6,000 in the preceding year, all of which was gone. He was put off by the Public Defender when he asked him about it, he said.

These revelations caused the press to take another look at Albert Tinnin's conviction for attempted murder of a woman in 1918.

That victim was the sister of the woman with whom Tinnin was living in San Francisco at the time. The two women had recently come into a shared inheritance of $100,000, all of which would have gone to Tinnin's live-in friend if her sister were dead. At Tinnin's trial for the 1918 attempted murder, Frank Egan had testified that the defendant was working as a process server in Egan's San Francisco office at the time of the crime and thus could not have been 200 miles away in Tehama County. The jury evidently didn't believe Egan and gave Tinnin ten years to life.

On the Thursday following his disappearance in the Hughes case, Egan turned up in a private sanatorium on Steiner Street where, according to his spokesman and attorney, Vincent Hallinan, he was recovering from a nervous breakdown. Egan, said Hallinan, couldn't remember anything that had occurred since the preceding Saturday. The following Monday, it was revealed that Tinnin had been in police custody since Wednesday, May 4, held incommunicado at the Whitcomb Hotel, where he was questioned by police. Soon afterward, as the authorities were closing in on him, Doran turned himself in to the police. Both ex-cons were held on parole violations; Doran was sent to San Quentin and Tinnin was lodged at the County Jail.

As the web of circumstantial evidence drew around Egan and his two suspected accomplices, Egan's defenders rallied to his cause. It was all a frame-up, Attorney Hallinan and others charged, engineered to abolish the office of Public Defender, which was unpopular in law-and-order circles for getting criminals off. The latter charge was lent some credibility by efforts to place a proposition on the ballot which aimed to abolish the Public Defender's office. As to the former, the conviction of radical labor activist Tom Mooney a decade earlier, resulting from a frame-up engineered by public utility companies and the District Attorney, with at least the tacit complicity of the Police Department, was still fresh in the public mind.

On June 4, as the grand jury was about to take up the matter, the case broke wide open. Verne Doran, Egan's chauffeur—who faced fifteen years on his parole violation, and still more time if convicted of a recent garage hold-up for which he was charged—decided to make a clean breast of it. Doran laid out the whole case for the authorities in gruesome detail. He and Tinnin had done the killing, he admitted, at the urging of Frank Egan. Egan had told him, Doran said, that Mrs. Hughes had been pressing him for money and threatening to take him before the Bar Association. Doran went along with the plan, he said, because he was afraid that Egan would send him back to San Quentin on some technical violation.

Egan had introduced him to Tinnin a week before the killing, he said. On the day of the killing he had borrowed the automobile from Postel as Egan requested and later in the afternoon went with Egan and Tinnin to Mrs. Hughes' home, where Egan had Tinnin ring the bell on a ruse, so he would recognize her later. Egan waited a block away. Tinnin and Doran met Egan later in his office, where Egan called Mrs. Hughes and told her he was bringing two friends for dinner. Later that evening, Tinnin and Doran went to the house while Egan established his alibi elsewhere. Expecting Egan, Mrs. Hughes opened the garage door to them, Doran said, and they drove directly in.

When the woman questioned them about Egan's whereabouts and refused to get her hat and coat to join them in going to him, Tinnin struck her several times, according to Doran, knocking her unconscious. Tinnin then placed her in front of the right front wheel and instructed Doran to drive over her, which he did. He then backed over her to make sure the job was done. They placed Mrs. Hughes in the car and drove to the Kenwood location and threw her out. Then they went to the Blackstone Hotel where they played ping-pong until 11:30 p.m., when Egan showed up and they reported that the job had been accomplished. The Grand Jury indicted all three suspects for murder and their trial began on August 8 in Superior Court 12, Judge Frank Dunne presiding. Assistant

District Attorney Isadore Golden appeared for the people; Vincent Hallinan represented Egan, and Nate Coghlan, a leading defense attorney of the day, appeared for Tinnin.

Golden opened for the prosecution by eliciting testimony from several witnesses describing how Egan had cozened Mrs. Hughes out of a house on Moultrie Street and used another woman to set up a dummy bank account through which he laundered Mrs. Weber's money. Other witnesses established the fact that Mrs. Hughes had almost $15,000 in life insurance with Egan as the beneficiary. Doran was the star witness for the prosecution, repeating in detail the story of how he and Tinnin had killed Mrs. Hughes at Egan's request. There followed a string of corroborative witnesses. One of Mrs. Hughes' neighbors identified Doran as the man she saw sitting in the Lincoln in front of the Lakewood address on the afternoon of the murder. Another woman who lived up the hill identified Egan as the man she saw standing in front of her house on the afternoon of the murder while, according to Doran, he and Tinnin made their exploratory visit to Mrs. Hughes' house. Still another neighbor testified that she had seen the Lincoln back out of Mrs. Hughes' garage about 9:30 p.m.

Police criminologist Frank Latulippe tied the physical evidence together, and Warren Louw described what he had seen on the night of the murder. The final and somewhat reluctant witness was Egan's stenographer, Marion Lambert, who testified that Mrs. Hughes had frequently called Egan at his office and that two days before her death she had come in and made a pest of herself.

The defense presented a cohesive case which pretty much covered the points addressed by the prosecution — if one chose to believe their witnesses. To counter the charge that Egan had milked Mrs. Hughes' accounts, the defense brought out that on many occasions Egan had made payments for her expenses. The main hurdle for the defense to overcome was Doran's confession. To do that they put Charles Colonna on the stand, a San Quentin convict who said that he met Doran on Mission Street a week before the murder and that Doran tried to interest him in burglarizing a woman's house out by Balboa Park. The implication was that Doran had done the killing himself during a bungled burglary attempt. Another defense witness, Doran's cellmate in the County Jail, testified that Doran had told him that he was going to give up Egan and Tinnin to save his own skin.

A Mrs. Burton Barren testified that Tinnin was with her in her room at the Californian Hotel from 7:30 to 10:30 p.m. on the night of the murder. Mrs. Egan testified she had spent the afternoon of the killing with her husband, so he could not have been with Tinnin and Doran at that time as Doran claimed. In a bold move, Hallinan called Egan himself to the stand as his final witness. By cleverly re-stricting his direct questioning to the day of the murder and the one preceding it, Hallinan was able to get Egan's adamant denial into the record while denying the prosecution the opportunity to cross-examine him about earlier events.

After rebuttal witnesses refuted Mrs. Egan's testimony and that of Doran's cellmate, the testimony came to an end. Attorney Hallinan had mounted his customary spirited defense throughout, and finished off by going to jail, not for the last time, on a charge of contempt for interrupting Prosecutor Golden during his closing arguments. On September 3, 1932 the case went to the jury which three days later returned a verdict of guilty of first-degree murder against both Egan and Tinnin. Their sentence was life in prison.

As the murder case unfolded the previous May, some had wondered at the ability of the police to move so quickly toward a resolution of what started out as a true "whodunit." After the verdict was in, the explanation was forthcoming. In May 1931 a man shot in a beer saloon at 110 Eddy Street sought treatment from Dr. Nathan Houseman, who was known by the police to have treated underworld characters in the past. At the urging of Captain Dullea, according to a bombshell revelation reported sympathetically in the *Examiner* on September 9, 1932, private investigator Ignatius McCarthy had installed a Dictaphone in Dr. Houseman's Flood Building office with wires running to his Monadanock Building office.

Several months later—and several months before the deed occurred—bored police inspectors monitoring the wire got an earful when they heard a discussion between Public Defender Frank Egan and Dr. Houseman, planning the intended murder of Mrs. Hughes. The opposition press had a field day. Their main question was: Why, if the police had knowledge of the murder before it happened, hadn't they prevented it? Captain Dullea responded that he had telephoned Mrs. Hughes about the threat but she discounted the possibility. He had also, he said, sent her — for reasons never explained — anonymous notes about the danger from Egan. As the months passed and nothing happened, the police became involved in other matters.

In the usual speculation following any major event, attorney Nate Coghlan opined that while he liked Charles Dullea personally, the police captain would soon be looking for other work. Alameda County District Attorney Earl Warren, of later Supreme Court fame as a civil libertarian, was asked what he would have done if he were Captain Dullea. He jocularly replied that he would have destroyed the transcripts and killed everyone who knew about them.

Members of the grand jury made noises about looking into the matter and the Police Commission considered doing so. In the end, they concluded that the whole affair was unfortunate and that the police shouldn't go around bugging people, but that it was really too late to do anything about it. Coghlan's prediction about Dullea proved wrong, he went on to an illustrious tenure as chief of police.

At first, the defense considered appeals and a new trial, but that soon ended, presumably because now that all was known, a second trial might have resulted in a death penalty. Doran went to prison on a manslaughter conviction and was paroled two years later. Tinnin and Egan waited more than twenty-five years for their release. In 1957, Tinnin finally admitted that he had committed the murder with Doran at Egan's bidding. It was Doran who knocked out Mrs. Hughes, he said. Otherwise his crime companion's story was correct. Shortly afterward, Tinnin was granted parole.

Egan never admitted to the crime and claimed that Tinnin had confessed only to expedite his own release. Over the years, Egan made several futile attempts to seek an executive pardon and was finally paroled in October 1957. His object, he said in a post-release interview, was to clear his name. He died four years later, still protesting his innocence.

I had occasion to interview Vincent Hallinan in the early 1990s, more than half a century after the most famous San Francisco murder of the early 1930s, and I asked him about Egan's claim of innocence, which some still claimed to support. Hallinan just smiled and rolled his eyes.

AFTERWORD

When news of America's victory over Japan reached San Francisco on Tuesday, August 14, 1945—90 years to the day after the riot that followed President Abraham Lincoln's assassination— the city erupted into several days of riotous "celebration." Over the next two days, 11 people were killed, more than 100 hospitalized and the downtown district of San Francisco was trashed. Rioters rampaged through the streets, unchallenged by any organized response from the police department. On the third day, the police department finally cancelled days off for its members and a joint police/military force was organized to deal with further rioting.

Criticism was swift in coming. "Civil and police authorities," said one observer, "despite all pious talk . . . about how prepared the city was to handle any situation that developed, proved themselves criminally lacking in foresight and totally unprepared to handle the situation that developed." District Attorney Edmund "Pat" Brown hurriedly announced a grand jury inquiry to find out what had gone wrong and who was responsible. "The past is the past," said the deputy police chief, "and if the police have made mistakes the thing to do is admit it."

But nobody admitted much of anything. In the post-war euphoria, the whole embarrassing matter was quickly forgotten. The grand jury investigation led nowhere, and the police administration returned to its regular routine.

But times were changing in ways that only the most prescient could have discerned. There had been many riots in the city's history, from the Gold Rush anti-Latino disorders mounted by the Hounds, to the Hoodlum riots of the 1870s and the labor troubles of the early twentieth century. All previous riots had some ostensible purpose or cause, traceable to some sort of grievance, legitimate or not. But the

V-J day riots were the first of what could be called recreational riots, having no discernible cause other than a general predisposition to raise hell. Nobody much thought about it at the time, least of all police authorities but the disorders of August 1945 augured the emergence of a very different city and a set of events with which the police department often found themselves ill-equipped to deal.

Over the next several decades the demographics of the city changed dramatically, from a largely neighborly mix of multi-generational ethnic European Americans, first to a town which now included large numbers of Easterners who first came to see the city on their way to Pacific postings in World War Two and were attracted enough to want to make the city their home. In later years the demographic center of gravity shifted still further with the arrival of large numbers of peoples of color and gays.

San Francisco, along with the rest of the nation and often in the forefront, became involved in the disorders which attended the quest for racial justice and opposition to what was seen as an unjust war. The city was also witness at first hand to the youth rebellion of "Summer of Love" as well as the sometimes turbulent emergence of a a gay civic identity. All the while, the city was plagued by an increasing surge of violent crime.

Through all this, the police department went through several spasms of wrenching change as it tried to adapt to the new configuration while still adhering to its timeless mission of keeping the peace and enforcing the law. It was not always pretty to look at.

But that's another story.

Index

262

Kevin Mullen was "born and raised" in San Francisco where he attended local parochial schools. After military service (82nd Airborne Division) he joined the San Francisco police department in 1959. He served for 26 years in almost all ranks and divisions, retiring in 1986 from the position of deputy chief. Since then he has researched and written about the San Francisco criminal justice system, past and present. He now resides in Marin County with his wife, Jeannie.

Also by Kevin Mullen

Let Justice be Done: Crime and Politics in Early San Francisco (Reno: University of Nevada Press, 1989)

Dangerous Strangers: Minority Newcomers and Criminal Violence in San Francisco (New York: Palgrave-Macmillan, 2005)

Check your local books store or for ordering information:

Go to www.sanfranciscohomicide.com

Or inquire at

Noir Publications
448 Ignacio Blvd. #202,
Novato Ca 94949